CAMBRIDGE

Brighter Thinking

Democracy and Nazism: Germany, 1918–1945

A/AS Level History for AQA
Student Book

Nick Pinfield

Series Editors: Michael Fordham and David Smith

**FOR
REFERENCE ONLY**

CAMBRIDGE
UNIVERSITY PRESS

University Printing House, Cambridge C

Cambridge University Press is part of the University of Cambridge.

It furthers the University's mission by disseminating knowledge in the pursuit of education, learning and research at the highest international levels of excellence.

www.cambridge.org
Information on this title: www.cambridge.org/9781107573161 (Paperback)
                www.cambridge.org/9781107573208 (Cambridge Elevate-enhanced Edition)

© Cambridge University Press 2015

First published 2015

A catalogue record for this publication is available from the British Library

ISBN 978-1-107-57316-1 Paperback
ISBN 978-1-107-57320-8 Cambridge Elevate-enhanced Edition

Additional resources for this publication at www.cambridge.org/ukschools

Cambridge University Press has no responsibility for the persistence or accuracy of URLs for external or third-party internet websites referred to in this publication, and does not guarantee that any content on such websites is, or will remain, accurate or appropriate. Information regarding prices, travel timetables, and other factual information given in this work is correct at the time of first printing but Cambridge University Press does not guarantee the accuracy of such information thereafter.

Message from AQA

This textbook has been approved by AQA for use with our qualification. This means that we have checked that it broadly covers the specification and we are satisfied with the overall quality. Full details of our approval process can be found on our website.

We approve textbooks because we know how important it is for teachers and students to have the right resources to support their teaching and learning. However, the publisher is ultimately responsible for the editorial control and quality of this book.

Please note that when teaching the A/AS Level History (7041, 7042) course, you must refer to AQA's specification as your definitive source of information. While this book has been written to match the specification, it cannot provide complete coverage of every aspect of the course.

A wide range of other useful resources can be found on the relevant subject pages of our website: www.aqa.org.uk

Contents

About this Series

Cambridge A/AS Level History for AQA is an exciting new series designed to support students in their journey from GCSE to A Level and then on to possible further historical study. The books provide the knowledge, concepts and skills needed for the two-year AQA History A Level course, but it's our intention as series editors that students recognise that their A Level exams are just one step to a potential lifelong relationship with the discipline of history. This book has further readings, extracts from historians' works and links to wider questions and ideas that go beyond the scope of an A Level course. With this series, we have sought to ensure not only that the students are well prepared for their examinations, but also that they gain access to a wider debate that characterises historical study.

The series is designed to provide clear and effective support for students as they make the adjustment from GCSE to A Level, and also for teachers, especially those who are not familiar with teaching a two-year linear course. The student books cover the AQA specifications for both A/AS Level. They are intended to appeal to the broadest range of students, and they offer challenges to stretch the top end and additional support for those who need it. Every author in this series is an experienced historian or history teacher, and all have great skill in conveying narratives to readers and asking the kinds of questions that pull those narratives apart.

In addition to high-quality prose, this series also makes extensive use of textual primary sources, maps, diagrams and images, and offers a wide range of activities to encourage students to address historical questions of cause, consequence, change and continuity. Throughout the books there are opportunities to criticise the interpretations of other historians, and to use those interpretations in the construction of students' own accounts of the past. The series aims to ease the transition for those students who move on from A Level to undergraduate study, and the books are written in an engaging style that will encourage those who want to explore the subject further.

Icons used within this book include:

 Key terms

 Speak like a historian

 Voices from the past/Hidden voices

 Practice essay questions

 Chapter summary

 Thematic links

About Cambridge Elevate

Cambridge Elevate is the platform which hosts a digital version of this Student Book. If you have access to this digital version you can annotate different parts of the book, send and receive messages to and from your teacher and insert weblinks, among other things.

We hope that you enjoy your AS or A Level History course, as well as this book, and wish you well for the journey ahead.

Michael Fordham and David L. Smith
Series editors

1 The establishment and early years of Weimar, 1918–1924

In this section, we will look into:

- the impact of war and the political crises of October to November 1918; the context for the establishment of the Weimar Constitution; terms, strengths and weaknesses

- the Peace Settlement: expectations and reality; terms and problems; attitudes within Germany and abroad

- economic and social issues: post-war legacy and the state of the German economy and society; reparations, inflation and hyperinflation; the invasion of the Ruhr and its economic impact; social welfare and the social impact of hyperinflation

- political instability and extremism; risings on the left and right, including the Kapp Putsch; the political impact of the invasion of the Ruhr; the Munich Putsch; problems of coalition government and the state of the Republic by 1924.

Political crises and the impact of war

The crises of October to November 1918

In the spring of 1918, it looked for a short time as if Germany might have achieved the impossible and won the Great War. Russia had been defeated. The German army's major offensive on the Western Front that spring enjoyed a brief initial success of a kind unseen since August 1914. It soon became clear, however, that it had failed to achieve the intended breakthrough. This was to prove Germany's last major offensive, and the losses of troops and **matériel** left military heroes, Hindenburg and Ludendorff, after 1916.

Germany's forces severely weakened. In the summer of 1918 the army command began to realise that the war was lost. On 29 September 1918 Ludendorff informed Paul von Hintze, the German Foreign Minister, that the Western Front might collapse at any time and that any request for a ceasefire should come from a civilian government. Clearly the army wanted to shift the blame for defeat onto civilians.

The crisis in military discipline

Yet a month later the German Imperial Navy's High Seas fleet was ordered to confront the blockading Royal Navy fleet. This would have been its first action since the indecisive 1916 Battle of Jutland. Rumours that the war was ending were circulating. The sailors of the Imperial German Fleet had grievances about their conditions and had **mutinied** in 1917, demanding an end to the war. On that occasion firm intervention, arrests and executions had ended the trouble. This time, when the sailors refused to obey the October 1918 command to sail pointlessly into danger, the authorities adopted the same approach, arresting 300 mutineers in Wilhelmshaven. In November the Wilhelmshaven example was followed in Kiel, but there, ships and buildings were seized and the red flag of **revolution** was raised.

The mutineers formed revolutionary committees. Many of these committees were formed of workers, sailors, soldiers and political activists. They often lacked structure, order and direction, but they did represent a new form of political action. The delegates were elected by their fellow sailors.

The revolutionary committees spread from Kiel across Germany. The authorities could not stop this spread. Sometimes the committees concentrated on local issues, sometimes on national ones, but all reflected anger with a leadership that had led Germany into a long and difficult conflict, causing misery and suffering to millions.

The crisis in the economy

The impact of the First World War (1914–1918) on the civilian population of Germany had been considerable, and alongside the patriotic fervour of some, an increasingly embittered and rebellious attitude was developing towards existing authority. The sailors at Kiel were not alone, and the public mood was shifting towards them. The German military leadership had anticipated a fairly short war; taking their lead from the experts, the Imperial government too had expected the war to be over quickly. After all, the preceding conflict, the Franco–Prussian War

Key terms

Matériel: military supplies.

Mutiny: refusal by armed forces personnel to obey an order or orders.

Revolution: change that takes place suddenly and unexpectedly, often despite opposition, usually by violent means.

of 1870–1871, had lasted ten months. Initially, as German troops swept through Belgium and attacked France, these assumptions seemed correct. The advance halted, however, and was replaced by static trench warfare on the Western Front. The lack of German planning for a long conflict now became apparent. **Total war**, the dominant military idea, required the involvement of the entire population in the war effort.

In practice this meant that priority was given to supplying the military; the civilian population consequently suffered badly as the war dragged on.

The German government did achieve some success in controlling the wartime economy. The pre-war Imperial German government had already modestly extended the control it exercised in society and the economy; the wartime government accelerated this process. A War Raw Materials Department (*Kriegsrohstoffabteilung, KRA*) under the industrialist (and future government minister) Walther Rathenau had been established as early as August 1914. Even by the end of the war at the end of 1918, Germany had not come to the end of its reserves of raw materials. The wartime government had established maximum prices for foodstuffs, then introduced requisitioning and finally rationing. They started with bread, as Germany was not self-sufficient in grain and had to import 40% of its needs. There was not enough food to eat, and the situation got worse as the war dragged on. Complex bureaucratic machinery was needed to administer all these controls; the idea of a more interventionist government thus became established in German society and politics.

Germany's heavy reliance on imported food was exposed as a major weakness. The British **blockade** of the North Sea ports, through which most food imports had to pass, had been very effective.

In addition, the winter of 1916–1917 was especially harsh and the potato harvest was poor. This period became known as 'the turnip winter' because this vegetable, usually used as fodder for animals, had to be eaten by many as a substitute for bread and potatoes. The situation was made even worse by the switching of almost all factory production to the output of military items. Most garment factories now produced uniforms, resulting in shortages of clothing. Many miners had been conscripted into the army, so the mines were understaffed and coal was in short supply. Those food supplies that were available to the civilian population consisted mainly of bread and potatoes, and it became ever harder to buy any meat. The availability of dairy products such as butter, cheese and eggs was about a fifth of that in peacetime.

There were of course **profiteers**, **black-marketeers** and other unscrupulous people who took advantage of the situation, and the wealthy could always afford scarce items.

In rural areas it was usually possible to grow your own food and supplement the ration with eggs and chickens, but for the majority of Germans these were grim times. There was much standing in queues. As the war dragged on, these miseries became worse. Diseases of malnutrition appeared. Writer G.J. Meyer states that, according to one report at the time, 80 000 children had died of starvation in 1916.[1] But it was not just malnutrition and hunger that killed: bodies weakened by an

Key terms

Total war: a war in which every part of the economy prioritises the war and the needs of the military.

Blockade: a campaign to disrupt trade and communication in order to prevent the movement of imports in such a way as to deprive the targeted place of necessary supplies.

Profiteer: someone who takes advantage of a crisis such as a war or famine to make money.

Black-marketeer: someone who buys and sells goods on the 'black market', dealing in goods in a way that breaks the law, such as not paying an import tariff or without taking account of a rationing system.

ACTIVITY 1.1

Consider the question: 'Could the German government have controlled the economic situation in 1918?' Using the information given here, plus whatever else you can find out for yourself, write one short paragraph to address each of the following:

1. the economic situation in Germany, 1918

2. the German government's actions in response – what they prioritised and what that tells you about where they thought the most pressing problems lay

3. the problems about which the German government could do little or nothing.

 Key terms

Kaiser: German word for emperor.

Kaiserreich: Imperial Germany (1871–1918), a German state dominated by Prussia and ruled by Prussia's king as emperor.

Chancellor: a figure with authority over certain organisations such as head of government.

inadequate diet were much more vulnerable to disease. It has been calculated that nearly half a million more civilians died in Germany during the First World War than would have been the case in peacetime.

As the years went by, the stresses on society in Germany became more and more marked. A characteristic of pre-war Imperial Germany (the **Kaiserreich**) had been the elevation of the **Kaiser** to the pinnacle of German society. As the war went on the power of Kaiser Wilhelm II faded, to be replaced by that of the new military heroes, Hindenburg and Ludendorff, after 1916.

The crisis in society

Habits of good order and unquestioning obedience to authority were deeply ingrained in the society of Imperial Germany. This attitude was largely maintained in the disciplined army but less so in the civilian population as the war dragged on; as people at home became more and more weary of deprivation, rationing and standing in queues, they became increasingly resentful. In 1917 there was even a series of strikes, supported reluctantly by the trade unions, for better conditions at work. In October 1918 new drafts of conscripted German soldiers were still being sent to the front, even though it was clear to the German High Command that the war was lost. The surge of optimism that followed the German army's victory on the Eastern Front of 1917 and the initial successes of the 1918 spring offensive on the Western Front had faded into bitterness.

By late 1918 ordinary people in many cities, including Berlin and Munich, had become more open to the arguments and ideas of revolutionary political groups. Winter was approaching and the effective British blockade of the North Sea coast was still in place. Many people felt hungry, bitter and angry. In particular, they blamed the national leadership for their problems. This included even the Kaiser and his top generals. The revolutionary committees would not have spread as they did throughout Germany in the autumn of 1918 unless these grievances had become intolerable for many.

The political crisis: chancellors come and go

The scale of the political crisis at the end of the First World War is indicated by the frequency with which new **chancellors** took office (Figure 1.1).

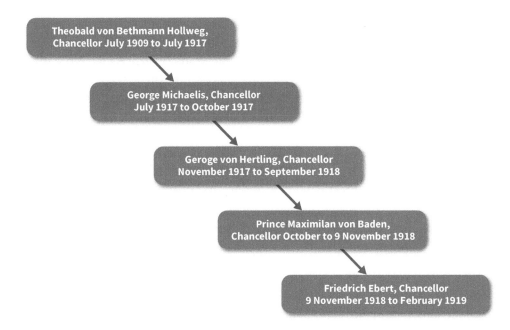

Figure 1.1: Changes in the German chancellorship during the First World War.

The military crisis lay behind the many changes of chancellor: the army High Command pushed to get rid of Bethmann-Hollweg, but although those that followed were their own candidates, the High Command quickly tired of them. Faced with civilian unrest, brewing mutinies and the generals' pessimism about the military situation, the army now advised the emperor to appoint a respected liberal, Prince Maximilian von Baden as German chancellor in October 1918. He had been critical of the conduct during the war by the generals including Ludendorff and Hindenburg; the emperor and his advisers hoped that he would have the credibility to command the respect of the increasingly revolutionary civilian population and the mutinous elements within the armed forces.

In the Reichstag, the hope was that the liberal Prince Maximilian would be able to draw the **Social Democrats** into government.

Ludendorff wanted to see a range of moderate and left-wing political parties in government in order that they could shoulder the responsibility for admitting Germany's defeat and later, all being well, be blamed for it. The new chancellor formed his cabinet: it was a mixture of liberals, Social Democrats, deputies from the conservative Roman Catholic Centre party, and people who were not members of any political party. This meant that for the first time the German government commanded a majority in the Reichstag. Later the same month, the **constitution** was altered so that for the first time in German history the chancellor and government were accountable to the Reichstag, not to the Kaiser. In addition, Prince Maximilian announced an amnesty for political prisoners. Having put his own political house in as good order as possible, Prince Maximilian entered negotiations with the USA in search of the most reasonable peace terms possible. For the Social Democrat party (SPD), the political truce of 1914 had become ever harder to sustain and had indeed split the party. Now with Prince Maximilian in the chancellery, politics was moving in ways they could support.

ACTIVITY 1.2

Our responses to these events might be shaped by our own views. For example, some people will instinctively side with the revolutionaries, just as others will instantly respond to patriotic speeches from history. It is fine to have the opinions that these responses imply, but you need to:

1. support them with information
2. show you have understood contrary views and can both explain them and explain why you disagree with them.

Read the following question and think about its implications. Draw up an essay plan, noting the points you want to make and the evidence you would use to support your views.

'Do you regard the spread of revolutionary committees from Kiel across Germany in October 1918 as a healthy sign of democratic decision-making or a step towards the politics of violence?'

Key terms

Social democrats: a left-wing political movement campaigning for political reform especially allowing all men, or all adults, to vote in elections; influenced by the ideas of Karl Marx; contains both constitutional and revolutionary traditions

Constitution: the written set of rules for how a country is governed; laws can only be passed if they do not conflict with the principles set out in the constitution.

Key terms

Abdication: renouncing a position of power or authority, stepping down from such a position

Republicanism: a political point of view preferring an elected or appointed head of state e.g. a president to a hereditary one, e.g. a king

Tsar: Russian word meaning 'emperor'.

The political crisis: the Kaiser's abdication

The burning topic of discussion in the German leadership was **abdication**. Few of them actually wanted this outcome. Prince Maximilian von Baden was a member of the ruling German nobility, heir to Frederick II, Grand Duke of Baden. He was a liberal, believing in managed political and social reform. The SPD leader Friedrich Ebert was the leader of the moderate wing of the SPD; he had supported the war effort and seen two of his sons killed. He was not a **republican** or a revolutionary and, like Prince Maximilian, he would have preferred an outcome with a constitutional monarchy. Wilhelm II himself agreed with enormous reluctance. His family, the Hohenzollerns, had ruled as kings of Prussia for centuries and as emperors of a united Germany for decades. He was a proud, sometimes arrogant and hasty man. All three men, however, knew that the previous year Russia had seen two revolutions. The Kaiser's cousin **Tsar** Nicholas II had abdicated before being shot by revolutionaries. The unrest in Germany seemed at the time to be similar to the revolutionary mood in Russia in 1917.

On 3 October 1918, events had also forced the Tsar of Bulgaria (who had family connections to both the Kaiser and his new chancellor) to abdicate; he stepped down peacefully and left the country, his son becoming the new Tsar. The contrast with Nicholas II was no doubt cautionary. On 7 November, the Bavarian King Ludwig III, increasingly unpopular because of the war, left the country and took refuge in Austria. Finally, the Kaiser was told by the new Chief of the German General Staff, General Groener, that he could no longer rely on the support of the army. The Kaiser's abdication was announced on 9 November 1918, even though the Kaiser himself did not sign a formal abdication letter for another few days. Perhaps learning from the fatal experience of his Russian cousin, he slipped over the border with his family into permanent exile in the Netherlands on 10 November. His abdication letter was sent from Amerongen in the Netherlands at the end of November 1918.

This resignation was of enormous political and social significance in Germany. The head of state – who was Commander in Chief of the armed forces and who appointed the chancellor – was gone. It was immediately clear that Germany would need a new constitution. This raised the question of legitimacy and legality: who was the government? And whose job was it to say who the government was? In the longer term, it opened to debate the way in which society and social classes worked. For many Germans who had grown up in Imperial Germany before 1914, the Emperor had been at the top of the pyramid, the head of society; loyalty to the Kaiser was taught to almost all Germans from birth. With the abdication, the top of the social pyramid was gone: that brought the whole of the social structure into question. What would the role of the existing social elites be: would they retain power or would power pass to others, and if so by what mechanism?

Thematic link: survival of social elites and conservative forces in Germany

The political crisis: revolution, republic and armistice

The Kaiser's abdication opened the door to a further change of government. Prince Maximilian von Baden had concluded, and others agreed, that only a Social Democrat government, with SPD leader Friedrich Ebert as chancellor, could succeed in negotiating with the Allies and preventing Germany from disintegrating. Again, events in Russia were a warning: there, one revolution had led to a second, then to a civil war and to the secession of parts of the country. Prince Maximilian resigned as chancellor and handed the role to Friedrich Ebert on 9 November 1918. Admitting that the event was 'an odd ceremony', historian V.R. Berghahn argued that this was an act of great political significance.[3] It was an attempt by the anti-revolutionary, reform-minded Prince Maximilian to make political changes within a framework approximating constitutional continuity. It was an extraordinary and unconstitutional step – but then, with the Kaiser gone, who was to say what was or was not constitutional anymore? As chancellor, Prince Maximilian was the nearest thing the country had to a head of state, so he acted like one.

ACTIVITY 1.3

1. List the individuals and groups who wanted Kaiser Wilhelm II to abdicate in 1918.

2. List those who were opposed to his abdication.

3. What power or authority did each of these have?

4. Taking the two lists into account, why do you think Wilhelm II abdicated in November 1918?

5. What alternatives, if any, do you think he had?

 Voices from the past

Kaiser Wilhelm II

Wilhelm's reign began in 1888 and ended in 1918 with this letter he sent from exile:

Figure 1.2: Kaiser Wilhelm II, German Emperor and King of Prussia until his abdication on 9 November 1918.

I herewith renounce for all time claims to the throne of Prussia and to the German Imperial throne connected therewith.

At the same time I release all officials of the German Empire and of Prussia, as well as all officers, non-commissioned officers and men of the navy and of the Prussian army, as well as the troops of the federated states of Germany, from the oath of fidelity which they tendered to me as their Emperor, King and Commander-in-Chief.

I expect of them that until the re-establishment of order in the German Empire they shall render assistance to those in actual power in Germany, in protecting the German people from the threatening dangers of anarchy, famine, and foreign rule.

Proclaimed under our own hand and with the imperial seal attached.

Amerongen, 28 November, 1918

Signed WILLIAM[2]

Discussion points

1. Which groups is Wilhelm addressing in his letter of abdication?

2. What is the nature of the crisis he describes?

3. What image of the German state does this letter communicate?

Key terms

Reform: change that takes place over the course of time, usually with widespread agreement, usually by constitutional means

Reichstag: the elected federal assembly or parliament of unified Germany; the building where that assembly met.

Socialist: a left-wing political movement campaigning for political reform especially allowing all men, or all adults, to vote in elections; influenced by the ideas of Karl Marx; contains both constitutional and revolutionary traditions.

Coalition: a government including members of more than one political party and thus committed to implementing more than one political programme or set of ideas.

But what would happen next? Three broad directions were advocated by different people.

Friedrich Ebert believed that he was now the legitimate political heir of Prince Maximilian and as such had a mandate to form a government and introduce social and political changes. The nature of the state should be decided by the **Reichstag** as the representative body. The future could be as a republic (like France and the USA) or as a constitutional monarchy (like the UK).

Social Democrat Philipp Scheidemann believed that with the Kaiser gone, Germany was now a republic. When crowds gathered outside the Reichstag building he urged Ebert to address them. When Ebert did not do so, Scheidemann did from a balcony in the Reichstag and proclaimed a republic had been formed. Ebert was furious that Scheidemann had made this announcement before there had been any discussion.

The **socialist** Karl Liebknecht had recently been released from prison. He believed that a revolutionary process was under way comparable to what had happened in Russia the previous year. Shortly after Scheidemann's speech to the crowds, Liebknecht proclaimed the founding of a Free Socialist Republic from a window of the Berlin City Palace where the Kaiser and his family had previously lived.

In the event, Ebert formed a cabinet not purely because Prince Maximilian had shaken his hand but also because as SPD leader he met with Independent Social Democrat (USPD) leaders the same day. Only a month earlier, Prince Maximilian had sought to widen his support and increase his legitimacy as chancellor by building a **coalition** with people to his left, the SPD. Now Ebert was doing the same thing.

As a result of his meetings with the USPD, Ebert was able to appeal not only to the Reichstag for support and confirmation in office, but also to the Workers' and Soldiers' Councils of Berlin. This was the body that called itself the national representative of the numerous revolutionary committees. Its members were thus the spokespeople for the mutineers, the strikers and the discontented. Ebert had not wanted them to meet at all, but he needed their support too and he got it the next day, on 10 November.

This might sound surprising, given the divergence between Ebert's aims and theirs. However, the SPD was the left-wing party that was best known to the German working class. Those who had lost faith in the SPD over its wartime policies looked to the USPD, which now seemed reconciled to Ebert's leadership. Ebert was now a chancellor who had sufficient credibility both inside the parliamentary system and outside it to be able to set about his task with some authority. As chancellor, he was able to use the structures of the existing civil service for the business of governing the country. He was Prince Maximilian's political heir, so he could reconcile the establishment on the political inside to radical change. Ebert was also chair of the *Rat der Volksbeauftragten* (Council of the People's Deputies). This provisional Government contained three SPD and three USPD members. Ebert could reconcile the radicals outside this framework to a process of **reform** and prevent mass support being given to the revolutionaries.

Ebert still needed to know what the people who had held power under the Kaiser, and whose power had not been removed, would do next. In particular he wanted to know what the army would do. General Groener telling the Kaiser he could no longer depend on the army's support was a key moment for the end of imperial rule. Ebert received a telephone call from Groener late on 10 November. The General later reported that he had told the chancellor that he was willing to support Ebert's government, but the army had to be taken care of, and he and Hindenburg wanted to head off any drift to revolution. In what has become known as the Ebert–Groener Pact, the two men agreed that the government would support the officer corps; discipline and order had to be maintained in the army. The government would also ensure that the army's food supplies were protected. In return, the army would back up the government in the fight against Bolshevism. Groener was already that rare thing, a soldier with whom the SPD felt they could do business. This trust dated back to events in 1917 when Groener interested himself in the welfare of the munitions workers. Realising that their pay and conditions affected their **productivity**, he had put forward the radical proposal that they be given a role in management. Such a proposal was next door to the SPD's own policies; Groener's name was one they would have remembered. Groener was perhaps the least hostile of the top military leaders to **social democracy**. He resigned from the army soon after and served as a minister in a number of Weimar governments, including for defence, transport and the interior.

Meanwhile things were also moving quickly with the war. On 7 November, Hindenburg telegraphed the Allies' supreme commander Foch asking for a meeting to arrange a ceasefire. A team of representatives had been sent straight away. The following day, 8 November, the German team saw the terms of surrender. They attempted to negotiate, but the Allies changed almost nothing. The Germans registered their protest but they signed at 5 a.m. on 11 November 1918. By this time the government that had sent them had ceased to exist. A ceasefire on the Western Front came into effect six hours later at 11 a.m. The following day, 12 November 1918, the Council of People's Deputies announced that several restrictions on liberty, such as censorship and restrictions on the right to assemble, were ended. Various wartime laws were abolished. The eight-hour working day would be introduced, as would new unemployment- and sickness-benefit schemes. New houses would be built. Food supplies would be restored. New elections would be held under a system of **proportional representation** in which all men and all women could vote. The country was going to be freer and more prosperous. The grievances of the mutineers, strikers, rioters and demonstrators would all be addressed.

There has been plenty of debate about the events of November 1918 and the constitutional discussions of January 1919. Their significance depends partly on your political point of view. Fifty years later, journalist Raimund Pretzel (who adopted the pseudonym Sebastian Haffner while in exile in London during the Second World War in order to protect his family, who were still in Germany) reflected on those events and asked whether they deserved the label of 'revolution'. He argued that what happened was more than a short-term failure of the police and army, it was a true revolution, replacing one political system with a different one.[4]

 Key terms

Productivity: the amount workers produce in a given time.

Social democracy: a left-wing political movement campaigning for political reform especially allowing all men, or all adults, to vote in elections; influenced by the ideas of Karl Marx; contains both constitutional and revolutionary traditions.

Proportional representation: an electoral system whereby the number of seats a political party holds in an assembly closely reflects the number of votes cast for that party in an election.

Thematic link: authoritarianism and democracy

ACTIVITY 1.4

The vocabulary in which we talk and write about historical events can affect our ability to reach a balanced, accurate interpretation. Find out about the following terms:

revolutionary	radical	counter-revolutionary
reactionary	conservative	monarchist
nationalist	social democrat	socialist
communist		

To which of the following people could you apply any of those terms and why?

Friedrich Ebert	Philip Scheidemann	Prince Maximilian of Baden
Erich Ludendorff	Paul von Hindenburg	Wilhelm Groener
Karl Liebknecht		

Key terms

Constitutional Convention: A conference held to debate and design a reformed constitution.

Democracy: a political system in which all citizens are able to choose their government, usually through an electoral process.

Militarism: a belief in the importance of the army; a tendency to depend on the army to solve diplomatic problems.

Freikorps: German word meaning 'free corps'; an armed paramilitary group of nationalistic anti-Republicans, usually ex-soldiers, many of which were formed after November 1918.

The Weimar Constitution

The context for the establishment of the Weimar Constitution

The new republic possessed a constitution drawn up in 1871 for a state headed by an emperor. Clearly this situation could not be left unaddressed. Accordingly a Constitutional Convention was called to draw up a new constitution that would reflect Germany's new status as a republic, but would also enshne in law the values of those politicians who were remaking the state, attempting to turn it into a liberal **democracy**.

About 220 kilometres south-west of Berlin in a part of Germany called Thuringia lies the small town of Weimar. It was here that the **Constitutional Convention** of the new German Republic started meeting in January 1919, only two months after the abdication of the last Kaiser.

One reason for the choice of location was that Weimar was associated with German culture. Johann von Goethe, Germany's most famous writer, lived and worked there in the late 18th and early 19th centuries, as did the poet and dramatist Friedrich Schiller, both prominent in the movement we now call *Weimarer Klassik* or Weimar Classicism. Philosopher Friedrich Nietzsche spent his final years there. Thus, while Berlin was associated with Prussian **militarism**, Weimar brought to mind the finest German cultural works of the past. Another reason for the choice was that Berlin was still not a safe place. There had been serious unrest in Berlin earlier that month with the Spartacist Revolt, a general strike and street violence from 4 to 15 January 1919, suppressed with great violence by the army and a *Freikorps* group. The latter were volunteer, armed paramilitary units, mostly composed of ex-soldiers, formed to suppress disorder on the streets in general and to fight against **communism** in particular. They operated with the full support of the government led by Chancellor Ebert.

The Weimar Constitution: terms, strengths and weaknesses

The 1919 Constitution was drafted by the liberal politician and lawyer Hugo Preuss, with valuable comments from others, notably the authority on constitutional law Gerhard Anschütz. It had many provisions, but in brief it declared Germany to be a democratic parliamentary republic. The Reichstag would be elected by all men and women aged 20 or over (while voting age in the UK was 21 for men and 30 for women). There were to be fixed-term parliaments with elections every four years. It guaranteed freedom of religion, speech, the press and political activity (unless subversive). The Constitution was signed and became law in August 1919. The state itself continued to be known as the *Deutsches Reich* (German Empire). But because of the constitutional conference's location, Germany 1919–1933 is known to history as the Weimar Republic.

A great deal of attention has focused on Articles 22 and 48 of the Weimar Consitution. Article 22 stated that the voting system for members of the Reichstag was to be proportional representation (PR). PR is a voting system in use in 80 or so countries today, including Australia, Sweden and Switzerland. Its appeal is that it can offer some representation to minority views and is said to improve levels of participation in elections. It means that the balance of opinion in the assembly is like that in the electorate itself. However, critics argue that it usually produces coalition governments that are not as decisive as the 'first past the post' system in use in UK national elections at the time of writing. The Weimar Constitution adopted a form of PR that allowed even the smallest political parties the chance to win seats in the Reichstag or state parliaments. Article 48 laid out the provision for the use of emergency powers. The Weimar Constitution is by no means the only one to include such powers, which in case of national crisis permit a President to suspend the constitution, often with a time limit, and rule by **decree**.

The danger of such powers is related to a definition of 'national crisis'. The problem in particular with the Weimar Republic was the frequency with which these powers were used. President Friedrich Ebert, Social Democrat and lifelong opponent of **autocratic** rule, used Article 48 no less than 134 times himself. His successor Hindenburg used them too. And so did Hindenburg's successor, one Adolf Hitler.

Was it a badly conceived constitution? Historian Richard J. Evans did not think so: 'All in all Weimar's constitution was no worse than the constitutions of most other countries in the 1920s and a good deal more democratic than many.'[5] Eric D. Weitz agreed:

'A less divided society, and one with a more expansive commitment to democratic principles, could have made the constitution work.'[6]

ACTIVITY 1.5

On two pieces of paper, note down the arguments you would use in a debate about the Constitutional Convention:

1. What do the circumstances in which the Constitutional Convention met tell you about the project?

2. Was this a necessary step in building a liberal democracy or an unrealistic activity?

Key terms

Communism: a left-wing political point of view or party believing in the working class taking political and economic power through revolution.

Decree: a law issued by a head of state, not formulated by an elected government and debated by an elected assembly.

Autocracy: a political system in which a single figure possesses unrestrained power.

The peace settlement

Expectations and reality

In the spring of 1919 delegates of the victorious Allies met in Paris to discuss in detail the peace terms to be presented to Germany. There were delegates from 32 countries present, but all the major decisions had been taken by the so-called 'Big Four', USA, Britain, France and Italy (Figure 1.3). A year before, in January 1918, US President Woodrow Wilson had made an important speech stating his 'Fourteen Points'. These should in his view have formed the basis for a relatively mild treatment of Germany. Wilson wanted to create a democratic, prosperous Europe with free trade, one in which conflict was resolved by discussion rather than by aggression. These Fourteen Points gave some hope to Germany that their treatment in Paris would not be as harsh as some feared. France, Britain and Italy, while not wishing to offend their most powerful ally, the USA, took a less generous view of the appropriate terms of the peace treaty to be presented to Germany.

Figure 1.3: The leaders of the 'Big Four' at the Paris Peace Conference in 1919: from left to right, David Lloyd George (UK), Vittorio Emanuele Orlando (Italy), Georges Clemenceau (France) and Woodrow Wilson (USA).

The German team was headed by Count Ulrich von Brockdorff-Rantzau, the Foreign Minister. In January, Ebert and Scheidemann had approached him about joining the government. Brockdorff-Rantzau accepted conditionally upon a return to constitutional order. Germany's civilian delegates to Paris at the end of April 1919 believed that they were going to negotiate appropriate terms for peace. The Allies, especially France and Britain, thought otherwise. They had in mind an ultimatum; Germany could accept the terms offered, or it could return to fighting the war. German hopes that the more conciliatory signs given by President Woodrow Wilson on behalf of the USA might mean acceptable peace terms proved unfounded. The German delegation was kept waiting for two days and treated with little respect. On 7 May 1919, far from the negotiation for which the delegates had hoped, they were presented with a number of non-negotiable demands that the Allies had agreed following their discussions in Paris since January 1919. It was a repetition of the manner of the meeting to arrange an armistice in November the previous year.

The German delegation was given just three weeks to accept the terms. They protested at what they saw as the harshness of these terms, but in the end they had little choice but to accept them, signing at Versailles on 28 June 1919 (Figure 1.4). The German army had been demobilised by January 1919 and the British maintained their North Sea blockade. French and Belgian troops were on Germany's borders ready to attack. Brockdorff-Rantzau's warning to Ebert and Scheidemann notwithstanding, Germany's ability to fight a war had collapsed and the Allies (and the German delegates and their government) all knew it.

Figure 1.4: The Treaty of Versailles (English version).

Terms and problems

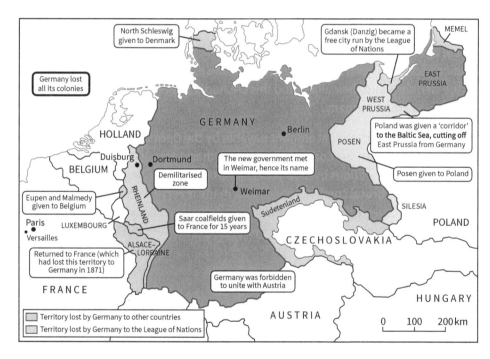

Figure 1.5: German losses of territory under the 1919 Treaty of Versailles.

Under the terms of the **Treaty of Versailles**, Germany was to accept the loss of around 13.5% of its 1914 territory (shown in Figure 1.5). Alsace–Lorraine was returned to France, having been seized by Germany in the Franco-Prussian War of 1871. The Saarland, an area rich in coal, was given to France for 15 years, after which a plebiscite was to be held to determine its future. Belgium gained the territories of Eupen and Malmedy. More land was lost in the east to the newly created countries of Poland, which gained Posen (Poznań) and West Prussia, and Czechoslovakia, which gained the Sudetenland. Poland was given a corridor to

ACTIVITY 1.6

Clearly the German delegates to the Paris conference had been unrealistic in April 1919 when they expected a negotiation of terms. But who else had misread the situation?

1. Create a list of the steps which led from the 1918 'spring offensive' to the armistice and on to Germany's representatives signing the document.

2. In each case, note who took those steps.

3. Later, nationalist right-wing political parties would blame Jews and Communists for Germany's signing the Treaty of Versailles. Whose responsibility do you think it was?

Key term

Treaty of Versailles: The treaty ending the First World War signed between Germany and the Allies in 1919.

ACTIVITY 1.7

1. List the key articles of the Treaty of Versailles and note the nature of the German objection to each one.

2. Find out about the two men who signed on behalf of Germany, Johannes Bell and Hermann Müller. Why do you think they were chosen? Who else could or should have been sent to sign?

3. Write a short paragraph about the 'war-guilt clause' quoted above.

Key term

Reparation: payment made by e.g. state as punishment for wrongdoing e.g. war crimes.

the sea that divided East Prussia from the rest of Germany, and the city of Danzig (Gdansk) became a 'free city' under the control of the newly formed League of Nations. Germany's overseas empire was distributed among the Allies, primarily Britain and France. Altogether this meant that some 7 million people were no longer German citizens. The loss of territory was a considerable blow to German national pride, and this was exacerbated by enforced cuts to the military. The army was restricted to 100 000 men with a ban on heavy artillery, gas, tanks and aircraft. The navy was to be restricted to vessels of under 10 000 tons, with no submarines. Under Article 180, the Rhineland on Germany's western border was to be demilitarised, with the demolition of any fortresses or military field works in the area. The effect of this was that Germany was not in a position to defend itself against possible future invasions.

These Treaty provisions caused outrage among many Germans, but of the 440 Articles of the Treaty, the one that caused the most indignation in Germany was Article 231, the so-called 'war-guilt clause':

The Allied and Associated Governments affirm and Germany accepts the responsibility of Germany and her allies for causing all the loss and damage to which the Allied and Associated Governments and their nationals have been subjected as a consequence of the war imposed upon them by the aggression of Germany and her allies.

Article 231 outraged Germany and laid the ground for a decade and a half of political, economic and social trouble. It put the entire blame for starting the war on the Germans and their allies, and this created a legal basis on which to claim **reparations** from Germany.

It was agreed that the actual amount payable by the German government was to be fixed by a Reparations Commission no later than 1 May 1921 and that Germany would pay the reparations over 30 years. For a country needing to rebuild its economy after a brutal conflict, reparations made it very difficult indeed for Germany to recover. Brockdorff-Rantzau, the delegation leader, returned to Berlin in disgust. The German delegation, however, had no choice but to sign.

Attitudes among the allies

There were influential allied voices who felt that the terms of the Treaty of Versailles were too harsh. Notable among them was John Maynard Keynes, a distinguished economist and academic in the UK. His book on the subject was called *The Economic Consequences of the Peace*; published late in 1919, it was contemporary to the discussions and the treaty. It sold 100 000 copies in the UK and was released in the USA the following year. It is said to have influenced public opinion in the USA and had a part in their decision not to join the new League of Nations. Keynes had attended the Paris Peace Conference as a British Treasury delegate. He argued that the reparations payments demanded by the victorious Allies were unreasonably harsh. He called the Versailles treaty 'a Carthaginian Peace'. He meant by this an unduly harsh and punitive settlement imposed by the victors on the vanquished. The name comes from ancient history, when Rome had set out not merely to conquer its rival Carthage, but to destroy it permanently. He concluded, 'but who can say how much is endurable, or in what direction men will seek at last to escape from their misfortunes?' Other economists have since analysed the Treaty of Versailles and have concluded that the reparations demanded were not unreasonable under the circumstances and that the need for payments had only a relatively small effect on the German economy. Opinions clearly vary. What is not in doubt, however, is that almost all Germans believed that reparations payments were a real burden on the German economy and a grossly unfair one.

Belgium and France were the two countries that had suffered the most damage as a result of the war. This was especially serious for Belgium as hers was a relatively small economy. The only way that Belgium could undertake necessary repairs to war-damaged **infrastructure** and buildings was by seeking a substantial loan from the Allies, a sum that was part of reparation payments demanded of Germany with 5% interest added. For France, this had been the second time in 43 years that it had been invaded by the German army. To the governments and populations of France and Belgium, these provisions were in the Treaty of Versailles to compensate for their past suffering and to ensure their future security.

Attitudes within Germany

In Germany public sentiment about the Treaty of Versailles was very different. Many resented the **demilitarisation** of the Rhineland, restrictions on German armed forces including on the manufacture of aeroplanes, submarines and new weapons systems, and the ceding of territory to France, Belgium and others. There was almost universal anger and resentment about the 'war-guilt clause' (Article 231) and the level of reparations likely to be demanded by the Allies. This anger was skilfully exploited by the political parties then existing, mainly nationalistic and conservative, that opposed the Weimar Republic. They successfully linked the government, and by extension the institution of the republic, to the treaty and its hated clauses. The army moved swiftly to distance itself from their own advice in 1918 to the Kaiser and government that the war was lost, and to place the blame for military defeat on politicians back home in order to preserve some elements of its battered reputation. The **Dolchstoss** theory was that the German army had never actually been defeated in 1918 but had been 'stabbed in the back' by cowardly and probably Marxist civilian politicians back home. This account of events, despite being nonsense, became a **propaganda** staple for the many violent extremist political groups already forming in Germany.

Economic and social issues

Post-war legacy and the state of the German economy and society

The First World War created nearly full employment in Germany. The Army High Command had declared that all German men between 17 and 60 were to be liable for military and civilian service, and this meant that workplaces – factories, farms, mines, steelworks, railways, offices, banks, schools – lost many of their male employees, which in turn created job opportunities for women. In addition, the

Key terms

Infrastructure: the services and systems which unpin the economy and society of a state, including bridges, power-distribution networks, railways, roads, telecommunications and water supplies.

Demilitarisation: removal of armed forces e.g. Army from an area.

Dolchstoss: German word meaning 'dagger thrust' or 'stab in the back'; the view that the German army was not defeated in the First World War but that left-wing civilians surrendered and signed a peace treaty in an act of treason.

Propaganda: communication especially in politics intended to persuade through emotional appeal not through explanation, information or argument.

wartime economy had created a large bureaucracy, and many more civil servants were employed.

The changes in society

The fact that many women found jobs in factories and offices represented a major social change from pre-war Imperial Germany. Before the war women were expected to remain at home, looking after their husbands and children, tied to domestic work, attending church and maintaining an unquestioned loyalty to the Kaiser. Added to this, as German **casualties** in the war mounted alarmingly, many women were widowed.

Single women were less likely to find husbands, and some became less able and less willing to behave as the pre-war society of Imperial Germany expected. Furthermore, beside the million or so German soldiers killed in the First World War, many more returned home wounded and often disabled. These facts changed assumptions about a society based on the family unit. It was now not an uncommon sight, especially in the cities, to see wounded ex-soldiers begging at street corners. For many families, women were now breadwinners.

The state of the German economy

The German economy was badly disrupted by the First World War, then by defeat and again by the terms of the Treaty of Versailles. Germany lost significant territory in the Treaty, both in the east and in the west. The wide corridor of land that had gone to Poland left the remains of East Prussia cut off from the main body of the country. As well as France taking Alsace–Lorraine, French troops also occupied the Rhineland region for a time. Germany's colonies had been a valuable source of raw materials and a useful captive market for its manufactured goods: they had all

Key term

Casualty: dead or injured especially in war.

Voices from the past

Paul von Hindenburg

The expression *Dolchstoss* was used by von Hindenburg when questioned by a Reichstag committee of enquiry into the war. He didn't invent it but he did make it famous:

An English general said with justice: 'The German army was stabbed in the back.' [*Die deutsche Armee ist von hinten erdolcht worden.*] No guilt applies to the good core of the army. Its achievements are just as admirable as those of the officer corps. Where the guilt lies has clearly been demonstrated. If it needed more proof, then it would be found in the quoted statement of the English general and in the boundless astonishment of our enemies at their victory.[7]

He thus ignored the fact that it was the army – he and Ludendorff – who had advised suing for peace terms in November 1918 and had known since the summer of that year that the war was lost.

Historians, who rarely accept this theory, call it the *Dolchstosslegende* ('stab-in-the-back legend'), but at the time many people seem not to have doubted it.

Discussion points

1. What is Hindenburg trying to achieve with the claims he makes here?
2. What do you think were the motives of those who took up this *Dolchstoss* theory?
3. What were the consequences of its becoming accepted over time as a historical and political fact by many Germans?

gone. The blockade by the British Royal Navy of the North Sea coast was initially still in place, leading to shortages of the imports that industry and agriculture (as well as consumers) needed. Food was in short supply again in the grim winter of 1918–1919. In the countryside there was growing discontent. The revolution had largely been an activity of urban areas, and all the talk of strikes and shorter working hours made little sense on farms. According to historian Gerald D. Feldman, there was a belief that profiteers, including Jews, were taking advantage of food shortages, making money while farmers and peasants were not.[8]

To complete the misery, the world was in the grip of the influenza pandemic of 1918 and 1919. Deaths from influenza in Berlin climbed throughout September 1918 from 2% of the population to peak at the end of the month at 4%, before falling back to 2% by 9 November 1918. Poverty, malnutrition and insanitary living conditions were major factors in the spread of this disease. Conditions in the wartime trenches could also have been an important factor in the population's vulnerability to this viral attack.

Millions of Germans were on the move from late November 1918. These were not only soldiers returning to Germany from years of fighting but also the women workers in factories who were summarily dismissed to give the men their jobs back. In large manufacturing operations like Krupp of Essen in the Ruhr, this change was rapid and not always welcomed by employers. By the end of November 52 000 workers had left Krupp's Essen factory, many of them female employees being laid off. It took some time for these factories to switch back to peacetime production from wartime manufacturing demands. Krupp, for example, had been a principal supplier of equipment and munitions for the German army. Meanwhile the terms of the Treaty of Versailles had demanded Germany surrender a vast amount of matériel – not just submarines and surface ships, but also railway stock, locomotives and trucks. This was a major blow to the country's infrastructure.

Reparations, inflation and hyperinflation

Hanging over the government and people was the question of reparations, the money that Germany would have to pay the victorious Allies in compensation for the war. The sum demanded was 132 billion **marks**, equivalent to £6.6 billion.

Reparations were only paid to the western Allies. Russia had not formed part of the Paris conference, despite having been an Ally in 1914, as it had lost the war in 1917, suffered political collapse and become a Bolshevik state. Germany was able to sign the Treaty of Rapallo with Russia in April 1922. Each country renounced all territorial and financial claims on the other. This meant cancelling any question of reparations arising from First World War damage.

The first reparation payment was made in full by Germany in June 1921, but as hard currency was required, increasingly worthless marks had to be used to buy foreign currency with which to pay. In order to start paying off this huge sum and to purchase foreign currency, the Reichsbank, the state's central bank, printed large numbers of banknotes. The bank's action was followed by prices climbing as more money chased fewer goods. Between June 1921 and January 1924 the Weimar Republic experienced a period of increasing **inflation**. The mark had been

Key terms

Marks: German currency or money; its name changed after each of a series of currency reforms e.g. Goldmark, Reichsmark, Rentenmark, Deusche Mark etc.

Inflation: The consequence of too much money in the economy compared with the supply of products and services; the obvious effect is that prices rise.

Key terms

Hyperinflation: a process by which prices rapidly go up in leaps, making goods and services far more expensive on a day by day basis

Middle class: a social group possessing less property and political power than nobility but more than working class and so in the middle of society; dependant on working to earn a living, so unlike nobility, but works in employment requiring higher levels of education (professions and management of business), so unlike working class

stable enough before this, at about 60 marks to the US dollar. During the first part of 1922 the rate had risen to 320 marks per dollar, and by November 1923 it had soared to an unsustainable 4210 500 000 000 marks per dollar. The inflation rate reached its highest point in October 1923, 29 500%. This meant that prices of goods in shops, including bread and other essentials, doubled every four days. In Germany there were rumours of foreign speculators, profiteers and bankers. In turn, because reparations were at first set in marks, the Allies believed that Germany had deliberately engineered this inflation as a way of reducing payment.

We tend to view this **hyperinflation** as disastrous, but we should remember that while many suffered, some did profit. The main losers were those who held cash assets, as these quickly declined in value.

Landlords who received a fixed rent from tenants found that their income soon became meaningless. Similarly, those on a fixed salary or pension were receiving income that was in practice worthless. The value of savings diminished fast. It was the **middle classes** who tended to have such savings, and they were particularly badly affected by the hyperinflation. However, there were some who benefited from hyperinflation.

Just as it wiped out the value of savings, so too it wiped out the value of debt. This meant anyone who had borrowed money could repay the loan very quickly. This was a particular benefit for businesses who had borrowed money to buy assets that held their value. The working classes were not all so badly affected by hyperinflation, as they received weekly wages that would soon be spent before prices rose again. Overall, however, the hyperinflation had a devastating effect on the people of Germany, and the memory of it remained with people for many years.

By the middle of 1923 it was clear that a new currency was needed to 'reboot' the Germany economy. The new currency was called the Rentenmark and it came into use on 16 November 1923. The Rentenmark was tied to the value of the US dollar, giving the currency the stability it needed. The financial situation settled and the alarming period of hyperinflation ended. It was not the first time a country has experienced hyperinflation, nor the most severe, but it was a prominent example, in part because of its political consequences. The many enemies of the Weimar Republic used the financial crisis as further evidence of the supposed inability of the government to protect German interests and way of life.

The invasion of the Ruhr and its economic impact

Hyperinflation made it impossible for Germany to make its reparation payments. France was not willing to accept payment in worthless currency and so sent troops into the Ruhr in January 1923 to begin requisitioning goods in lieu of payment. They were to stay two and a half years. The Ruhr valley, near the western border with France and Belgium, was the industrial powerhouse of Germany. From Duisburg in its west, a series of heavily industrialised cities ran eastwards to Dortmund, including Essen, home to the main factory of Krupp. It was an area rich in coal, and was the centre of iron and steel production in Germany. Belgium and France were determined that Germany pay reparations in full. Both countries believed that Germany was attempting to use the hyperinflation as a way of meeting their repayments without too much difficulty, so the seizure of the Ruhr and a demand that future reparations payments were to be made in goods and commodities was a way to achieve their aim. They invaded the area on January 1923 and took control of factories and mines, assuming that these would continue to work as before.

The occupation lasted from January 1923 until late August 1925. The invasion was met by an angry campaign of passive resistance by local Germans. Over 100 Germans were killed by the French and Belgians during the occupation. France and Belgium, however, did succeed in making their occupation of the Ruhr pay and to that limited extent their dramatic invasion had worked. In Germany itself, the occupation could well have contributed to the hyperinflation of 1923, although the extent of this contribution has been disputed. Loss of revenue from Germany's most productive industrial area certainly did not help its struggling economy.

The Weimar Government was furious and called for a general strike in the Ruhr and a campaign of passive resistance. Factories shut down and mines closed. Transport came to a halt. There was no cooperation with the invaders. Once again the German economy was badly hit, this time from the effective closure of its most important industrial area, but the public finances of France and Belgium suffered also. Faced with high unemployment and worsening hyperinflation the new government, led by Gustav Stresemann, called off the campaign of passive resistance in the Ruhr in September 1923, and then declared a state of emergency. Demonstrations, riots and attempted seizures of power continued throughout Germany. It remained a time of serious civil unrest.

Social policies in Weimar Germany and the impact of hyperinflation

Family policy

One estimate from the Bavarian and Reich Statistical Office in 1920 by Fritz Burgdorfer was that Germany had lost 12 to 13 million people, civilian as well as military, because of the war. This would mean the population was nearly one fifth smaller. Such estimates are notoriously hard to make, but whatever the precise figure the government of the Weimar Republic was greatly concerned with this population decline. The fact that made it particularly pressing was that the birth

Voices from the past

George Grosz

The artist George Grosz (1893–1959) remembered these difficult times:

Lingering at the shop window was a luxury because shopping had to be done immediately. Even anadditional minute meant an increase in price. One had to buy quickly because a rabbit, for example, might cost 2 million marks more by the time it took to walk into the store.[9]

Discussion point

In what ways does this source help us understand the economic situation during Weimar Germany's period of hyperinflation?

What do you think were the objectives of the family policies of the Weimar governments? Remember, they might have had several objectives, and some of these objectives could have been contradictory.

1. List possible objectives and gather evidence that suggests these were important to the government.

2. Was there a change of priorities over time?

rate was already falling, from 27.5% in 1913 to 25.7% in 1920, so there was no prospect of a population boost unless effective incentives were offered to families to have more children. This might seem quite an abstract matter, but it was one that the Weimar Government turned its attention to, and it was also one to which Hitler later alluded several times. In speeches given when Germany annexed adjoining territory before the outbreak of war, he would announce the increased size of the Reich and its population. Clearly he believed this was a matter to which the listening crowds would respond.

An emphasis on family was already incorporated in the Weimar Constitution. Article 119 protected the sanctity of marriage, confirmed the protection of motherhood and promoted population growth, although Article 121 did give children born out of wedlock equal rights. Beyond the constitution, the coalition government headed by SPD chancellor Gustav Bauer attempted to respond to the falling birth rate through family policy, with a wide range of social welfare programmes. These included tax benefits, improved maternity leave and better healthcare to combat the high infant mortality rates of the time in Germany. Pregnant wives and daughters who did not have insurance but who had a husband or father who did could also claim some support. However, these measures had only limited success, especially for working-class women, partly because of financial concerns and partly because of the difficulty of making the lifestyle changes required. There was no other significant family policy initiative by the Weimar Government until after 1924, but many of their policies in this area were undermined by the clear preference given to state employees and civil servants, to the exclusion of workers in other sectors of the German economy such as agriculture or industry.

In 1923 the state officially adopted *Muttertag*, based on the American festival of Mother's Day, itself a secularised version of the English church festival of Mothering Sunday. Those who wanted to see women free to enter the workforce and participate in professional and political life were unenthusiastic, seeing it as a retrograde step, a return to Imperial Germany's values of *Kinder, Küche, Kirche* (children, kitchen, church). To this basic phrase *Kaiser, Keller, Kammer* and *Kleider* (emperor, cellar, room and clothing) had sometimes variously been added. The list clearly implies domesticity, with the addition of piety or patriotism. Despite the radical political changes under way, these three or more 'K's were still seen by many as the proper set of priorities for a woman.

Health provision

Health provision in Weimar Germany was patchy, and there was no truly comprehensive or national system. Instead, the delivery of healthcare was often undertaken by State governments. In Prussia, for example, a large state that had become a stronghold for the SPD with the introduction of the universal right to vote under the Weimar Constitution, a duty was placed on local authorities to provide affordable homes and to enforce minimum standards of hygiene. Many doctors were becoming used to working for the state rather than being in private practice, although national laws about this were not introduced until after 1924. Progressive social welfare legislation was a marked feature of the Weimar Republic from the start. The government introduced legislation in 1919 extending health insurance to several groups such as wives and daughters without their own income or those unable to work owing to disability. Further legislation was passed in 1919 limiting the working week to 48 hours. These were the steps that many of those participating in the strikes and supporting the revolutionary committees had been demanding.

Youth policy

In 1922 the Imperial Youth Welfare Act was passed by the Reichstag, to coordinate all youth-related social welfare programmes. Under its provisions, all children had the right to an education. In addition, all States and municipalities were to set up youth offices responsible for child protection. However, the activities of voluntary groups operating outside the formal national political framework were just as important for youth development as this government legislation. For example, the *Wandervogel* operated from 1896 and was officially founded in 1901 in Berlin; it encouraged young people to go out into the countryside, to develop independence of spirit. It was relatively unstructured and romantic in inspiration. The Boy Scout movement was an import from Britain that had reached Germany in 1906. Founded by a British war hero, it had a military format, with uniforms and flags. A national umbrella organisation for youth groups emerged after 1919. The Youth Movement (*Bündische Jugend*) combined the *Wandervogel* and scout traditions and methods. As Lisa Pine points out in her study of *Education in Nazi Germany*, after the First World War these groups became less free-spirited than the *Wandervogel*. Activities became more formalised and uniform more common. Instead of bringing young people together, which had been part of the pre-war vision, the new groups divided them. Political parties and churches increasingly created their own youth movements. These groups were a significant influence on young people: membership amounted to 5 to 6 million in Weimar Germany.

Social welfare policy

It is something of a tribute to the long-standing concern for those less fortunate in German society that the development of a social welfare system continued in the early years of the Weimar Republic, despite the economic hardships of the time. Ever since the unification of Germany in 1871, a national system of social welfare had been seen by successive governments of Imperial Germany as a priority. Because the 1914–1918 war effort required the active participation of the German working class, the political influence of that class grew. This led to greater social protection and better industrial dispute resolution, with the appearance of a number of voluntary employee committees. These efforts to improve worker participation and dispute resolution were expanded in the Weimar period.

There was a significant extension of the social welfare system during the Weimar period. The Ebert government issued a decree in February 1919 stating that the state would take over responsibility for aid to wounded service personnel and their dependents. It continued the wartime establishment of a nationwide network of state and district welfare bureaus to coordinate social services for war widows and orphans. In so doing, the government was responding to a campaign by veterans' associations. In 1920 the benefits due to war victims were added to the social welfare system. In 1923, at the height of hyperinflation, unemployment relief was consolidated into a regular assistance programme that was financed by employers and employees. The same year of 1923 saw a new law for the social insurance for miners put into effect. This consolidated the administration of insurance provision for miners into a single agency instead of over 100 separate agencies as before. Although the focus of discussion on this period has often been on the plight of formerly comfortable middle-class families, with their now-worthless savings, forced to sell their possessions – furniture, heirlooms, books, clothes – many working-class families also suffered in Germany from the hyperinflation of 1922–1923. Unemployment rose sharply, and it has been calculated that by 1924 real wages had dropped in their purchasing power by 74% from 1913.

In the more challenging context of an inflationary economy, poverty grew, but the ability of the state to meet the expectations it had itself created did not. Detlev Peukert argued that the social provision created by democratic governments was in fact a reflection of their ambitions for social control, to extend the reach of the state far beyond what pre-war governments would have thought appropriate or even possible.

The 'welfare state' aspect of Weimar was, he argued, driven not by a concern for individuals at all, but by a desire to control. His argument was that when at the end of this period the **Nazis** came to power, they were able to retain the inherent controlling and disciplining aspect even while throwing aside the democratic framework.[10]

The government's most pressing task was to establish itself as legitimate, and to ensure that the various groups in the country who possessed power supported it. A clear threat came from the lack of order on the streets. Some of this lawlessness was simple criminality, some of it was revolutionary activity. (The dividing line is not always clear.)

Political instability, uprisings and extremism

Power and authority in the Weimar Republic

The coalition governments knew that social order had to be re-established in order to defend political order and prevent the kind of collapse that Russia had experienced in 1917. They did not have a monopoly on power; they needed the support of the traditional elites in Germany (see Figure 1.6).

Key term

Nazis: contraction for *Nationalsozialistiche Deutsche Arbeiterpartei*, a German expression meaning 'National Socialist German Workers' Party' (NSDAP).

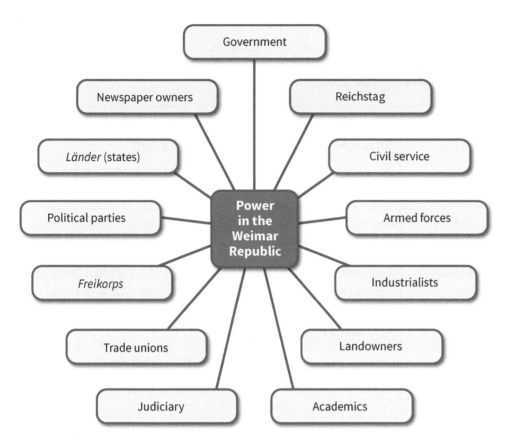

Figure 1.6: Groups with power in the Weimar Republic.

On the other hand, the events of 1918, with defeat, abdication and abrupt political change, had been a frightening reminder of the previous year's developments in Russia. The ruling German elites were alarmed, and although they were by no means sympathetic either to the Social Democrats or to the Weimar Republic that the SPD brought into being, they hated the idea of revolution even more. The 19th-century Germans Karl Marx and Frederick Engels had both thought in the middle of the previous century that a communist revolution would happen in an industrialised country such as Germany. In 1918, the middle and upper classes began to be afraid that Marx and Engels had been right. The deal done to knit the SPD and the traditional ruling elites together was **pragmatic**. When the reasons for the deal changed, it would begin to unravel.

 Key term

Pragmatism: moral principle favouring choices being based on the relative practicality of the options available than basing them on other moral or religious principles.

Sort this list of political parties in the Weimar Republic onto a scale showing how left- or right-wing they were.

BB	*Bayerischer Bauernbund*, Bavarian Farmers' League
BVP	*Bayerische Volkspartei*, Bavarian People's Party
DDP	*Deutsche Demokratische Partei*, German Democratic Party
DNVP	*Deutschnationale Volkspartei*, German National People's Party
DVP	*Deutsche Volkspartei*, German People's Party
KPD	*Kommunistische Partei Deutschlands*, Communist Party of Germany
NSDAP	*Nationalsozialistische Deutsche Arbeiterpartei*, National Socialist German Workers' Party (formerly DAP, German Workers' Party)
SPD	*Sozialdemokratische Partei Deutschlands*, Social Democrat Democratic Party of Germany
USPD	*Unabhängige Sozialdemokratische Partei Deutschlands*, Independent Social Democratic Party of Germany
Zentrum	*Deutsche Zentrumspartei*, German Centre Party

The army and the *Freikorps*

Lack of political stability breeds extremism, and Germany in the early years of the Weimar Republic was anything but politically stable. Following the armistice on 11 November 1918, the soldiers began their weary march back into Germany. They were demoralised, defeated, bitter and exhausted. There was no warm welcome in the towns and villages through which they passed. The authorities in these places were concerned mainly with getting them to move on. A greater contrast with the levies of optimistic soldiers who had marched proudly to war in 1914, to the cheers of excited and enthusiastic crowds, could not be imagined. Demobilisation was rapid. Eight million or so soldiers had returned to Germany from the fighting in November 1918. Just one million men were left in the army by January 1919. Most returned to their home villages, towns or cities to live out their lives in peace, but some had very different plans. Inevitably with such rapid demobilisation, many simply left without completing any formalities, sometimes taking their weapons with them.

Some of these armed, trained and battle-hardened soldiers found a ready welcome from one of the many extremist political parties that were forming in Germany at this time. Some moved into one or other of the paramilitary groups operating on the extremes of German politics at this time. One of the most prominent was the *Stahlhelm*, named after the steel helmets worn by its members. This association of First World War veterans held militaristic rallies, was nationalistic and **monarchist**, and actively sought physical confrontation with Communist Party (KPD) supporters.

In this period the *Stahlhelm* was outside the formal party system but acted as a security service for the German National People's Party (*Deutschnationale Volkspartei*, DNVP), with whose right-wing views it was in sympathy. Some ex-soldiers joined a *Freikorps* group such as the *Freikorps Hülsen* (Figure 1.7). These various volunteer militias, formed largely of ex-soldiers and led by former army officers, together numbered more than 250 000 men in 1919. Relations between these groups, the army and thus the government were close.

Key term

Monarchist: political point of view or party believing in monarch e.g. a king being head of state or head of government

Figure 1.7: *Freikorps* recruitment poster. The caption reads: 'Protect your Homeland! Join the Freikorps Hülsen'.

The army itself had declared its willingness to offer conditional support. The Ebert–Groener Pact dated from as early as 10 November 1918, when the Kaiser had barely crossed the Dutch border, revolutionary crowds were cheering Liebknecht, and Ebert was still hoping to debate the future shape of German politics in the Reichstag. However, the author of the pact, Groener, resigned from his post and from the army in September 1919, although Ebert tried to persuade him to stay on. The *Freikorps* were still less predictable than the army. They were not centralised. They might be depended on to supplement the army's interventions. But the army–*Freikorps* combination was a major force in German polity and it was not clear that the government was fully its master. Their loyalties would only become clear as different crises of political order arose. And, in a series of crises in which the army and *Freikorps* paramilitary groups responded to a number of outbreaks

Figure 1.8: Hermann Ehrhardt and his *Freikorps* Brigade, Berlin, March 1920.

Key terms

Coup: French word meaning 'blow'; the attempt to change government by force rather than persuasion; putsch.

Putsch: An attempt to change government by violence rather than democratic methods.

of disorder throughout December 1918, their actions ensured the survival of the Weimar Government.

Risings on the left and right

The Spartacist Revolt and the Bavarian Soviet

In January 1919, a small, radical political group, the Spartacus League (*Spartakusbund*), tried to spearhead a revolution. The revolutionaries, led by Rosa Luxemburg and Karl Liebknecht, called themselves 'Spartacists' after the gladiator Spartacus who led a slaves' revolt in ancient Rome. Luxemburg and Liebknecht had been on the radical wing of the SPD; Liebknecht had been the only member of the Reichstag to vote against funds for the continuation of the war, in December 1914. He and Luxemburg left the SPD in 1917 to form the Independent Social Democratic Party of Germany (USPD). The Spartacus League, though, was never an organised political party but rather a small group of revolutionary activists. On 8 January 1919 the insurgents had seized some key points in the city. Ebert called in a combination of the German army and *Freikorps* to suppress the uprising, which they did with considerable violence. By 15 January it was all over. Liebknecht and Luxemburg were captured by the *Freikorps* and shot.

Four months later, in May 1919, left-wing activists declared the Bavarian Soviet Republic, centred on the major city of Munich. This too was brutally suppressed, and again the government's agent in this was a combination of 30 000 army and *Freikorps* including the *Marinebrigade Ehrhardt*. This was a noted *Freikorps* group named after its leader Hermann Ehrhardt (see Figure 1.8). Again women and men thought to have been involved were summarily executed, usually by *Freikorps* units.

The political impact of the Kapp Putsch and the Ruhr Uprising

An attempted seizure of power in March 1920 in Berlin led by Wolfgang Kapp and General Walther von Lüttwitz gave the government's relationship with the army a far more severe test than had the Spartacists or the Bavarian Soviet. Kapp, a Prussian civil servant, was politically active as a prominent monarchist and nationalist. Lüttwitz broadly shared his political views.

Given that he was a serving army officer in charge of a key military group, his participation in this attempt to nullify the 1918–1919 revolution in Germany and destroy the Weimar Government was significant. As the **coup** leaders attempted to take over Berlin, the army, now commanded by General Hans von Seeckt, stood by for several days. Seeckt disobeyed a direct order from his superior the Minister of Defence Gustav Noske to suppress the uprising and sat firmly on the fence to await developments. This refusal to act forced the Weimar government to flee. Once again the Ehrhardt Brigade was active among the forces of repression (from a left-wing perspective) or defending order and the rule of law (from a right-wing perspective). Seeckt had little time for the Weimar Government, but wanted above all to preserve the reputation and unity of the army. However, the **putsch** lacked the popular support it needed to succeed. A general strike in Berlin brought the city to a standstill and the putsch fizzled out.

A direct result of the Kapp–Lüttwitz Putsch was an uprising in the Ruhr area in March and April 1920. In response to a call by the trade unions and Social Democrat members of the Weimar Government, the Ruhr Uprising took place in this key industrial area. There were strikes, marches and demonstrations. The response of the army and *Freikorps* units to events in the Ruhr contrasts tellingly with their actions in Berlin during the Kapp Putsch. While participants and leaders of the right-wing putsch were treated with notable leniency, the Ruhr Uprising was suppressed by the army and *Freikorps* with considerable brutality. The leaders were given death sentences and there were illegal summary executions as well.

Thematic link: authoritarianism and democracy

The assassinations of Walther Rathenau and Matthias Erzberger

Matthias Erzberger was a member of the Centre party and had signed the Armistice in November 1918. He served in the Scheidemann cabinet and following Scheidemann's resignation became deputy chancellor under Bauer. He had been wounded by an attacker in 1920, following a libel case against the right-wing (and **anti-Semitic**) DNVP's Karl Helfferich. Erzberger was a hate figure as a signatory to the armistice, and his tax reforms had done nothing to endear him to the right wing. The press had attacked him savagely.

The Ehrhardt Brigade had been banned after the Kapp Putsch of 1920 but had formed a secret group in their Bavarian hideout, the *Organisation Consul* (OC). On 26 August 1921 two OC members (ex-Navy officers and ex-members of the Ehrhardt Brigade) shot Erzberger in the Black Forest. Supporters then helped them leave Germany to avoid prosecution.

Their next target was Walther Rathenau, who had just negotiated the Treaty of Rapallo with the Soviet Union, enabling economic and political cooperation with a major Marxist power. Rathenau was a leading industrialist, writer and politician whose father, Emil Rathenau, had founded the electrical engineering company Allgemeine Elektricitäts-Gesellschaft (AEG), and he was a prominent Jewish businessman. He had run the War Raw Materials Department during the First World War. He was a founder of the German Democratic Party (*Deutsche Demokratische Partei*, DDP), a nationalist, but a liberal and a democrat. Rathenau was Foreign Minister in the second Joseph Wirth cabinet from early February 1922. His also being a wealthy and successful Jew made him a hate figure and a target. The treaty with the USSR only added to the attacks on him in the right-wing press. In late June 1922 he was assassinated by two ultranationalist extremists, again OC members, formerly part of the Ehrhardt Brigade.

Friedrich Ebert intended to stand in presidential elections that year, as Rathenau had been widely respected and the response to his assassination was that more people seemed to rally around the republic. Stresemann's advice was that the political situation was too unsettled for a campaign. Accordingly Ebert's term was extended by a two-thirds majority vote in the Reichstag. The extension itself would have been unconstitutional, but the majority vote met the demands of the

Key term

Anti-Semitic: hostile to Jews.

ACTIVITY 1.11

What do you think are the most significant aspects of the assassinations of Rathenau and Erzberger? Write down a set of bullet points of those things you think important. You might find it helpful to comment on things to do with the religion, ethnicity, social class, political party or group membership of the victims and of the assassins.

Article which specified how changes to or, as in this case, departures from the Constitution could be made.

The Hamburg Rising

After Berlin and Munich in 1919 and the Ruhr area in 1920, there were further left-wing attempts to seize power, but they were short-lived and supported by small numbers only. An example is the events in Hamburg in October 1923. Here, the regional Communist Party leadership was ordered to begin an uprising. The rebels attacked police stations in order to seize weapons. The membership of the local party was about 14 000 people; that only 300 of them took part in the supposed uprising says a great deal about the lack of unity of purpose. Nevertheless, that a body of sympathy existed in working-class districts for revolutionary action is shown by the fact that local people came out to help build barricades and to give the rebels food. The rebels held their positions for several hours before, realising the hopelessness of their position, they departed quietly, leaving the police to retake what were now undefended barricades. Estimates suggest that about 100 died, another 300 were injured and 1400 were arrested.

The political impact of the invasion of the Ruhr

All Allied occupations of areas of Germany were a continuous grievance for nationalists of all kinds, not just for the extremist political parties. When in January 1923 French and Belgian troops occupied the Ruhr region, there were protests locally and nationally. Since November 1922, the chancellor had been businessman Wilhelm Cuno, who led a coalition of the DDP, the German People's Party (*Deutsche Volkspartei*, DVP), the Centre and several economists who were not party members. His government's intention was to tackle inflation and the issue of reparations. The French and then Belgian invasions led the government to cease all payment of reparations to France and Belgium. Mine owners were ordered to deliver no more coal to either country. Civil servants were instructed to take no orders from the occupying forces. Having ordered a strike, the government had the job of paying the strikers. At a stroke they had created a new source of expense just when circumstances had deprived them of a source of income. Inflation went up (just what the government didn't want) and the value of the mark went down.

In August, the opposition SPD tabled a motion of no confidence while expressing its willingness to cooperate with a replacement government. This time the president invited Gustav Stresemann of the DVP to form a coalition. In addition to his own party the DVP, the DDP and the Centre (all of whom had been represented in the non-party Cuno cabinet), Stresemann included the SPD and two independents. The French and Belgian troops' occupation of the Ruhr area gave additional energy to the development of nationalist politics and contributed significantly to the growth of political extremism. Centre-right political parties such as the Catholic Centre Party and the DVP moved to the right and divided into factions. Further to their right, conservatives had already formed an umbrella group in 1922, the United Patriotic Associations of Germany (*Vereinigte Vaterländische Verbände Deutschlands*, VVVD). With over 130 member organisations, the VVVD was intended to coordinate right-wing political activities with the aim of overturning both the Treaty of Versailles and the Weimar Constitution. The events of 1923 boosted its appeal and it continued in existence for another ten years, withering away eventually due to inadequate resources but also due to the National Socialist German Workers' Party (*Nationalsozialistische Deutsche Arbeiterpartei*, NSDAP) increasingly becoming the vehicle for right-wing political aspirations.

Nationalist groups were angered by the presence of foreign troops on German soil, and public opinion in general was outraged at this latest national humiliation. In particular, newspapers carried stories of rapes and murders carried out by black soldiers. The allegations were particularly directed at Senegalese *Tirailleurs* (infantry) who were recruited from all over French colonial territories in west Africa, not just Senegal, and who formed a significant part of French occupation forces after 1919. This propaganda was picked up by most of the political parties and had the effect of inflaming nationalist sentiment in Germany still further. The fact that some local women married black French soldiers and others had affairs with them suggests a rather different situation.

The invasion also had consequences abroad, not that Belgium or France paid much attention to this. Splits between the victorious Allies now became clearer. France and Belgium, who had suffered so much in the First World War, continued to take a hard line over Germany. However, Germany won a degree of sympathy in Britain and the USA. The British Labour Party condemned the French and Belgian action, denouncing what it called 'French imperialism' and blaming an unduly vengeful and short-sighted public mood in France and Belgium. In the USA, further away from the conflict, there was a greater emphasis on the need to build a strong, peaceful and democratic Germany in the best interests of all. A plan for tackling the German economic crisis became easier to sell to the American public: formulated by a committee headed by US banker Charles Dawes, it offered substantial loans and deferral of reparations payments (we will examine this in the next chapter).

In September 1923, the decision of the Stresemann government to wind down opposition to the Ruhr occupation itself led to a right-wing attempted putsch in Spandau and Küstrin, fortresses near Berlin. Soldiers whose association with the armed forces was concealed, because their actions were illegal under the Treaty of Versailles, rebelled with the aim of bringing down the government and installing a military dictatorship. Members of the regular army moved in and arrested the leadership of the rebellion. It was all over quickly and most of the rebels were released. An amnesty was agreed and punishments were minimal or nonexistent. A further and more famous putsch attempt took place two months later in Munich.

The Munich Putsch

With French and Belgian troops in the Ruhr area of North Rhein–Westphalia, and unrest and disorder in Munich as elsewhere in Bavaria, the Bavarian Prime Minister declared a state of emergency at the end of September 1923. The Bavarian state government was in the hands of the monarchist Bavarian People's Party (*Bayerische Volkspartei*, BVP) and resented the political complexion (and indeed existence) of the federal government. The disorders of the time were a handy excuse to impose martial law. An activist had briefly seized power in Munich on hearing news of the Kapp Putsch in Berlin. This was the context of uncertainty in which the NSDAP attempted to seize power by force.

On demobilisation from the defeated Bavarian army in 1919, Austrian-born Corporal Adolf Hitler was used by the military to keep an eye on some of the many politically extreme groups that were being formed all over Germany at this time. Hitler's patch was Munich, a hotbed of both left- and right-wing political extremism. His spying duties took him to the meetings of a small political group who met for discussions in various beer halls, the German Workers' Party (DAP). He became interested in the ideas he heard discussed and occasionally he spoke himself. He was an effective speaker with a magnetic effect on his audience. He joined in 1919; the size of the party at this time is indicated by the fact that Hitler became its 55th member. The following year the party added the words 'national socialist' to its name, becoming the National Socialist German Workers' Party (NSDAP). The NSDAP was highly critical of many aspects of the Weimar Republic. Although small, it had the support of retired army general Erich Ludendorff, hero of the First World War, and others holding ultraconservative and monarchist views. For them, the *Dolchstoss* theory was a strong motivational force.

 Voices from the past

George Grosz's friend, Klaus

The artist George Grosz had a school friend called Klaus who had evidently become a teacher by the 1920s. His attitude to French black colonial soldiers is revealing, and so is the way he influenced his class in the Ruhr in 1923:

Day after day I had to suffer the sight of French black troops marching from the one-time garrison city of

Diez to their training place at Altendiez. ... I taught the children under my care never so much as to look at these black fighters. If, by chance, they happened to pass by the school during recess, teachers and pupils would turn their backs and remain standing like pillars of salt. [11]

Discussion point
What light does this source cast on attitudes to the Ruhr occupation, the occupation of the Rhineland, and the Treaty of Versailles?

Figure 1.9: Adolf Hitler's DAP membership card.

Although small and little known outside Bavaria at this point, early in November 1923 the NSDAP and its now leader Hitler decided to attempt an armed insurrection in Munich to take advantage of the outrage among the German population, and especially among extremist groups, caused by the occupation of the Ruhr. Perhaps the NSDAP members were inspired by the so-called 'March on Rome' in 1922 of Benito Mussolini and the Italian Fascists, in some ways their Italian counterparts. In any case, in November 1923, after rallying in a *Bierkeller* (beer hall), Hitler, Ludendorff and their supporters took to the streets in what is sometimes called the Beer Hall Putsch.

There were just a few hundred armed NSDAP members. Hitler and his followers were easily arrested by Bavarian police and army units loyal to the Weimar Government. Sixteen NSDAP members and four Bavarian policemen were killed. The putsch failed and over a couple of days, police and loyal army units rounded up the leaders. The 1923 Munich Putsch might not have seemed of major significance at the time; subsequent events have elevated its importance to historians. Hitler was arrested and put on trial for armed insurrection. For the first time the failed coup attempt and the well-publicised trial brought him a degree of national fame.

Hitler feared that the outcome of the trial would mean deportation back to his native Austria, but the judge at his trial for treason declared that anyone 'who thinks and feels like a German' should remain in the country. Hitler was therefore fined 500 Reichsmarks and sentenced to five years in prison. In fact, because of some time already spent on remand, he had just eight months left in rather comfortable imprisonment in the fortress of Landsberg am Lech before his release for good behaviour. He spent his time receiving visitors and working on his memoirs entitled *Mein Kampf* (My Struggle).

The leniency of Hitler's treatment and the sympathy of many in the army underlines the degree of support for nationalist and autocratic government that still existed in Germany in 1923. The NSDAP had powerful friends in Bavaria and in the army, and Ludendorff was still popular among nationalists. This leniency was among the reasons for the fall of the Stresemann federal government. The SPD contrasted the response of the government to treasonable left-wing activism in Thuringia and Saxony with its response to treasonable right-wing activism in Bavaria.

 Thematic link: survival of social elites and conservative forces in Germany

---

 Voices from the past

Adolf Hitler

As his trial at the People's Court in Munich in 1924 came to an end, Hitler made the following address to the court:

I aimed from the first at something a thousand times higher than being a minister. I wanted to become the destroyer of Marxism. I am going to achieve this task and, if I do, the title of minister will be an absurdity as far as I am concerned. …

At one time I believed that perhaps this battle against Marxism could be carried on with the help of the government. In January, 1923, I learned that that was just not possible. The hypothesis for the victory of Marxism is not that Germany must be free, but rather Germany will only be free when Marxism is broken. At that time I did not dream that our movement would become great and cover Germany like a flood.

The army that we are building grows from day to day, from hour to hour. Right at this moment I have the proud hope that once the hour strikes these wild troops will merge into battalions, battalions into regiments, regiments into divisions. I have hopes that the old cockade will be lifted from the dirt, that the old colours will be unfurled to flutter again, that expiation will come before the tribunal of God.

Then from our bones and from our graves will speak the voice of the only tribunal which has the right to sit in justice over us.

Then, gentlemen, not you will be the ones to deliver the verdict over us, but that verdict will be given by the eternal judgment of history, which will speak out against the accusation that has been made against us. I know what your judgment will be. But that other court will not ask us: Have you committed high treason or not? That court will judge us, their quartermaster-general of the old army, its officers and soldiers, who as Germans wanted only the best for their people and Fatherland, who fought and who were willing to die. You might just as well find us guilty a thousand times, but the goddess of the eternal court of history will smile and tear up the motions of the state's attorney and the judgment of this court: for she finds us not guilty.

Discussion points

1. Summarise what Hitler is saying. What do you think are his key messages?
2. 'The Munich Putsch had no effect on the Weimar Republic and contributed nothing to the rise of the NSDAP. Far more important was Hitler's trial.' To what extent do you agree?

Problems of coalition government and the state of the republic by 1924

Many of those with power and authority were not natural allies of the Social Democrats; some were more likely to pay attention to the SPD's partners in government. Ebert's cabinet, the first government of the republic, was SPD-led, but it was a coalition with the more radical USPD. Although the SPD was the largest party in the Reichstag, it had no absolute majority. Its relationship with its coalition partner the USPD experienced both political and personal strains and was not built to last. Scheidemann's cabinet brought in the **liberals** of the DDP and the Centre party, which at this stage occupied the conservative centre ground of German politics (it would later become more right-wing).

This coalition was clearly less left-wing than the government that had managed the constitutional crises of 1918. The Bauer administration that followed Scheidemann's resignation maintained an SPD–DDP–Centre coalition, as did the Müller administration.

The SPD had never held power before and despite involvement in Prince Maximilian's cabinet had little experience of government or of taking responsibility for basic services or responding to strikes. In addition, there were conflicts of priorities and political programmes. Trade unions expected the government to increase social welfare and intervene to support workers. Industrialists wanted as little government interference as possible. Some on the left wanted to see land reform, but landowners opposed this as it directly and adversely affected them. All of these groups had representatives in the Reichstag, and sometimes in government.

One of the areas in which left-wing and centre-left parties made themselves unpopular with some of society's more powerful people was taxation. Those on the centre-left of German politics wanted to see some redistribution of wealth in society, achieved through the tax system. In July 1919, the DDP's Erzberger, serving in the Bauer cabinet (he had previously served in the Scheidemann cabinet) put through the Reichstag a reform of the tax system. One aspect of this was a lighter tax burden on households with lower incomes. In addition, the government raised more money from those with higher incomes, wealth and inheritance. December 1919 saw additional taxation of wealth, as did March 1920. These steps did nothing to make the government popular with the better-off, the influential and powerful.

In June 1920, the Republic had its first Centre party chancellor, Konstantin Fehrenbach, and for the first time the SPD found itself in opposition. Fehrenbach's cabinet had members from both his own Centre party and the DDP, both parties being veterans of coalition with the SPD. He introduced others from the DVP. This changed the flavour from centre-left to centre-right; the DVP was a liberal party and favoured the return of the monarchy. After Fehrenbach, Joseph Wirth's first administration retained the Centre and DDP, brought the SPD back into government and omitted the DVP. His second cabinet introduced one member from the regional agrarian Bavarian Farmers' League (*Bayerischer Bauernbund*, BB), which was right of centre in its views. The parties of the two Stresemann

Key term

Liberals: a 19th-century reform movement which emphasised free trade and a process of constitutional political change.

cabinets were the DVP, SPD, DDP and Centre, and the first two governments of Wilhelm Marx continued to draw on these parties, although omitting the SPD.

So, there were several consistent features of these coalitions in this period. First, Governments were not long-lasting: Stresemann, for example, was chancellor for three months; halfway through he resigned and was asked to form a new administration. This gave the impression that the country was not being properly and authoritatively governed. Second, the Centre party was continuously in government. The Centre was essentially a middle-ground party: it could form agreements with both left and right. In addition, its priorities included looking after Roman Catholic Church affairs, including church schools.

These were matters on which other parties were largely willing to cooperate, as they were not matters of left–right disagreement. Accordingly several parties could work successfully with the Centre. Although there appear to be numerous changes of chancellor and government, the changes were not always as great as they appear. There was a high degree of continuity both of individuals and policies: although the deck was often shuffled, the cards remained the same. This might have helped build the feeling that, despite democratic elections, the voters were not able to put a government into office nor vote it out of office. There was thus a disconnect between the electors and the elected.

These parties of government (notably the DVP, SPD, DDP and Centre) shared a fear of violent disorder. For all of them, security was paramount and German streets must be kept peaceful. Some historians argue that this fear alone would have been strong enough for them to be willing to support the suppression of any armed threat to the Republic by the police, army and *Freikorps*, whether or not Chancellor Ebert and General Groener had made a deal in 1918. The tendency of parties was to find allies within the centre ground. Because some parties, including the KPD on the left and the DNVP and NSDAP on the right, were fundamentally opposed to the underlying political values of the Republic, it was largely impossible for them to participate in coalition governments. As a result, the left–right debates which are characteristic of most democracies were permanently undermined. The KPD, tutored by Moscow, treated the SPD as a right-wing party and later (in the 1930s) dubbed them 'social fascists'.

Right-wing parties such as the DNVP and the NSDAP denounced social democracy and persisted with the *Dolchstoss* version of the November 1918 surrender by the German army. By attacking social democracy, they were attacking the republic itself. The NSDAP fought the SPD and KPD in the streets as well as at elections. Meanwhile, the leniency of the army and courts to the right-wing extremists' attempts to seize power in the 1920 Kapp Putsch and the 1923 Munich Putsch, contrasted with the ferocity with which the 1919 Spartacist Uprising or the 1920 Ruhr Uprising were suppressed, reveals just how half-hearted their support for the Weimar Republic was. The economic instability of the Republic had also been demonstrated by the problems of inflation and hyperinflation. The Ruhr occupation and the continued rule of the Saarland by France under the terms of the Treaty of Versailles demonstrated that the Republic was unable to control its borders and defend its territory. In this, it had failed a basic test of government.

 Key term

Roman Catholic Church: member of largest of the Christian churches with administrative centre in Rome.

Timeline

1918	
January	Germany signed Treaty of Brest–Litovsk with Russia
September	General Ludendorff informed Paul von Hintze, Foreign Minister, Western Front might collapse at any time; von Hertling resigned the chancellorship, replaced by Prince Maximilian von Baden
October	Imperial Navy's High Seas fleet confronted the blockading Royal Navy fleet; mutinies and strikes; Prince Maximilian von Baden appointed chancellor, SPD joined cabinet; constitution changed, political power moved to Reichstag
7 November	Ebert demanded increased role in the government for SPD and further reform; calls for Emperor and crown prince to renounce throne; King of Bavaria abdicated
8 November	Kings and princes deposed
9 November	Prince Maximilian handed over the chancellorship to Ebert; Kaiser Wilhelm II's abdication announced; resignation of Chancellor Prince Maximilian von Baden; Ebert became chancellor; Scheidemann proclaimed a republic; Liebknecht proclaimed a Free Socialist Republic
10 November	Ebert formed government of his SPD and USPD; imperial family went into exile; Ebert–Groener telephone call
11 November	Ceasefire on Western Front
December	Spartacus League split from USPD
1918–1919	Influenza pandemic
1919	
January	Victorious Allies met at Versailles
4–15 January	Spartacist Uprising in Berlin
19 January	Federal elections in which SPD won nearly 38% of votes casted
January	Constitutional Convention began in Weimar
February	Resignation of Ebert as chancellor, appointment of Scheidemann by President Ebert
April	German delegation summoned to Paris; Bavarian Soviet Republic declared in Munich
May	Scheidemann opposed draft Versailles Treaty; Bavarian Soviet Republic ended by army and *Freikorps*
June	Treaty of Versailles signed; North Sea blockade lifted; Scheidemann resignedas chancellor, replaced by Gustav Bauer
August	President Ebert signed Weimar Constitution into law

1920	
March	Kapp–Lüttwitz Putsch in Berlin; Ruhr Uprising; Bauer replaced as chancellor by Hermann Müller
June	Federal elections; resignation of Müller as chancellor, replaced by Constantin Fehrenbach
1921	
May	Fehrenbach replaced as chancellor by Joseph Wirth
June	Inflation became severe
August	Erzberger assassinated
1922	
April	Germany signed Treaty of Rapallo with Russia
June	Assassination of Foreign Minister Walther Rathenau
November	Wirth replaced as chancellor by Wilhelm Cuno
December	Reparations Commission declared Germany in default
1923	
January	Germany found to have defaulted on its reparation; French troops invaded and occupied the Ruhr
August	Wilhelm Cuno replaced as chancellor by Gustav Stresemann
September	Bavarian Prime Minister declared state of emergency
October	Stresemann announced end of resistance to occupation of the Ruhr and state of emergency; hyperinflation reached 29 500%
November	Munich Putsch; Stresemann replaced as chancellor by Wilhelm Marx; Hjalmar Schacht appointed currency commissioner, later president of Reichsbank; Crown Prince Wilhelm visited Germany
1924	
January	Marx declared state of emergency, issued decree replacing trial by jury with trained and lay judges (Emminger Reform); end of hyperinflation
February	Start of Hitler's trial following Munich Putsch
March	Reichstag sought to discuss abolition of decrees; Ebert dismissed parliament to avoid discussion
May	Federal elections
June	Marx formed second cabinet
August	Dawes Committee produced proposals; Monetary Law allowed the exchange of one trillion mark note for one new Reichsmark
December	Federal elections; resignation of Marx; Hans Luther formed government; Hitler released from prison

Practice essay questions

1. 'Ebert created a democratic government for Weimar Germany only by relying in undemocratic elements.' Assess the validity of this view.
2. 'The payment of reparations was the most damaging requirement the Treaty of Versailles placed on Germany.' Assess the validity of this view.
3. To what extent did the hyperinflation have a detrimental effect on the lives of Germans in 1923?
4. With reference to the sources below and your understanding of the historical context, assess the value of these three sources to an historian studying the problems faced by the Weimar governments in the years 1918 to 1924?

Source A

From Hitler's speech in court in 1924 following the Munich Putsch, *Der Hitler-Prozess vor dem Volksgericht in Muenchen*, Part 2 Munich 1924 (translated in Noakes, J. and Pridham, G., *Nazism 1919–1945, Volume 1*).

The army that we are building grows from day to day, from hour to hour. Right at this moment I have the proud hope that once the hour strikes these wild troops will merge into battalions, battalions into regiments, regiments into divisions. I have hopes that the old cockade will be lifted from the dirt, that the old colours will be unfurled to flutter again, that expiation will come before the tribunal of God. Then from our bones and from our graves will speak the voice of the only tribunal which has the right to sit in justice over us.

Source B

Proclamation of the Workers' and Soldiers' Council, Kiel, 7 November 1918, *Zur Geschichte der Kieler Arbeiterbewegung, Gesellschaft fuer Kieler Stadtgerichte*, Kiel, 1983 (translated in Stackelberg R. and Winkle, S.A., *The Nazi Germany Sourcebook*).

Political power lies in our hands. A provisional provincial government will be formed, which will construct a new order in cooperation with the exiting authorities. Our goal is a free, social people's republic. Where workers' and soldiers' councils do not yet exist, we call on the population of the city and the countryside to follow our example and close ranks behind the new people's government and support its work for public welfare.

Source C

Proclamation of Wolfgang Kapp, 1920 (in Lee, S.J., *Europe 1890–1945*).

Empire and nation are in grave danger. We are speedily approaching the total collapse of the state and legal system. The people only vaguely sense the coming disaster. Prices soar without stopping. Misery is growing. Famine threatens. … The ineffective government, lacking authority and tied to corruption, is not capable of mastering the danger. … Militant Bolshevism threatens us with devastation and violation from the east. Is this government capable of fending it off?

Chapter summary

By the end of this chapter you should understand:

- the way in which Weimar Germany came into existence
- the context of the First World War, and the significance of the competing attempts to create a new kind of state
- the way in which the war ended, and the political implications of the different interpretations of those events being offered at the time
- how after four years of war, there were mutinies, food shortages and revolutionary committees, attempts to democratise and negotiations for a ceasefire
- that the Kaiser abdicated, a Social Democratic government formed; the government agreed with the army to maintain law and order; a committee drew up a new constitution, elections were held and a coalition government was formed
- that the Treaty of Versailles gave various parts of Germany to other countries, blamed Germany for the war breaking out, and ordered it to pay reparations, and that these terms brought widespread protest, but Germany had to accept them
- that German governments taxed richer people more and poorer people less, and provided improved social welfare
- how hyperinflation made all economic policy hard to pursue, left many people poorer than they had been, and took time to get under control
- how several attempts to seize power through political violence were put down by the army, Freikorps and police, and how left-wing rebellions were treated violently while right-wing ones were treated sympathetically
- the precipitation of strikes, an uprising and an increase in popularity of nationalist parties by the Franco-Belgian invasion of the Ruhr.

End notes

1 Meyer, G.J., *A World Undone*.
2 In Horne, Charles F., ed, *Source Records of the Great War Vol. VI* (National Alumni, 1923).
3 Berghahn, V.R., *Modern Germany*.
4 Haffner, S., *Die verratene Revolution – Deutschland 1918/19* (Hamburg: Stern-Buch, 1969).
5 Evans, R.J., *The Coming of the Third Reich*.
6 Weitz, E.D., *Weimar Germany*.
7 Shirer, W., *The Rise and Fall of the Third Reich*.
8 Feldman, G.D. *The Great Disorder*.
9 Grosz, G., *A Little Yes and a Big No* (New York: Dial Press, 1946)
10 Peukert, D., *The Weimar Republic*.
11 Abel, T., *Why Hitler Came into Power*.

2 The 'Golden Age' of the Weimar Republic, 1924–1928

In this section, we will examine the situation of Weimar Germany after it had recovered from its turbulent early period. We will consider the stabilising factors in the economy, investigate how well its political system was working, and learn about governments' domestic and foreign policies. We will examine the flourishing culture of the period. We will look into:

- economic developments: Stresemann; the Dawes Plan; industry, agriculture and the extent of recovery; the reparations issue and the Young Plan

- social developments: social welfare reforms; the development of Weimar culture; art, architecture, music, theatre, literature, film; living standards and lifestyles

- political developments and the workings of democracy: President Hindenburg; parties; elections, and attitudes to the Republic from the elites and other social groups; the positions of the extremists, including the Nazis and Communists; the extent of political stability

- Germany's international position: Stresemann's foreign policy aims and achievements including: Locarno, the League of Nations, the Treaty of Berlin, the end of Allied occupation and the pursuit of disarmament.

Economic developments

Stresemann

In the period 1924–1929, the economy of the Weimar Republic stabilised and even experienced modest growth. In the international field, Germany managed to regain its position to a remarkable extent. The key figure in these developments was Gustav Stresemann. Although Stresemann was chancellor for only a few months in 1923, he was foreign minister in every government from 1923 to 1929. He was an effective politician whose conservatism enjoyed fairly wide support.

Stresemann came from a lower-middle-class background in Berlin. He was the youngest of seven children; his father bottled and distributed beer. Gustav did, however, receive an excellent education. He spent time at the University of Berlin and then became active in politics in the state of Saxony, becoming a member of the Reichstag in 1907. Declared unfit for the army in 1914, he became leader of the National Liberal Party in 1917 and went on to help found the German Peoples' Party in 1919, becoming its chairman.

The Dawes Plan

When faced with a major crisis in Germany regarding reparations, the **Reparations Commission** turned to US banker Charles G. Dawes to find an answer. A committee was formed, consisting of two members each from France, Belgium, Britain, Italy and the USA, and chaired by Dawes. Their task was to find a workable plan that would ensure that Germany resumed reparations payments and calm the disturbed situation in Germany at the time.

In August 1924, the Dawes Committee put forward its plan. The main provisions of the Plan were:

1. Evacuation of the Ruhr by Allied troops.
2. Rescheduling of reparations payments starting with one billion marks in the first year rising to two and a half billion marks by year five.
3. Reorganisation of the Reichsbank (the German central bank) under Allied supervision.

Germany had little choice but to agree.

The Dawes Plan was put into effect from September 1924. It relied heavily on the offer by a consortium of US banks led by the Morgan Guaranty Trust Company, under the supervision of the US State Department, to loan Germany 800 million marks, enough to allow it to resume reparations payments and to stabilise the economy. The repayment schedule required of Germany was set at a very high level. The plan did provide short-term economic benefits to Germany, but it made the German economy heavily reliant on foreign markets and economies. Britain and France had their own debts to the USA. As a result, money flowed from Germany to the European allies and then on to the USA in two sets of repayments. This movement of money meant that the economic connections between the Western European economies and that of the USA became even tighter. The consequences were to become disastrously clear five years later.

Key term

Reparations Commission: In accordance with Articles 231–235 of the Treaty of Versailles, the Reparation Commission was directed to estimate damage done by Germany to Allied civilians and their property during the First World War and to formulate methods of collecting assessments.

Gustav Stresemann

Initially the DVP was seen as the opposition to the Social Democrats and to the Weimar Republic itself. Stresemann's own position was a somewhat ambivalent one. Although he himself had moved sharply to the right during and after the war, endorsing popular anger at the terms of the Treaty of Versailles and making no secret of his monarchist sympathies, he became prepared to work with the Weimar government for the time being, if only to free Germany from foreign occupation. As he put it to the exiled Crown Prince:

"First we must remove the strangler from our throat."

In this spirit he accepted the posts of chancellor and foreign minister of the coalition government in August 1923. Stresemann saw the solution to Germany's problems as combining domestic- and foreign-policy initiatives. Currency reform at home was imperative. But the relationship with Germany's neighbours, especially the Allies, also needed to improve, not least because war reparations were part of the economic problem, and the solution lay not in Germany's hands but in the Allies'. At home, the short-lived Stresemann governments, which included members from the SPD, DDP and Centre as well as Stresemann's own DVP, introduced into industrial relations a process of arbitration. Abroad, Stresemann worked to build a new set of treaties to normalise as far as possible the diplomatic situation.[1]

Hjalmar Schacht

Much of the responsibility for implementing the Dawes Plan fell to an economist called Hjalmar Schacht (see Figure 2.1). Schacht was not an apolitical bureaucrat. He had helped found the German Democratic Party in 1918. He was as bitter about reparations as anyone else in Germany. In November 1923 he had been appointed currency commissioner by President Friedrich Ebert, supported by Chancellor Gustav Stresemann, and had established the new interim currency, the Rentenmark, based on the mortgage of all German property. His success led to his appointment as President of the Reichsbank that same month, a post he retained until March 1931. Schacht was the representative figure in economic matters of the period 1924–1928 in Germany, sometimes called Weimar's 'Golden Age', a period of relative economic stability if not growth. His was a steady economic hand and a reassuring presence at the head of the Reichsbank for the Weimar government. He restored Germany's international reputation for financial control and he did this by keeping a very tight rein on money supply. He introduced a range of measures designed to stabilise the monetary position. Schacht believed that printing of money as a means of easing a monetary crisis had been a major factor in the hyperinflation of 1923. There was to be no more of it. Lending had encouraged speculators and contributed to business bankruptcies in Germany in 1923. Now there were strict controls on lending by banks and other institutions.

The huge US loan provided by the Dawes Plan of 1924 allowed much-needed investment in infrastructure and in the German economy generally. It underpinned

ACTIVITY 2.1

Divide a page vertically into two. In the left-hand column write the economic problems facing Germany in 1924. On the right, write down the proposals in the Dawes Plan. On this basis, how effective would you expect the Dawes Plan to be?

Schacht's reforms and reassured the international financial markets. In August 1924 the interim Rentenmark was replaced by the Reichsmark as the German currency. These were major changes for the German economy. Schacht was ruthless in applying the new rules restricting credit and the supply of money. As a result, the number of companies going bankrupt in Germany rose sharply from 233 in 1923 to over 6000 in 1924 as the new rules began to bite and poorly managed or inefficient businesses were no longer able to survive. Unemployment rose and people's spending power was sharply reduced. Such outcomes are usually highly unpopular among the general public, but so grim had been the hyperinflation of 1923 that most were prepared to accept the new measures.

Schacht recognised that German industry had to become more efficient and productive. In 1926 he was instrumental in persuading five of Germany's largest chemical companies, including BASF, Hoechst and Bayer, to merge, forming an industrial giant, IG Farben. This was achieved largely through providing the necessary funding. In its day the company was the largest chemical conglomerate and fourth largest industrial concern in the world (the others were all American). The company was a major employer in Germany. In the short term Schacht's measures did much to establish economic stability. By 1927 the cost of living had fallen, wages had increased in real terms and the government of the day felt sufficiently economically secure to introduce income guarantees as part of welfare legislation. New roads were built, as were schools and public buildings.

Industry

During the revolution of November 1918, employers' organisations and trade unions had succeeded in negotiating an agreement. Employers recognised the right of trade unions to represent the views of the workers and negotiate pay settlements. As a result, trade unions backed away from earlier demands for nationalisation and workers' control of industry. During the same period, membership of trade unions shot up. This went some way to stabilise the world of urban work. Meanwhile, as the terms of the Treaty of Versailles removed several regions from Germany, the German domestic market suddenly shrank. As well as losing about an eighth of its geographical area, the country lost about 20% of the coal, iron and steel industry and 6–7% of the processing of raw materials industry. The invasion of the Ruhr area had removed an important industrial area from governmental control.

Over time, Franco–German economic and political relations gradually improved. The 1925 evacuation of the occupying troops from the Ruhr helped in this process. The following year the two countries signed an agreement on potash and formed an aluminium cartel. Representatives of heavy industry in Germany and France were joined by those of Luxembourg and Belgium for an agreement on raw materials. However, the world economic context was not favourable. Across Europe the population had fallen, which meant that the market had shrunk. New competitors, notably Japan, were able to undercut German's manufacturers. Germany was not producing as much and was not exporting as much as it had done before the war.

With the economy stabilised, or at least apparently stabilising, the agreements hammered out in 1918–1919 came into question. Employers argued that they were restrictive and undermined efficiency, productivity and, thus, prosperity. During the mid to late 1920s, the length of the working day (which had been settled as eight hours) and the role of the trade unions (which had been agreed as the voice for collective bargaining) were both challenged. Employers succeeded in removing the force of law from the eight-hour day; it remained the norm, but longer days became possible. A DVP–SPD–DDP–Centre coalition introduced into industrial relations a process of arbitration. In the case of strikes, an outside arbitrator would come in to listen to both sides and then issue a binding ruling by which both sides had to abide or be in breach of the law. The intention was to restore peace to the German economy, in which the currency chaos had undermined employer–employee relationships. From being a rarity, government intervention became the norm. Eberhard Kolbe suggested that this indicates that employer–employee relations had deteriorated and the two sides' attitudes had hardened.[3] In 1923, decisions tended to favour employers; from 1924 they took a more middle line. As trade unions were growing weaker, the arbitration process became a protection for employees and as such a cause of resentment by employers.

November and December 1928 saw the Ruhr Ironworks dispute, perhaps the most famous industrial dispute in the history of Weimar Germany. The employers rejected the ruling of the arbitrators and locked out 220 000 workers. This was a stand against organised labour, but also against the authority of the federal government. A compromise was reached, but it took time, and the experience left industrialists less convinced that the Weimar Republic could be trusted with the economy.

Krupp

Krupp AG is a German steel firm specialising in armaments. Its experiences help us understand the industrial situation in Weimar Germany's 'Golden Age'. Krupp AG was one of the largest employers in Germany. The main factory was located in Essen in the Ruhr region, the industrial powerhouse of Weimar Germany and the area occupied by French and Belgian troops from 1923 to 1925. Krupp had been the main manufacturer and supplier of armaments to the **Reichswehr**, the German armed forces, in the First World War: the large mortars used to bombard frontier fortresses in Belgium and France in 1914 were made by the company.

It switched to peacetime production in 1918, including railway engine and carriage manufacture. Its motto was '*Wir machen alles*' (We make everything). After the First World War, the firm sacked 70 000 workers, many of them women, but with generous severance pay and the provision of good welfare services, including a war veterans' dental hospital.

Bertha Krupp had inherited ownership of the company on the death of her father Friedrich and was the sole proprietor from 1902 to 1943. However, it was unusual for a woman to be in such a position, and Kaiser Wilhelm II suggested that she marry Gustav von Bohlen und Halbach, a diplomat from a family of East Prussian nobility. Gustav Krupp von Bohlen und Halbach (as he became on his marriage in 1906) was a monarchist, a conservative and a determined opponent of the Treaty

ACTIVITY 2.2

What do the stories of Gustav Krupp and Krupp AG tell us about the situation in Germany 1924–1928? List some details that you think are significant and comment briefly on them.

As you progress further in working with this book, revisit this list and add further comments, linking the details you have highlighted to the topics you are studying, notably developments in society, the economic situation and politics, and Germany's international context.

of Versailles. He ran the company from 1909, throughout the Weimar period and most of the Nazi period, until retiring owing to poor health in 1943.

Neither Gustav nor Bertha Krupp were supporters of the republic. However, Gustav was a believer in proper social and political order, so he worked with the Weimar government and treated President Ebert with the respect due to his office. At the same time he worked in secret with the Reichswehr to evade the restrictions placed by the Treaty of Versailles on German military development, designing and manufacturing new weapons for them including tanks and artillery. In 1921 and 1922 he bought companies in Sweden and the Netherlands to manufacture arms for neutral countries. In common with much German industry, Krupp AG did well enough in the period 1924–1928. Arms were openly designed for and sold to neutral countries and were secretly produced for the Reichswehr.

Gustav Krupp became a national hero in 1923 when he arranged a lavish funeral for some victims of the French occupation of the Ruhr. He was tried and imprisoned by the French. From 1921 to 1933 he was a member of the Prussian State Council. The Krupps were part of the established elite of Germany, and their power and influence in German society, economy and politics under the Kaiser, during the republic and then under the Nazis (and later too) says something about the ability of the ruling class – the upper leadership of the armed forces, senior members of the judiciary, the landowners and industrialists – to survive change and prosper.

Agriculture

Germany's agriculture had been hit hard by the First World War. It was heavily dependent on manure as fertiliser, and the drastic wartime reduction in livestock herds left farms short of this resource. After the war there was a shortage of fodder, so increasing the herd size was something that could only be done slowly. Imported fodder and fertiliser helped with these twin problems, but imports only increased slowly and both added to costs. A combination of the use of artificial fertilisers (made by the new, German-invented Haber–Bosch process) and the slow growth in the number of animals meant that production gradually crept up. In addition to the war itself, poor harvests in 1916 and 1917 had reduced dairy and meat production. As the war ended, the country was only producing 50% of pre-war butter and 60% of pre-war meat quantities. The land losses that came as a consequence of the Treaty of Versailles also meant that Germany lost about 15% of its pre-war agricultural production.

The agricultural sector was impoverished by a severe drop in prices in 1921. Less affected than industry by the period of hyperinflation, farmers were hit again in 1925–1926 when a global grain surplus caused prices to plummet. While imports of fodder and fertiliser helped farmers, they were harmed by imports of food, as these came in at prices too low for them to compete. The obvious solution, to modernise and improve productivity, was easier said than done: change is usually expensive in the short term even if it pays dividends in the longer term. In agriculture, change meant investing in farm machinery such as tractors, but this was a mixed blessing for, although it increased productivity, it did so at the cost of lower rural employment. Farmers often had to borrow money to buy technology, and sometimes lost their farms if they failed to repay their debts. In 1928 farmers held several demonstrations against these foreclosures and the low prices they were receiving for their products. These demonstrations tipped over into riots.

The tendency of governments to respond to rural problems by providing subsidies to the agricultural sector was politically and socially understandable. But it increased government expenditure without increasing productivity. Another policy, of introducing protectionist **tariffs**, protected farmers but hit consumers. By the later 1920s, German agricultural production was increasing, but even in 1929, it was still at less than three-quarters of its pre-war levels.

The extent of recovery

The period between 1924 and 1929 was more settled economically than the one that preceded it in Germany. However, even with the recovery, there were economic problems. The manic economic activity of the inflationary period was followed by a slowdown that hit some companies particularly hard. The insatiable demand for goods on which to spend the vast excess of *Papiermarken* ended when the latter were replaced by the smaller denomination *Rentenmarken*. This left some companies starved of income and in some cases struggling to pay their bills. In a period of inflation, debts are not a problem: by the time you come to pay them the numbers mean less than when you incurred them. When inflation drops, buying habits have to change. Bankruptcies climbed steeply. In 1924 there were 5700 bankruptcies. In 1925 there were 10 800. Over the 18 months of the second half of 1925 to the first half of 1927, there were 31 000. As a result, in many fields of economic activity – banking, industry, commerce and farming – the talk was of rationalisation. This meant that, to survive, firms cut costs; and the biggest cost for most of them was the wages bill. They laid off workers, unemployment rose, the tax base of the government fell and the welfare bill grew.

The economy of Weimar Germany was nevertheless in relatively good shape by 1929. The hyperinflation of 1923 was over and industrial growth had resumed, albeit on a modest scale, largely thanks to the Dawes Plan of 1924, with the stabilisation of the currency, restructuring of reparations payments and huge financial loans from the USA. German industry seemed to have recovered well and the country was achieving levels of production comparable with those before the war. As such, Germany was becoming the world's second greatest industrial power after the USA. Wages had begun to rise again and those Germans who were in work now enjoyed a higher standard of living. The hated reparations were at least being paid off. Exports were increasing again. The government was even able to increase both wages for state employees and welfare benefits.

Many of the state's major assets – the Reichsbank, the national railways and many industries – had been used as collateral for the huge US loans, but even so, compared with what had gone before, times were good. No wonder this period is known as the Golden Twenties (*die Goldenen Zwanziger*). A population of nearly 65 million benefitted from the Weimar Republic's liberal reforms, although unemployment remained stubbornly high at about 2 million. There was even a resumption of trade, internal as well as overseas, although as with industry the growth was relatively modest. Schacht, the Republic's currency commissioner

Key term

Tariff: a tax applied to goods when they are imported.

ACTIVITY 2.3

Make notes comparing the Dawes Plan and the Young Plan. Put them into the economic context and ask yourself whether they were exercises in postponing Germany's problems or genuine attempts to solve them.

and president of the Reichsbank, played an important role in the stabilisation and growing international confidence in the new currency, the Reichsmark. The removal of foreign troops from the important industrial area of the Ruhr negotiated under the Dawes Plan in 1924 provided a significant industrial boost. At the same time, the real value of wages (their purchasing power) grew every year after 1924. In 1927 they rose by 9% and by a further 12% in 1928. Unemployment was high, but for those who did have a job, Germany's workforce was now the best paid in Europe.

The reparations issue and the Young Plan

It became clear to the Allied Reparations Commission after 1924 that Germany was unable or unwilling to make even the rescheduled reparations payments laid out in the Dawes Plan of 132 billion marks. US industrialist Owen D. Young, a member of the Dawes Committee, was asked early in 1929 to form a new committee to consider the problem and to suggest a solution. The Young Committee met in the first part of 1929 and agreed a package of measures they thought to be both fair to Germany and acceptable to the Allies. Reparations payments were to be reduced by 20% to 112 billion marks over 59 years. There was little expectation that this sum would be paid in full but the annual payment of 2 billion marks was, they hoped, a feasible sum. This was especially so as they had agreed to split this annual payment into two parts – one third unconditional and two thirds that could be postponed until later. This latter part did attract interest but, as with the Dawes proposals, it was to be managed by a consortium of leading US banks. These were quite generous terms, but they were never put to the test. Between their agreement in mid-1929 and their formal adoption in January 1930, the Wall Street crash had occurred in the USA and the world was plunged into economic crisis.

Social developments

Social welfare reforms

Throughout the Weimar period, welfare bureaucrats, social reformers and charities argued over the most effective way to relieve poverty. Different governments adopted different approaches, but there was a high degree of continuity. Governments intervened in several areas that affected life for millions of Germans. The National Welfare decree of February 1924 created a public assistance programme, and in 1925 the accident insurance programme was reformed, making certain occupational disorders insurable. By the end of 1923, governments had already added the benefits due to war victims to the social welfare system, consolidated unemployment relief into a regular assistance programme and consolidated the administration of insurance provision for miners into a single agency. Finally in 1924 a modern system of public assistance came into effect, replacing the old Poor Relief laws of the 1870s. Even so, there was still great poverty and difficulty for many in Germany during hyperinflation, and some historians argue that employers used the economic crises to take back many of the concessions made to workers in the radical years 1918–1919.

Under the 1927 Unemployment Insurance Law, workers and employers contributed to a national unemployment welfare scheme. The law created the

National Employment Placement and Unemployment Insurance Office. The scheme started well, but the Great Depression, which was only two years away, was to undermine this and other such social insurance schemes. Also in 1927, the second Wilhelm Marx government banned sacking pregnant women, something which had been an almost universal practice across the Western world. Radically, it covered both married and unmarried women. Excluded from the ban were women in domestic service or agricultural work, and also those working for companies with three or fewer employees.

Housing

Successive Weimar governments were active in the provision of affordable housing, The Weimar Constitution (Article 155) declared that the state must 'strive to secure healthy housing to all German families, especially those with many children'. Weimar governments initiated several innovative schemes in an attempt to secure this aim. They employed leading architects and planners to devise ways of alleviating the chronic shortage of decent and affordable houses in Germany in the 1920s. These governments also did what they could directly to stimulate house and apartment building by means of significant government investment in housing, tax breaks, land grants and low-interest loans. The result was impressive. Between 1924 and 1931 more than 2 million new homes were built and nearly 200 000 more were renovated. One estimate is that homelessness in Germany had been reduced by 60% by 1928. Whatever the precise figure, a major inroad had been made into an important social problem.

A good example of housing that offered residents access to light and air was the Berlin-Britz development, built 1925–1927. The architects Bruno Taut and Martin Wagner designed a large horseshoe (*Hufeisen*) housing complex with rounded corners and stairwells, and interior sightlines into other apartments that the architects hoped would encourage a sense of community among residents. A fine example of collaboration between modern architects and commercial enterprise is provided by the Schocken department stores designed by Erich Mendelsohn, of which the best known are the stores in Nuremberg (built 1925–1926), Stuttgart (1926–1928, Figure 2.2) and Chemnitz (1927–1930). The department-store chain of I. Schocken Sons, founded by Simon and Salman Schocken, was by 1930 the fourth largest department store chain in Germany, with some 20 stores nationwide. Their clean lines and lavish use of artificial light marked these buildings out. Despite the appearance of luxury in the designs, the Nuremberg department store at least was intended to provide for a mainly working-class public.

 Thematic link: social welfare

Figure 2.2: The Schocken department store in Stuttgart, 1928.

Key term

Protestant: group of Christian churches stemming from a church-reform movement in the 16th century with a tendency to be more closely linked to individual nationalities and states than e.g. Catholic church

Education

Before the 1918 revolution, most German children attended schools which were publicly funded but linked to a specific faith; most were **Protestant** or Catholic, but some were Jewish. Religious groups were deeply suspicious of reform in education, but with the change from empire to republic, change was on the political agenda.

Social Democrats, German Democrats and educational reformers in the German Teachers' Association (*Deutscher Lehrerverein*) and the smaller German Women Teachers' Association (*Deutscher Lehrerinnenverein*) were to some extent agreed on a reform programme for education. The plan was to create an education system in which children from a variety of faith backgrounds were educated together in secular schools. There was also a desire that children from different social classes be educated together in one place, with equal opportunities for development, and that boys and girls be educated in the same subjects and with the same expectations.

Beginning with government decrees and moving on to the Weimar Constitution, private preparatory schools were banned, teaching in schools had to be interfaith and tolerant, and religion was to be a school subject like any other. The secularising 1919 Constitution also elevated teacher training to university level and banned school prayers. These measures and declarations did, of course, offend conservative-minded educators and the churches, who had until 1919 provided almost all elementary education in partly state-funded schools. The extra parliamentary opposition from the churches and the faith schools was channelled through the Catholic School Association (CSA) and the Protestant Parents' League. These became powerful pressure groups, and their vociferous opposition to reform influenced the ruling SDP to become lukewarm on the issue. The power of pressure groups of this kind was evident in the 1926 campaign against pornography or 'filth and trash writing'.

In addition, and unsurprisingly, the Centre Party made education an item on the agenda of negotiations with other parties when governments were being formed. At the same time the SPD encouraged parents to register that they did not want their children to attend religious education lessons. Reform-minded elementary teachers did succeed in getting important changes in educational provision at elementary level introduced. The elite preparatory schools were indeed abolished. Four-year basic schools (*Grundschulen*) were introduced; these were intended to lead on to higher education for any children for whom that was appropriate, regardless of social background. The reformers also promoted a learning-based and child-friendly tone in the classroom, in contrast to the traditional **authoritarian** atmosphere.

They introduced active learning in place of the fact-based rote learning that had been standard. In addition, about 200 experimental schools abandoned corporal punishment and grades.

The record of educational provision by the state during the Weimar period was mixed. Between 1921–1922 and 1926–1927, the number of students registered in state elementary schools dropped by about a third, although by 1931–1932 at least part of that loss had been made up. At secondary level too there was a drop in registration in the same period, although here the change was smaller. Enrolments for universities, polytechnics and other higher-education colleges went up, and the proportion of women attending climbed from about 7% in 1921–1922 to about 17% in 1931–1932. This was in line with Weimar government policies. Weimar schools changed less than the ambitious reform programme set out in the constitution proposed. This was because the radicals in the SPD and the moderates in the DDP had a wide political agenda that they wished to take forward in German society, while the Centre Party was willing to compromise in several other areas but not on confessional schools. The Centre Party was therefore an effective force in the Reichstag and in government for the aims of the CSA and the Catholic Church.

The development of Weimar culture

Weimar Germany was a period of change for many aspects of culture. Remarkable experiments were conducted, and new ways of writing, painting, dancing and so on were introduced. It was such a radical period that we are still working through many of the ideas today.

Dance
Marie Wiegmann (Mary Wigman as she became better known) was born in 1886. A dancer and choreographer, she is one of the most influential figures in the history of modern dance. After suffering a nervous breakdown in 1918 she opened her own dance school in Dresden in 1920. Here she taught what has become known as 'Expressionist' dance, a style with an emphasis on free and uninhibited movement.

Key term

Authoritarian: a political point of view or system in which the government has the authority to take decisions without consultation and the power to enforce them, and the population is expected to obey instructions from the government without questioning them.

ACTIVITY 2.4

What does the conflict over education and educational reforms tell us about the bigger political picture in Germany at this time?

1. Draw up a list of the reforms.

2. What were the reformers trying to achieve?

3. What were opponents of the reforms trying to prevent?

Figure 2.4: *Berlin Street Scene* (1913) by Ernst Kirchner.

 Key terms

Expressionism: An artistic movement that emphasised the expression of the artist's subjective feelings and experience. Expressionism developed in Germany during the Weimar period.

Dada: An artistic movement that produced nonsensical or satirical art in reaction to the traditional values that had enabled the horrors of the First World War.

She rejected the formality and costume of classical ballet, in particular the wearing of *pointe* shoes and the style they demand (see Figure 2.3). She was also a pioneer in the use of dance as therapy for all sorts of physical and mental disorders. In 1930 she toured the USA with her dancers to great acclaim, and in 1931 a school of dance was founded by her disciples in New York.

Figure 2.3: This depiction of Mary Wigman dancing was drawn by the Expressionist artist Ernst Kirchner in 1933.

Art

Ernst Kirchner was one of a group of Weimar artists whose style is known as 'Expressionist' (Figure 2.4 shows an example). **Expressionism** means more than expressing emotions. It suggests showing what things feel like more than what they look like. It also means exploring the deeper, darker hidden inner life that people rarely share with one another and often do not admit to themselves.

George Grosz was another well-known artist of the Weimar period. He was critical of the work of Expressionists like Ernst Kirchner because of what he regarded as a lack of realism in their work. He was one of a group of artists known as the New Objectivity movement. Together with his friend and fellow artist Otto Dix, Grosz is best known for his savage and critical depictions of Weimar life. His pictures lampoon German institutions and characters. They show us the irreverence and disrespect for authority that is one aspect of Weimar culture.

Another artist critical of the Weimar period was Hannah Höch, a member of the **Dada** movement. *Dada* is an informal French word for a hobbyhorse, but the word also suggests the early sounds a baby makes. The Dadaists rejected labels or names and hated the very idea of 'meanings'. They wanted their art to speak for itself, to provoke, offend and cause outrage. Höch was a pioneer of photomontage: cutting up photographs and placing the pieces together.

Like the Dadaists, but with a more Expressionist approach, Käthe Kollwitz was deeply critical of militarism as a solution to national problems. Her dislike grew out of her despair at the damage inflicted by the 1914–1918 war, in which one of her sons was killed. She had a great concern throughout her life for the hungry, poor and victims of war. A versatile artist, she was a sculptor, engraver and painter. Perhaps her best-known graphic works of the Weimar period were the posters *Germany's Children Starve, Bread* and *Never Again War*, all of 1924. Like Dix, she produced political art, but unlike him she created more obviously campaigning images.

Architecture

As we have already seen, architecture flourished in Weimar Germany. The work of Erich Mendelsohn was especially prominent. He is often associated with encouraging a consumer society, famously with his designs for the Schocken department stores, cinemas and even a hat factory. An architect who could not be accused of commercialism was Bruno Taut; as well as the *Hufeisen*, he was responsible for the *Onkel Tom* housing development in the Berlin suburbs, which similarly provided modern affordable apartments and remains an Art Deco landmark.

Perhaps the best-known art movement in Weimar Germany, however, was the **Bauhaus** school, which combined crafts and fine art. It was founded by the Berlin architect Walter Gropius in 1919. To start with, the school had no architecture department, but later it became famous for combining craft, architecture and design into one seamless whole. From 1919 until 1925 it was housed in Weimar, then in Dessau until 1932. *Bauhaus* literally means 'house of construction', and building technology was fully integrated into the Bauhaus approach. Its principles were very influential in the development of design, perhaps the most important of the 20th century, embracing furniture, cutlery, door handles, bathroom taps and pepper pots as well as buildings and building materials. The very influential German architect Ludwig Mies van der Rohe was Director of the Bauhaus school 1930–1933.

Music

Austrian-born Arnold Schoenberg was a leading composer, teacher and musical theorist active in Germany in the 1920s, having settled in Berlin before 1914. His early works were in a late-Romantic style, but in the 1920s he developed the 'twelve-tone' method of musical composition, perhaps the most important influence on 20th-century music. This was music without the tonal centre or musical 'home' that audiences were used to; as a result, audience members could not tell what any piece of music would do next. His students included Alban Berg and Anton Webern, both of them of enormous importance and influence in their own right in the history of modern music.

As a measure of stability returned to Weimar Germany, creative people had to become used to a new phenomenon – mass culture. The wide appeal of jazz was shown by the clubs and cabarets of Berlin. Its popularity took off after 1924

 Key term

Bauhaus: A Modernist style of design, art and architecture named after the school that has had a strong and lasting influence on design.

when German radio started to play it regularly and German bandleaders like Eric Borchard and Stefan Weintraub had success. US stars such as Paul Whiteman, a regular visitor to Berlin after 1926, were always popular in Germany. Composers such as Paul Hindemith, Ernst Krenek and above all Kurt Weill adopted aspects of jazz in their work.

Jazz's connections with African-Americans and also the unpredictability of its improvisatory element contributed to its being strongly disliked by social conservatives. This response was later supported by the NSDAP government.

Drama

Music and drama both flourished in the Weimar period. They came together in the collaboration of the playwright Bertolt Brecht and the composer Kurt Weill, notably on *The Threepenny Opera* (*Die Dreigroschenoper*). This was an adaptation in German of a 'ballad opera' by the 18th-century British writer John Gay. The plot, of criminals and prostitutes plotting robberies, greatly appealed to Brecht, and the fact that it had used popular tunes of the day caught Weill's imagination. Their work challenged conventional ideas of propriety and of the very idea of theatre itself. It was a typical product of Weimar – challenging, innovative, unconventional – and wildly successful in Germany and all over the world. By the time that Brecht fled Germany in 1933 it had been translated into 18 other languages and had been performed over 10 000 times.

Musically the score is heavily influenced by jazz. The songs 'Mack the Knife' and 'Pirate Jenny' have proved particularly popular, being often covered. The German composer and violinist Paul Hindemith, who was appointed a professor at the Berlin Hochschule für Musik in 1927, was influenced by Bertolt Brecht's social engagement when he wrote his 'Music for use' (*Gebrauchsmusik*) pieces.

Film

For early German cinema, the Babelsberg studios in Berlin and the company UFA were central. In 1926 F.W. Murnau's silent Expressionist classic *Faust* was released, followed in 1927 by Fritz Lang's silent Expressionist science fiction epic *Metropolis*. Lang went on to direct M (1931), a disturbing and powerful talking picture allegedly based on the story of Peter Kürten, a notorious child killer dubbed 'The Monster of Düsseldorf'. Another famous example of later Weimar cinema was *The Blue Angel* (1930). Directed by Josef von Sternberg and freely adapted from a novel by Heinrich Mann, it starred Emil Jannings as Professor Unrath and it made a star of Marlene Dietrich, who played the part of a nightclub singer.

Society in Weimar Germany varied enormously depending on where it was observed: Bavaria was (and still is) very different from Berlin. However, in general the period was frenetic and exuberant, and people – women and men – had previously unheard-of freedoms of speech, of thought and, of religion. Those of a traditional cast of mind, who looked back to the social certainties of Imperial Germany, were dismayed. Marlene Dietrich herself had started out as a theatre violinist, before moving on to working as a chorus girl, singing and dancing. Her image in her most famous films at this time …, sexually ambiguous (she was herself bisexual), ironic and mocking …, tells us something about the new freedoms of Weimar culture, although even in Berlin, Dietrich's membership of a boxing club is likely to have raised eyebrows.

Literature

Alfred Döblin's 1929 novel *Berlin Alexanderplatz*, one of the most innovative and important novels about Weimar Germany, is set in a working-class area of Berlin in the 1920s. Whatever the Jazz Age had to offer those who could afford to partake of it, life was still grim for inhabitants of such areas. Döblin was a doctor in working-class Berlin and he knew about the struggle for survival in these areas from personal observation.

In contrast to Döblin, who was not well known at the time, Thomas Mann was acclaimed both in Germany and internationally; he was awarded the Nobel Prize for Literature in 1929. He was born in Lübeck in north Germany in 1875, into the comfortable upper-middle-class life that he described in his first major novel *Buddenbrooks* (1901). He wrote many novels, essays and short stories including the novel *The Magic Mountain* (*Der Zauberberg*), which was started in 1912 but only published in 1924. It used the imagery of illness and health to open up questions about the way society works and the importance of individuals pursuing spiritual development.

 Voices from the past

Oswald Spengler

Oswald Spengler was the author of the highly influential book *The Decline of the West (Der Untergang des Abendlandes)*. Its first volume was published in Germany in 1918; Volume 2 followed in 1922. Spengler ranged widely through historical periods in an attempt to show that all civilisations and cultures flourish and then die by unchangeable laws. By 1926 it had sold 100 000 copies in Germany alone, a remarkable figure for a book of this kind, and had been translated into many languages.

I saw the present – the approaching World-War – in a quite other light. It was no longer a momentary constellation of casual facts due to national sentiments, personal influences, or economic tendencies endowed with an appearance of unity and necessity by some historian's scheme of political or social cause-and-effect, but the type of a historical change of phase occurring within a great historical organism of definable compass at the point preordained for it hundreds of years ago.

Spengler was not a professional historian and his work received a cool reception in academic circles in Germany. However, it was widely influential if only poorly understood in some cases. Spengler did reflect on the idea of race but he rejected the biological definitions then current and emphasised the connection of race with landscape, comparing it to a plant with roots.

If, in that home, the race cannot be found, this means the race has ceased to exist. A race does not migrate. Men migrate, and their successive generations are born in ever-changing landscapes; but the landscape exercises a secret force upon the extinction of the old and the appearance of the new one.

Discussion points

1. To what extent do these two extracts help us to understand how people thought about Germany's situation following the First World War?
2. To which developments can you relate Spengler's ideas?

ACTIVITY 2.5

Make notes on:

1. the campaign against 'filth and trash'
2. the campaign against reforms in education.

What connections do you notice between them? What do these campaigns, and the opposing campaigns, tell us about Weimar society and politics?

Censorship

The Weimar Constitution (Article 118) had declared, 'No censorship will take place.' The only exception was film, to ban pornography. However, various groups outside the Reichstag, including teachers, the churches, social workers and socially conservative groups of all kinds, campaigned vigorously against what they called 'trash and filth writings' (*Schund- und Schmutzschriften*) poisoning the minds of young people. The churches (Protestant and Catholic) were prominent in this campaign, as were a number of pressure groups of teachers, social workers and parents, anxious, as they saw it, to preserve the morals of young people. This 'filth and trash', they believed distracted them from reading the classics of German literature. These dreadful works, so it was claimed, were often written by foreign, explicitly Jewish, authors. One Protestant minister defined *Schund und Schmutz* as rooted in 'Jewish Manchesterism', a turn of phrase that, as Margaret F. Steig has noted, combines anti-Semitism, anti-free-market capitalism and anti-British sentiments in one phrase.[4] One of the leading campaigners, Hermann Popert, a Hamburg juvenile court judge, was greatly concerned, he declared, with the overstimulation of young minds caused by reading 'filth and trash'.

On the other hand, some of Germany's leading thinkers and writers condemned this campaign as blatant censorship and a clear violation of the constitution. Thomas Mann wrote:

Every literate and knowledgeable person recognises that the need to protect our youth from filth and trash … is nothing more than a pretext. The law's drafters want to use the law's penetrating power against freedom, against intellect itself.[5]

The different situations of books, films and the lively cabaret scene in Berlin's nightclubs formed part of the debate. The 1926 *Gesetz zur Bewahrung der Jugend vor Schund- und Schmutzschriften* (Law for the Protection of Youth from Trash and Filth Writings) introduced the censorship of printed materials specifically in the interest of youth welfare. Nothing could be censored on political, social, religious or ethical grounds. The new law was controversial, as it seemed to many to go against Article 118 of the Constitution, and took three readings in the Reichstag and a mixed majority before it could become law.

A governmental board was set up by the minister of the interior in cooperation with the state governments. This board scrutinised newly published books and had the power to ban any deemed unsuitable. In the event the new law did not have much effect. By spring 1932 only 114 titles had been placed on the banned list. It only applied to book distribution and therefore was after publication. However, the fact that a liberal principle of the Weimar Constitution had been breached was one sign among many that the constitution and the republic had many enemies.

Science

Innovation in science needs a willingness to rethink established and accepted ideas, the freedom to experiment without limitations. The spirit of Weimar, its open-mindedness, lack of deference, and tolerance of criticism, created the sort of atmosphere in which science could flourish.

Perhaps the most famous scientist in this or any other period was Albert Einstein, Director of Physics at the Kaiser Wilhelm Institute (KWI) in Berlin–Dahlem between 1914 and 1932. His revolutionary work on relativity and quantum theory had transformed physics and altered the consensus that had existed since the time of Isaac Newton in 17th-century England. Werner Heisenberg was another theoretical physicist and one of the main pioneers of quantum mechanics. He is perhaps best known for the uncertainty principle, put forward in a scientific paper he published in 1927. This asserts that there is a physical limit to the precision with which certain pairs of properties of a particle, such as position and momentum, can be defined. Heisenberg was awarded the Nobel Prize for Physics in 1932. He was a lecturer (*Privatdozent*) at Göttingen University, 1924–1927, and then a professor at Leipzig University. Because he insisted on teaching about the work of Jewish scientists like Einstein, he was criticised by a group of German physicists who supported *Deutsche Physik* (German physics), an anti-Semitic group who, even in the early 1920s, were opposed to the very concept of quantum mechanics ('too Jewish', they believed).

Popular culture

Culture means different things to different people. As well as the arts and sciences, there is also the world of sport and the day-to-day lives of individual people. Here too there are stories to be found that tell us a lot about the experience of living in Weimar Germany. Football club Bayern Munich had been founded by members of a Munich gymnastics club in 1900 and enjoyed considerable success, at first locally. They won the South German championship in 1926 and again in 1928. Their first national title came in 1932 under coach Richard Kohn when they beat Eintracht Frankfurt 2–0. As Kohn and the club president Kurt Landauer were both Jewish, the team would later be taunted by rival fans as a 'Jews' club'. Kohn and Landauer both left the country during Nazi rule.

In 1920 the Weimar Republic offered opportunities to many groups for free expression, such as Socialist Youth group (*Sozialistiche Arbeiter Jugend* or SAJ). The SAJ was the youth wing of the SDP, who gathered in Weimar that year and were popular for folk dancing.

Another activity popular in Germany in the 1920s was naked gymnastics for both women and men. Hans Surén was the most popular author in this field. His books became well-known in Germany in the 1920s. His book *Man and the Sun (Der Mensch und die Sonne)* (1924) was published in no less than 61 editions over the next two years. It is a nice example of new and old combining: the German state both before 1918 under imperial Hohenzollern rule and after 1933 under Nazi rule was in favour of athletics, sport and the outdoor life. But the combination of this ongoing tradition with *Nacktkultur* (naked culture) was a peculiarly Weimar one. A former army officer and an officer's son, Surén himself later joined the Nazi party and agreed to alter his book to suit changing times.

Living standards and lifestyles

In the decades after 1945, historians did not examine the middle period of the Weimar Republic with the attention it deserved. Understandably, the priority at that time was to demonstrate the wickedness of the Nazi regime in Germany

ACTIVITY 2.6

What features do you notice that the different aspects of culture in Weimar Germany have in common? Create a spider diagram showing the different characteristics (you might want to think about, for example, issues to do with tradition and innovation, authority and rebellion, group and individual). Having created the diagram, think about how you might be able to use the ideas in an essay about Weimar society more widely.

from 1933 to 1945. One way to do this was by contrasting it with the regime that preceded it, the Weimar Republic. It became the norm to divide the Weimar years neatly into three sections, a peaceful, prosperous and culturally rich middle period sandwiched between two troubled and turbulent periods. Historians could not ignore the economic and social problems of the first Weimar period (1919–1924) and the last (1929–1933), but they argued that in 1924 the Weimar Republic entered a 'Golden Age'. The image of Weimar citizens in this middle period suggests confident, independent thinkers enjoying new social freedoms and adequate disposable income. It is unlikely, though, that such people were typical of Germans as a whole, either in their standard of living or their attitudes. Other Germans continued to struggle to make ends meet, to the extent of going hungry. Helped by the Dawes Plan of 1924, the German economy had largely stabilised. However, unemployment remained high, and workers knew that if they did not accept a job on the terms offered, there were numerous others who would do so. That being the case, trade unions were reluctant to call strikes. Nevertheless, the strong tradition of social and industrial welfare survived the governments' shifts from centre-left to centre-right.

Since the 1980s, some re-evaluation of this middle period (1924–1928) has taken place. It has become clearer that developments in such things as social welfare reform or longer-term economic problems have a greater continuity that does not fit neatly into these three periods. In addition, some research has focused on the continuities between the Weimar Republic and the Nazi regime that followed. Here family and youth policies, welfare reform and the willingness of the state to become involved in the many activities of ordinary Germans have been studied in detail. Nevertheless, despite acknowledging the willingness of Weimar governments to intervene in private family matters, some historians deny any clear continuity between Weimar and Nazi family policies. They point out that Weimar policymakers did not try to dictate what families or individuals did. Women, for example, were neither ordered into the workplace nor back into the home. They were offered a measure of support in motherhood, but also the right to pursue university studies or employment outside the home.

Political developments and the workings of democracy

This middle period of the Weimar Republic was, in political terms and on the surface, a quiet one. There were no revolutions, attempts to seize power by force, invasions, strikes or other emergencies like those that had plagued Germany 1918–1923. There was, however, a slow drift of both parties and voters away from the centre ground, making politics increasingly argumentative and compromise harder to find. Many political parties were right-wing: nationalist, conservative, militarist or monarchist. However, of these several were centre-right. Most politicians on the right and even the centre ground of German politics had little emotional or intellectual engagement with democracy and the Republic. This included the DVP's Stresemann, whose conservative and monarchist views were well known. They often presented their views as plain common sense, in contrast to parties of the left who were 'ideological'.

 Key term

Ideology: set of ideas and ideals that underpins and gives shape to e.g. a policy or political programme.

These parties of the right were therefore hostile to the very idea of the Weimar Republic. Only a fading fear of violent revolution on the Russian model prevented their active hostility to the Republic.

Weimar political parties

Weimar politics was a noisy debate to which several political parties contributed. Often they had overlapping names and policies. Table 2.1 lists the descriptive vocabulary from which they drew their names.

Arbeiter	Workers
Deutsch	German
Demokratisch	Democratic
Kommunistisch	Communist
National	National
Sozialdemokratisch	Social democratic
Volk	People
Zentrum	Centre

Table 2.1: Examples of vocabulary used in German party names.

Most political parties built their names by choosing words from this list. With a couple of exceptions, their names were calculated to communicate their commitment to Germany and its people. Most parties, and many of their deputies, were new to the business of politics, and all of them were new to government. Even the SPD had had only been in government during the closing days of the First World War. When Germany was a monarchy, the Kaiser appointed the chancellor and the chancellor appointed the government, none of them being members of political parties or the Reichstag. Under the Kaiser, the Reichstag discussed, commented and complained, but the government could largely ignore it. The first time a chancellor had been a member of a political party or had included Reichstag deputies in his cabinet was in the closing stages of the First World War. Before this, government had been in the hands of **aristocrats** and of soldiers and civil servants who were close to or part of the aristocracy themselves.

None of the parties of the Weimar Republic ever commanded a majority of the votes in federal elections, and thus they never commanded a majority in the Reichstag. Every Weimar government was thus a coalition. As a result, the business of government and legislating required different parties to negotiate agreements and compromises throughout the Weimar period. For the electorate (which, like the parties, was new to the business of democratic politics and government), this gradually created disillusionment, as the party they voted for failed time and again to put its programme into practice. Not all of the political parties supported the existence of the Republic. Several of them wanted to see it replaced. The state thus faced threats to its existence within the Reichstag itself.

 Key term

Aristocrat: a member of the nobility, from a family with a tradition of owning land and holding political power.

The Communist Party of Germany (KPD)

On the left of German politics was the KPD. The KPD was the largest and most important communist party in Europe after Russia's. It had been formed by the merger of the USPD's left wing with the Spartacists, both of which broke up in the early 1920s, leaving various splinter groups. The party rejected the Republic and its constitution as a bourgeois construct, and initially saw the way forward as being demonstrations and strikes, ultimately leading to an armed uprising. Contesting its first federal election in 1920, it gained about 2% of the votes cast. Its support grew and its vote share in the Weimar Republic settled at around 10%.

The Social Democratic Party of Germany (SPD)

The Social Democrats had been one of the main designers of the constitution and fully supported the Republic and its democratic system. Although the SPD was the largest party in the early years of the Weimar Republic, it never commanded a majority of votes at federal elections or seats in the Reichstag. Seen as a working-class party, it never attracted a substantial body of middle-class voters. With nearly 40% of the vote in the first federal election, it had spent the first few years as the senior partner in coalition governments. It was regarded with hostility by the right because of its left-wing history and policies, but also by those further to its left because of its compromises, beginning with Ebert's pragmatic decisions. The same tensions existed within the party itself; there were internal conflicts and gradually its voters deserted it, slowly at first and then in a rush, its vote share dropping from the 40% at the beginning of the Republic to 20% at its end.

One reason for the decline in the party's reputation and thus levels of support was the Barmat scandal of 1924–1925. The brothers Julius and Henry Barmat were importers and wholesalers accused of wartime profiteering. Julius had good social connections to the SPD leader in the Prussian **Landtag** (state government), but also to Ebert, Bauer and the SPD's national chairman Otto Wels. They did business with state institutions, the Prussian State Bank among them. They donated money to SPD-supporting newspapers. They lent money to leading SPD figures. The SPD leader in the Prussian Landtag served on various Barmat boards, though he did not accept a financial reward for doing so. The national postal office invested funds in a Barmat company, as did the Prussian State Bank. When the Barmat company with those funds collapsed, both institutions lost money. The Barmat brothers and various bank employees were arrested. Bauer issued denials that were proved false, and he was forced to resign from the SPD. Ebert was cleared of wrongdoing but was still too close to the scandal for comfort, and in the 1925 election would have been the object of sustained right-wing attacks. The fact that the Barmat brothers were Polish Jews and the politicians were Social Democrats confirmed all the right-wing parties' and groups' worst suspicions.

The German Democratic Party (DDP)

The DDP had been founded in November 1918, drawing on the left wings of the Progressive and Liberal parties. The DDP fully supported the Republic; DDP member Hugo Preuss had been one of the Constitution's main authors. He, Walther Rathenau and Max Weber were all DDP ministers in Weimar coalition governments. Of these, the sociologist Weber was very influential for generations of social historians. The party's electoral support came from middle-class

Key term

Landtag: German word meaning 'living space'; territory claimed by Hitler's Germany in eastern Europe.

intellectuals and small businessmen. It believed in a secular state, a more limited role for government in the economy than the SPD wanted to see, but also a fairer economy, with employer and employee put on a more even footing. (See, for example, Figure 2.5.) The DDP supported the creation of a League of Nations. Its willingness to compromise made it a frequent partner in government; but compromises also cost it support at the polls. Its support at the start of the Weimar period was at 17.3% and by the end was at about 1%.

The Centre Party

The Centre Party (*Zentrumspartei* or often just *Zentrum*) was the voice of the Catholic Church in Germany and tended to win about 15% of the vote in federal elections. It supported the constitution and was one member (with the SPD and DDP) of the Weimar Coalition. In theory a party of the centre ground, it aimed to have a pragmatic approach to many questions, which made it useful in coalitions. As a result it was a partner in the federal government for almost the whole of the Republic's life and provided five chancellors. However, in education it was unsurprisingly a vigorous defender of Catholic Church schools. The party was itself a coalition: one group supported the SPD project in extending the welfare state and Stresemann's policy of rebuilding international relations; another, more right-wing grouping was socially conservative, regarded social reforms with suspicion and believed in maintaining the rights of the states (*Länder*) at home and strongly defending national interests abroad. One prominent Centre politician was Wilhelm Marx, twice chancellor (1923–1925 and 1926–1928). His first term as chancellor lasted just 13 months, his second some two years under President Paul von Hindenburg, whose right-wing sympathies were well known. In the earlier part of the Weimar period, the left-liberal wing of the Centre Party tended to dominate. Later its conservatives held power and during Heinrich Brüning's chancellorship there was a distinct step towards a more authoritarian, less consensual and accountable administration.

The German People's Party (DVP)

The DVP was the successor to the right wing of the Liberal and Progressive parties of Imperial days. Its electoral and financial support came from industrialists and the upper middle class. It was not in favour of the Republic but did not seek to undermine it. Like the Centre Party, it emphasised Christian family values, but, unlike the Centre, it supported secular education. Domestically, it made the case for strong, authoritative central government. Abroad, it wanted the Treaty of Versailles revised. It was led by Gustav Stresemann, chancellor then long-serving foreign minister, who pursued a policy of 'fulfilment', meeting Germany's obligations while at the same time seeking to negotiate less harsh terms. Stresemann was unusual not just because he came from relatively humble origins to become the dominant politician of the period but because he was always prepared to compromise and conciliate. After his death the party became more openly hostile to the Republic, losing the support of those who believed in the democratic process without succeeding in attracting the mass vote of those who did not. Its vote accordingly dropped from a reasonably steady 10% to 1% in the final elections.

Figure 2.5: This 1924 poster reads: 'Nothing will sway us from the middle road. The German Democratic Party.'

The German National People's Party (DNVP)

The DNVP was a monarchist, conservative and anti-Semitic party. Initially the most significant of the extreme right-wing parties, it was hostile to the Republic, the democratic process and the Treaty of Versailles. It received support from large landowners east of the River Elbe but also from major industrialists. It originally saw itself as a potential partner with other right-wing parties and briefly served in government. It later regarded the NSDAP as the most suitable party for collaboration, joining the Nazis in coalition in 1933.

The National Socialist German Workers' Party (NSDAP)

The NSDAP (*Nationalsozialistische Deutsche Arbeiterpartei* or Nazi Party) was founded in 1919. Its first support came from the lower-middle classes in Munich. Under Adolf Hitler, it tried to establish itself as a force on the right of German politics through demonstrations and then, in 1923, a putsch. It was consistently nationalist and anti-Semitic, emphasising its opposition to the Treaty of Versailles and entirely rejecting the Weimar Republic and all the political parties that made up the democratic process. After the Munich Putsch had failed, Hitler abandoned the idea of an armed uprising, but not the use of street violence against political enemies. Its candidates received support around 2.6–6.5% until after the Wall Street Crash, when the economic context of politics changed dramatically and with that the fortunes of the NSDAP.

Regional and smaller parties

The Reichstag also contained parties with specifically regional powerbases. Notable among these was the Bavarian People's Party (*Bayerische Volkspartei*, BVP). This had been founded as a regional breakaway from the Centre Party. It adopted a more conservative stance than the Centre. Its support was limited to Catholics in Bavaria, where it dominated local politics. One of its aims was to keep the left out of government.

The Bavarian Farmers' League (*Bayerischer Bauernbund*, BB) was another Bavarian party. It dated from Imperial times and was a force in local politics (and occasionally in national politics) throughout the Weimar period.

The National Rural League (*Reich Landbund*) was also a farming-based party, this time with a powerbase east of the River Elbe. Its policies resembled those of the DNVP, with whom it often voted in Reichstag policy decisions.

The German-Hanoverian Party (*Deutsch-Hannoversche Partei*, DHP) dated back to Imperial times. In the Weimar Republic it stood for the interests of the area around Hanover, and was thus another conservative, federalist party.

As well as these (and other) regional parties, there were various parties that represented the interests of different social groups. These tended to come into existence when a group felt that larger parties were neglecting them. One of these was the Reich Party of the German Middle Class (*Reichspartei des deutschen Mittelstandes*), also known as the Economic Party of the German Middle Classes (*Wirtschaftspartei des deutschen Mittelstandes*, WP). This conservative party emerged when some supporters of the DNVP decided that that party spoke only for big business and landowners, and not sufficiently for the middle class, those people who were neither the wealthy bosses nor the unionised workers. The WP stood for less government interference and lower taxes.

President Paul von Hindenburg

Born in 1847 to an aristocratic Prussian father and a middle-class mother, Paul Ludwig Hans Anton von Beneckendorff und von Hindenburg spent most of his adult life in the Prussian and then German armies, retiring in 1911. Recalled from retirement in 1914, he became a Field Marshall, and Chief of the General Staff in the First World War from 1916. He retired again in 1919, a national hero. His role both in the defeat of Germany and the abdication of the Kaiser were kept from the German public, and his memoirs were a bestseller.

The 1925 presidential election

In February 1925, the President of the Republic, Friedrich Ebert, died. Ebert had been elected to office by the National Assembly following the first federal elections. Under the constitution, the new president had to be directly elected. The presidential elections that followed in March saw seven parties put forward candidates. The DVP/DNVP candidate won the most votes, but not a majority, so there was a second round of voting in April. Despite leading the poll, the candidate withdrew and the right-wing parties approached Paul von Hindenburg. Hindenburg was reluctant to agree, as victory would make him head of state, a position he believed belonged to the exiled Kaiser. Persuaded to stand as an independent (and possibly after seeking the Kaiser's permission), he received the support of the DVP and DNVP, as well as the smaller WP and NSDAP. The Catholic BVP, which might have been expected to back the Centre Party, threw its regional weight behind the retired soldier.

The SPD candidate (with the shadow of the Barmat scandal still hanging over the party) withdrew; the DDP candidate withdrew; both parties agreed to support the Centre Party candidate, former Chancellor Wilhelm Marx. The KPD candidate refused to do so and was thus the third candidate. Marx's support trebled in the second round of voting. The KPD vote largely held up, losing a few votes, presumably to Marx. But the winner was Hindenburg on just over 48% of the vote. Had the KPD withdrawn and backed the Centre, Marx might have narrowly won. The campaign made much of the idea that Hindenburg was coming out of a well-deserved retirement out of a sense of duty, not political ambition. He was in fact an apolitical candidate. No doubt many people supported him out of a matching sense of duty and perhaps a matching discontent with politics. He was above all a war hero around whom a mythology had gathered. Several historians have commented that his appeal was less that of a person (about whom people in fact knew little) and rather that of a charismatic myth.

Hindenburg's first term as president

Hindenburg's election was a clear victory for the nationalists, monarchists and militarists in German society. He was an honorary member of the *Stahlhelm*. Some of his supporters (such as the DNVP) might have expected Hindenburg to set about undermining the Republic or working towards its dismantling. In fact he took his oath of office seriously:

ACTIVITY 2.7

ACTIVITY 2.7

Review the information about the different German political parties from the period 1918–1933. You might want to find out more about some of them. Then write notes in response to the following questions about the parties:

1. What are their most prominent policies?

2. What do some of them have in common and what marks them out as different from one another?

3. Given the policies, which of the parties would you call left- or right-wing and why?

4. Given this analysis, where did the centre ground of Weimar German politics lie?

5. With this understanding, which of these parties seem to be supporters of the Republic and which seem to want to alter the nature of politics and the state?

I swear to devote my energy to the welfare of the German people, to increase its prosperity, to prevent damage, to hold up the Reich constitution and its laws, to consciously honour my duties and to exercise justice to every individual.[6]

He sought to abide by it throughout his two terms of office (1925–1934). Impatient with politics, its debates and crises, he kept his distance from day-to-day affairs by surrounding himself with advisers like a defensive structure. These included his son Oskar von Hindenburg, and Generals Groener and Schleicher. In addition, he inherited from Ebert the state secretary Otto Meissner. For many years historians tended to regard Hindenburg as a figurehead, and believed that Ludendorff had been the military genius in the First World War and that the political decisions during Hindenburg's presidency had been made by this group of advisers. More recently this view has been revised.

Hindenburg also inherited Ebert's belief in the supreme importance of maintaining order, where necessary using the emergency provisions of the constitution to do so. Four articles in particular set out the role of the president:

• Article 25: the president could dissolve the Reichstag
• Article 47: the president was head of the armed forces
• Article 48: the president could issue decrees with the status of law without taking them through the debates and votes of the Reichstag (the only limit on this power was that the Reichstag could vote to cancel them so long as the vote was carried by a majority)
• Article 53: the president appointed the chancellor and government.

In normal circumstances, the chancellor, with the support of the government and the Reichstag, took the lead in politics. In crises, the president stepped in and took over temporarily. What was unclear was the definition of a crisis (and of 'temporarily'). Ebert had intervened during the crises in the Ruhr area in 1920, and in Saxony and Thuringia in 1923. Soldier, monarchist and social conservative, Hindenburg might be expected not to hesitate to use his powers. During the relative calm of 1925–1929, he kept out of the detail of politics. He did, though, intervene during the campaign to seize princes' property without compensation. As the waters of government grew stormier, so he and his advisers exercised the presidential powers more.

Elections, and attitudes to the Republic among the elites and other social groups

Despite Germany's liberal constitution, republican structure and democratic process, the traditional elites had retained their power and influence in the major institutions of the state. These included the senior members of the army, churches, the state bureaucracy and the judiciary, and major landowners and industrialists. This was an unusual mixture and one that gave this period its particular character.

The armed forces

The Reichswehr was, as usual in German politics, a crucial element. The days were gone when Social Democratic Chancellor Friedrich Ebert could reach an understanding with a relatively sympathetic General Groener, the then commander of the Reichswehr. At this time, at least until his resignation in October 1926, the Reichswehr was commanded by General Hans von Seeckt, a traditionalist with little sympathy for the Weimar Republic. His downfall in 1926 illustrates both his lack of support for the Weimar Republic and the Republic's fragility. He invited the grandson of the former Kaiser to join Reichswehr manoeuvres wearing the uniform of the old Imperial First Foot Guards. He had received no permission from the government to do this. So clear an indication of monarchism from a servant of the Republic was unacceptable and Seeckt retired from the army under pressure later that year.

Royalty, nobility and the expropriation controversy

Weimar's major landowners were by and large those who had been landowners for years, even centuries. This included the **Junkers**, Prussian nobility from the north-east of the country with estates east of the River Elbe.

The most powerful of the landowners were kings and princes from the previous Imperial age, who had been deposed or had abdicated during the revolutionary period of 1918–1919. Many of them had retained their wealth and social status, abandoning only their hereditary political significance. Others had suffered seizures of property and been engaged ever since in court cases for compensation. Where compensation had been paid, the impact of inflation had complicated the settlement: land had held its value whereas currency had not. Periodically, there were calls for their property to be seized by the state without compensation. One campaign, spearheaded by the KPD, called for a referendum on the idea of 'expropriation' in 1926. The SPD, DDP and Centre Party supported the call. At a time of high unemployment, the campaign had mass appeal, and for the KPD it was a means of dividing the SPD leadership from its own voters. The campaign was opposed by individuals and associations representing the nobility, but also the churches' leadership, major landowners and large-scale industrialists, and the right-wing parties in the Reichstag and the states. President Hindenburg told the then Justice Secretary, the Centre's Wilhelm Marx, that the proposal to seize princes' property without compensation was in breach of the Constitution; the Luther government concurred. As a result a majority in the turnout of a referendum and a majority vote in the Reichstag would not be sufficient; the action would need a simple majority from the electorate. The NSDAP looked as though, swayed by the left-leaning Gregor Strasser, it might support the campaign, but Hitler crushed that idea. In the event, no law was achieved and the issue was handed back to the individual states to negotiate separately with the individual royal houses – the Prussian Landtag with the Hohenzollerns, the Bavarian Landtag with the Wittelsbachs and so on.

Other elite groups

Both the Protestant and Catholic Churches contained a range of political views. The Centre Party itself might adopt more conservative or liberal positions depending on the individual issue and also the waxing and waning of the left and right wing within the party.

The senior levels within state bureaucracy were staffed by people who had gained their education, training and experience before the revolution. They had

Key term

Junker: land-owning Prussian nobility with tradition of joining the officer class in the Army and the government's bureaucracy.

ACTIVITY 2.8

Write a short paragraph in response to each of the following questions:

1. From where did the Republic draw its support?
2. From where did the threats to the Republic come?
3. Given these different forces, how stable would you assess the Weimar Republic as being in the period 1924–1928?

cooperated with Ebert not least because he had been seen as Prince Maximilian von Baden's appointed political heir, the only basis for legitimacy at that point. Otto Meissner's career, though, is very telling. Born in modest circumstances, he had succeeded in his education and his career. In 1919 he was appointed acting adviser in the office of the president, working for the SPD's Ebert, becoming state secretary in 1923. When Hindenburg was elected he served him. From 1934, he worked for Adolf Hitler.

The senior judiciary consisted of people who had pursued careers in law under the Kaisers. Their cultural (and legal) frame of reference was accordingly monarchist and conservative.

The major industrialists tended to be from a different social class from the landowners and were essentially upper middle class, but could have connections by marriage with the nobility (as in the case of Krupp). They could also have at their disposal incomes comparable with the nobility. Some of them were based in the Ruhr region with its coal, iron and steel. Others were based in the ancient Baltic ports, such as Lübeck and Hamburg.

Other social groups

Many industrialists and businessmen did not operate on such as scale and had more limited financial resources. They were nevertheless socially conservative. They might be connected to the professional middle class, with its doctors, lawyers, academics and teachers. Slightly poorer than these were shopkeepers and small businessmen, office workers, and middle and junior management. The middle class (*Mittelstand*) did not see the wage rises that industry experienced during the better years. Nor were social welfare programmes always of relevance and use to them. Even when the unemployment rate fell, it fell more slowly and less far among the white-collar workers from this group than among the working class. As a result, these people often felt that they had been left behind by the Weimar Republic, and that they did not have a voice either in the trade unions or in the political parties.

Then there was the large working class, amounting to perhaps 40% of the total population. It included both the urban proletariat – working in industry, railways, ports and factories – and agricultural labourers. Workers in the towns and cities were often organised into trade unions. Those in the countryside rarely were. A great deal of politics in Germany was organised along class lines: people voted for the party that was intended to be the voice of their class in the Landtag or Reichstag. However, some allegiances were regional or confessional, with people voting for the party of their state or their church. Historians thus describe the political parties as falling under four headings: conservative, middle class, working class and Catholic.

The positions of extremists, including Nazis and Communists

The NSDAP

The NSDAP's leader, Adolf Hitler, had spent a relatively comfortable eight months dictating a book and receiving admiring visitors in prison after the failure of the Munich Putsch in 1923. He was now concerned with keeping everything legal. The

NSDAP contested elections to the Reichstag from 1924, at first with little success. Barred from putting up candidates as NSDAP in 1924 elections because of the putsch, their candidates stood for the 'National Socialist Freedom Movement' instead, but they received just 3% of votes cast. They contested the federal elections again in 1928, this time as the NSDAP because the ban had ended. They received even fewer votes this time, some 6.4%, giving them 12 Reichstag members.

Hitler was never a good organiser, and anyway his focus was on re-establishing himself as party leader after being out of circulation for eight months in Landsberg prison. Even so, the NSDAP continued to develop as a national party from 1925. It was still shunned by the respectable majority of Germans, who were deterred by the street violence in which the members engaged and had yet to learn to like Hitler's speaking style. However, the NSDAP was gradually emerging from the pack of far-right parties. The party had most electoral support in mainly Catholic Bavaria and in old industrial regions such as Thuringia. It also did well in rural mainly Protestant areas such as Schleswig-Holstein, Pomerania and East Prussia. Working-class areas in Berlin never swung behind the NSDAP, nor did the Ruhr area or Hamburg.

The Great Depression was the opportunity the NSDAP needed, and its vote suddenly climbed rapidly. Its collaboration with the DNVP had helped make it look like another party for which respectable people might vote. The DNVP found itself one of several parties which lost voters to the NSDAP. However, the NSDAP also attracted people who had not previously voted with its combination of anti-Semitism, anti-**communism**, opposition to the Treaty of Versailles, also to social divisions.

The last was the reason for Hitler's refusing to back the campaign for expropriation without compensation.

The KPD

The Communist Party had worked to push its share of the vote in federal elections up to about 10%. Like many political parties at the time it was becoming better organised, making increasingly skilful use of propaganda. It had a large and well-defended headquarters in Berlin and a national organisation with particular support in working-class areas such as some districts of Berlin. In the federal elections of May 1924 the KPD took nearly 3.7 million votes, a proportion of 12.6%. This put them in fourth place and brought them 62 seats in the Reichstag, a gain of 58. For the KPD, it looked like a breakthrough. The KPD leader and candidate for President in the 1925 election was Ernst Thälmann. He received nearly 2 million votes or 6.4%, succeeding in splitting the centre-left vote and letting in the right-wing candidate.

The Communists never succeeded in becoming a major force in Weimar politics, for various reasons. The SPD continued to command the largest share of the working-class vote. When that share broke down in the early 1930s, voters seem to have moved to the NSDAP rather than to the KPD. The KPD took its instructions from the Soviet government in Moscow. In the case of a referendum in Prussia, the KPD were ordered to oppose the SPD, which meant taking the same side

Key term

Communism: a left-wing political point of view or party believing in the working class taking political and economic power through revolution.

as the NSDAP. This Stalinist line, which Thälmann maintained, prevented the development of an anti-Nazi front on the left of politics until it was far too late.

Other extreme parties and groups

The USPD (the Independent Socialists) continued to operate as a party even after the Spartacist Uprising and the merger from which the KPD emerged. It put up candidates in the 1928 federal elections but won no seats. There were various leftist splinter parties. Like the USPD, the Socialist Workers Party of Germany split from the SPD (in its case, in 1931); it had about 20 000 members. What was left of the old USPD merged with it. Some of those discontented with the KPD also joined, but it never grew to a significant force. It is largely remembered today only for the fact that a future German chancellor, Willy Brandt, was a member as a young man.

The International Socialist Militant League was another SPD splinter group. It remained a small group of dedicated left-wing idealists. It did achieve one notable propaganda coup, which we will mention in a later chapter.

In addition, there was an anarchist movement in Germany dating back to the 19th century. Some of its members became prominent during the Bavarian Soviet and were arrested and prosecuted after that period of revolutionary activity. Again, the numbers involved and the influence on German politics were small.

There were also several paramilitary groups, but these only involved a small percentage of German population.

The extent of political stability

Compared with the revolutionary year 1918, and even the years of attempted putsches and uprisings 1919–1923, politics 1924–1929 had clearly become more stable. After 1923, there were no more attempted revolutions. The parties that supported the Republic were succeeding in gaining the support of the electorate in state and federal elections. However, that still left 30% of the votes cast going to parties that opposed the Republic, a substantial base on which those parties could build.

Away from, though connected to, the world of party and Reichstag politics, special-interest campaigning flourished. This was shown by the emergence of hundreds of different pressure groups pursuing targeted campaigns. They came from all across the political spectrum, but the majority were conservative and nationalist. Their activities were taken forward in posters, leaflets, petitions and letter-writing campaigns, marches, rallies and meetings. There were many large, national pressure groups, as well as small, local ones. One of the largest was the National Rural League (*Reich Landbund*). Established in 1921, it represented the interests of right-wing farmers and landowners, especially those from east of the River Elbe. Politically it was close to the DNVP. It had a strong central administration and a number of affiliated organisations. By 1924 it had some 500 district offices and by 1929 directly or indirectly controlled nearly 200 press outlets. Its membership was around 1 million. In some ways, these campaigns are the sign of a healthy democracy with an active citizenry.

Another sign of stability might be found in the fact that in the 1928 elections the right-wing DNVP, which was opposed to the Republic, lost much of the support and seats that it had gained in 1924 (when the Ruhr Occupation had inflamed nationalist feelings). The Communist vote also dropped a little, while the SPD vote rallied from its 1924 post-Barmat droop. However, some problems had not gone away. Unemployment was still dangerously high. This was a political as well as an economic problem. Paramilitary groups, fed by unemployment, still fought one another in the streets. In addition, some commentators at the time drew attention to the fact that in electing Hindenburg, the electorate had chosen as head of state someone fundamentally opposed to the nature of that state.

There was a great deal that was new in Germany: the political system, of course, but also the opportunities available to women. These developments meant that there were divisions between supporters and opponents of change. For as long as the economy was stable, the political debate over the nature and speed of change was manageable. Once the economy was unstable, these divisions could be exploited by extremists.

Germany's international position

Stresemann's foreign policy aims and achievements

From August 1923 Chancellor Stresemann's DVP was in a coalition government with the SPD and others. Stresemann was already the subject of some suspicion as a known monarchist. At the end of October 1923 he announced the ending of resistance to the occupation of the Ruhr. In November 1923, his administration was judged by some to have dealt too leniently with the Munich Putsch. The Social Democrats announced that they were leaving the Coalition, which then collapsed. The new chancellor, Wilhelm Marx of the Centre Party, put together a new coalition, appointing Stresemann Foreign Secretary, a post he was to hold in several governments until 1929.

Stresemann was as eager as most Germans to reverse what they regarded as the deeply unfair and onerous provisions of the Treaty of Versailles, especially the war-guilt clause and the reparations payments demanded by the victorious Allies. However, he also believed that Germany needed breathing space if it was to prosper again. As foreign secretary, he tried to achieve this aim by seeking to keep the Allies content by meeting the obligations placed on Germany by the Treaty of Versailles. This policy came to be known as 'fulfilment'.

In addition he wanted to settle all disputes over borders and defence with Germany's western neighbours, and help the country regain a respected place in international diplomacy. Stresemann always made it clear, however, that this policy lay in the field of reparations and the western borders. The eastern frontiers of Germany were not to be included, and recovery of lands lost to Poland in 1918 was to remain a high priority of German foreign policy throughout the Weimar period. Understandably this was of great concern in Poland but the Allies were far more concerned with their own future security. Finally he wanted to end the foreign occupation of German territory.

Locarno

The following year, 1925, in the lakeside town of Locarno in Switzerland a series of peace treaties were negotiated by all the major European powers, notably France, represented by foreign minister Aristide Briand, and Britain, represented by foreign secretary Austen Chamberlain. Gustav Stresemann represented Germany. Locarno was hailed at the time as in effect securing peace for Europe. Stresemann, on behalf of Germany, gave guarantees against any future aggression against France or Belgium, confirming its western borders. At the same time France and Belgium agreed not to attack Germany. All of these undertakings were to be guaranteed by the USA and Italy. However, Stresemann refused to do the same in the east. Germany would not renounce its claims to Danzig (modern Gdansk), other parts of Poland, and the Sudetenland (the German-speaking western fringe of Czechoslovakia). The treaties were a complex series of seven agreements. In recognition of their contribution to peace in Europe, Gustav Stresemann was awarded the Nobel Peace Prize in 1926 together with Aristide Briand. Austen Chamberlain and Charles G. Dawes had been awarded the 1925 prize.

The League of Nations

The admission of Germany to the newly formed League of Nations as a Permanent Member of the Security Council in September 1926 was a sign of international approval and a remarkable moment for Gustav Stresemann and Germany after the humiliations of 1919. It brought Germany the power to block any League of Nations proposal that might help to stabilise the economy of Poland or guarantee the security of its neighbours to the east.

The League of Nations had been established in January 1920 as a direct result of the Paris Peace Conference that brought the First World War to an end in November 1918. Its primary purpose was to end the use of conflict to settle international disputes. The main means were to be disarmament and collective security. The League had no armed force itself and so relied on the Great Powers to enforce its decisions if needed, to apply economic sanctions and so on. In addition it was concerned with drug trafficking, the arms trade, global health, prisoners of war and the protection of minorities.

Despite some early successes such as resolving the Åland Islands dispute between Sweden and Finland in 1921, an argument over the port city of Memel on the Baltic between Lithuania and Poland in 1924, and over the status of Mosul between Iraq and Turkey in 1926, the League of Nations did not succeed in truly fulfilling the terms of its mandate. Nevertheless, it was a bold and imaginative attempt to end conflict and to address other important international problems. At its height (in the mid-1930s), it had a membership of 58 countries, although the USA never joined.

There were several different agendas behind all of this diplomatic activity. France and Belgium had suffered much material damage and were deeply concerned that Germany should never be able to invade their countries again. The issue was simple – how to ensure that Germany remained weak economically and militarily despite its many evasions of the Versailles terms. Britain was somewhat less severe. On the one hand, Britain did not wish for a rival sea power nor did it want an enemy in France or on the Channel coast. The war had cost Britain dearly in lives and expense and it wanted reparations to be paid. On the other hand, a greatly weakened Germany might, as J.M. Keynes had argued, become so unstable as to launch another major war in Europe, and that was the last thing Britain wanted.[7] Also, a weakened Germany could never be a counterbalance to France or make for the stable Europe that Britain wanted as a major trading nation. The USA was reluctant to be drawn into the quicksands of European politics and had anyway always favoured a gentler approach to a defeated Germany. It was also the case that the USA was a major supplier of food and raw materials to Germany and was herself an important export market for German manufactured goods.

The Treaty of Berlin

In November 1917, a new revolutionary government took Russia out of the First World War. In March 1918, Germany and Russia had signed the Treaty of Brest–Litovsk, by which the defeated Russia lost a significant amount of territory to the Central powers (Germany, Austria–Hungary and Turkey) and agreed to pay reparations of 6 billion marks. The territory in the west of Russia that was surrendered consisted of areas conquered over centuries where subject peoples did not speak Russian. The Treaty was designed to ensure that German-speaking elites could take a leading role, but was only in force for just over eight months before Germany surrendered on 11 November 1918. In April 1922 Germany and Russia signed the replacement Treaty of Rapallo under which each renounced all financial or territorial claims on the other. This was reaffirmed and strengthened by the Treaty of Berlin in April 1926. These treaties established a measure of stability on the eastern borders of Germany.

The end of Allied occupation

Allied occupation of parts of Germany continued for more than a decade after the end of the First World War. Five divisions of the Belgian army were based in Krefeld, close to the Rhine to the north-west of Düsseldorf. British soldiers were based in Cologne on the Rhine, while between 25 000 and 40 000 French troops of the French Army of the Rhine, mainly French colonial troops, occupied a large part of the Rhineland.

As long-serving foreign secretary, Stresemann became the acceptable face of Germany on the international circuit. His cool intelligence, obvious competence and ability to control and communicate his indignation at what he regarded as the unfair treatment of Germany in 1919 all impressed at international gatherings. His first success was the negotiation with the USA of the Dawes Plan of 1924 to gain rescheduling of the reparations debt and the removal of French and Belgian troops from the Ruhr. This was in return for German assurances that rescheduled payments and the other terms of the Treaty of Versailles would be met. Here was the policy of fulfilment in action.

Although French and Belgian troops marched out of the Ruhr area in 1925, the Rhineland area on Germany's western borders with France and Belgium was occupied until 1930, and French troops left the much smaller Saarland only in 1935. These occupations of German territory were a grievance for nationalists of all kinds, not just for the extremist political parties.

ACTIVITY 2.9

1. List Gustav Stresemann's achievements in foreign policy.
2. Note briefly what each was intended to achieve in foreign policy terms.
3. Note briefly what each was intended to achieve within Germany.

The pursuit of disarmament

The Kellogg–Briand Pact (or *General Treaty for Renunciation of War as an instrument of National Policy*, as it was officially and rather clumsily called) was signed in Paris at the end of August 1928 by representatives of Austria, Belgium, Canada, Czechoslovakia, France, Germany, British India, the Irish Free State, Italy, Japan, New Zealand, Poland, South Africa, the UK and the USA. It gets its shorter name from the US secretary of state, Frank B. Kellogg, and the French foreign minister, Aristide Briand. It was widely adopted by other countries and was seen as a major advance in disarmament and the settlement of international disputes by peaceful means. It was signed on behalf of Germany by foreign minister Gustav Stresemann.

This pact was concluded outside the League of Nations. As an attempt to outlaw war it proved ineffective. Belligerent countries simply failed to declare war officially, as happened a few years later in 1931 with the Japanese invasion of Manchuria. All were less concerned with Germany's eastern borders, so that when Stresemann declined to establish a 'Locarno in Eastern Europe', there was little or no protest from the Allies, whatever their differences. In this sense Germany's eastern neighbours such as Poland, Czechoslovakia and the Soviet Union were not treated equally because they were denied the security guarantees given to France, Belgium, Italy, Britain and the USA. Nevertheless, Stresemann's contributions to diplomacy, including Germany's signing the Kellogg–Briand Pact and the other treaties, contributed to the country being treated as a reasonable partner in international discussions. Both the Dawes Plan of 1924 and the Young Plan of 1929 were drawn up during his time as foreign secretary and were made possible by his success in rehabilitating Germany.

Gustav Stresemann died of a stroke in 1929 at the age of 51. He had been a calming force in foreign policy but also a restraining and stabilising influence at home. His death left a gap in German politics which proved impossible to fill.

Timeline

1924	
January	Marx declared State of Emergency, issued emergency decree replacing trial by jury by trained and lay judges (Emminger Reform); end of hyperinflation
February	Start of Hitler's trial following Munich Putsch
March	Reichstag sought to discuss abolition of decrees; Ebert dismissed parliament to avoid discussion
May	Federal elections
June	Marx formed second cabinet
August	Dawes Committee produced proposals; Monetary Law allowed the exchange of one trillion mark note for one new Reichsmark
December	Federal elections; Marx resigned; Hans Luther formed government; Hitler released from prison

1925	
January	Marx replaced as chancellor of Germany by Hans Luther
February	Ebert died
March	First round of presidential elections
April	General Paul von Hindenburg won presidential elections
July	Belgian and French troops left Ruhr area
October	Locarno Treaties negotiated
December	Locarno Treaties signed; Hans Luther resigned as chancellor
1926	
January	Luther formed second cabinet
April	Treaty of Berlin
May	Luther resigned as chancellor, replaced by Marx
June	Referendum on expropriation of princes
September	Germany joined League of Nations
November	Seeckt allowed Prince Wilhelm to join Reichswehr manoeuvres; later Seeckt resigned as head of the army
December	Law for the Protection of Youth from Trash and Filth Writings; Marx's third cabinet ended
1927	
January	Marx's fourth cabinet
July	Unemployed Insurance Law passed
1928	
May	Federal elections
June	Marx's fourth cabinet ended, Müller became chancellor
August	Kellogg–Briand Pact signed
October	Hugenberg became head of DNVP
December	Kaas became head of Centre Party; farmers' demonstrations

Practice essay questions

1. 'Weimar Germany became a more cohesive society between 1924 and 1928.' Assess the validity of this view.
2. 'The German economy experienced a remarkable revival between 1924 and 1928.' Assess the validity of this view.
3. To what extent did the years 1924–1928 represent an era of political stability in Weimar Germany?
4. With reference to the sources below and your understanding of the historical context, assess the value of these three sources to a historian studying the stability of the Weimar Republic between 1924 and 1928.

Source A

A retired army officer recalling the culture of Berlin in the late 1920s (in Evans, R.J., *The Coming of the Third Reich* and Merkel, P.H., *Political Violence Under the Swastika*, Princeton: Princeton University Press, 1975).

Returning home, we no longer found an honest German people, but a mob stirred up by its lowest instincts. Whatever virtues were once found among the Germans seemed to have sunk once and for all into the muddy flood. … Promiscuity, shamelessness and corruption ruled supreme. German women seemed to have forgotten their German ways. German men seemed to have forgotten their sense of honour and honesty. Jewish writers and the Jewish press could 'go to town' with impunity, dragging everything into the dirt.

Source B

From the announcement by President Paul von Hindenburg on taking office, 12 May 1925. (in Lee, S.J., The Weimar Republic *Question and analysis in History*; Routledge London and New York).

I have taken my new important office. True to my oath, I shall do everything in my power to serve the well-being of the German people, to protect the constitution and the laws, and to exercise justice for every man. In this solemn hour I ask the entire German people to work with me. My office and my efforts do not belong to any single class nor to any stock or confession, nor to any party, but to all the German people strengthened in all its bones by a hard destiny. My first greetings go to the entire working population of Germany which has suffered much. It goes to our brothers outside the German borders, who are inextricably bound together with us by ties of blood and culture. … And it goes finally to our German youth, hope of our future.

Source C

From a speech given to an international audience by Gustav Stresemann in December 1925 regarding the signing of the Locarno Treaties. http://spartacus-educational.com/GERlocarno.htm

The sacrifices made by our continent in the World War are often measured solely by the material losses and destruction that resulted from the War. Our greatest loss is that a generation has perished from which we cannot tell how much intellect, genius, force of act and will, might have come to maturity, if it had been given to them to live out their lives. But together with the convulsions of the World War one fact has emerged, namely that we are bound to one another by a single and a common fate. If we go down, we go down together; if we are to reach the heights, we do so not by conflict but by common effort. For this reason, if we believe at all in the future of our peoples, we ought not to live in disunion and enmity, we must join hands in common labour. … In such co-operation the basis of the future must be sought. The great majority of the German people stands firm for such a peace as this. Relying on this will to peace, we set our signature to this treaty.

Chapter summary

By the end of this chapter you should understand the extent to which Weimar Germany had recovered from the political and economic disorder that characterised the years 1918–1923. You should be aware of changes in society, including social welfare reform and cultural developments. You will have gained further insight into the workings of the political system, and its strengths and weaknesses. You will be aware of how foreign and domestic policies affected one another. You have learned about:

- problems in the economy and the Dawes and Young Plans to solve those problems, including the continuing issue of reparations
- social welfare reforms put into place by different governments; the exciting and challenging new developments in Weimar culture; the issue of varied living standards and lifestyles
- the different programmes of moderate and extreme political parties, the significance of the election of Hindenburg as president, and the attitudes of different social groups to the Republic
- the work done by Gustav Stresemann to change Germany's international position, including the range of treaties signed with some countries, but also the significance of Stresemann not signing treaties with other countries.

End notes
[1] In Paxton, R.O. and Hessler, J., *Europe in the Twentieth Century*.

[2] Schacht, H., *Account Settled* (London: George, Weidenfeld and Nicolson, 1949).

[3] Kolbe, E., *The Weimar Republic*.

[4] Steig, M.F., *The Origin and Development of Scholarly Historical Periodicals* (Tuscaloosa: University of Alabama Press, 1986).

[5] In Beutin, W., Ehlert, K., Emmerich, W. *et al, A History of German Literature: From the beginnings to the present day* (Stuttgart: Metzlersche Verlagsbuchhandlung, 1989).

[6] Hindenburg's election was a clear victory for the nationalists.

[7] Keynes, J.M., *The Economic Consequences of the Peace*.

3 The collapse of democracy, 1928–1933

In this section, we will examine the breakdown of German politics under the impact of the Great Depression. This period includes the rapid rise of the Nazis from a fringe party to a party of government. We will consider how Hitler came to be appointed chancellor. We will look into:

- the economic, social and political impact of the Depression: elections; governments and policies
- the appeal of Nazism and Communism; the tactics and fortunes of the extremist parties, including the role of propaganda
- Hindenburg, Papen, Schleicher and the 'backstairs intrigue' leading to Hitler's appointment as chancellor
- political developments: the Reichstag fire; parties and elections; the Enabling Act and the end of democracy; the state of Germany by March 1933

The economic, social and political impact of the Depression

All economic historians commenting on the causes of the **Great Depression** of the 1930s highlight the role of the **Wall Street Crash** at the end of October 1929, when share values tumbled on the US stock exchange. However, some also

 Key terms

Great Depression: A sustained, severe, worldwide economic downturn that lasted from 1929 until the late 1930s.

Wall Street Crash: A sharp drop in share prices that began in the stock market of Wall Street, New York, on Black Tuesday, 24 October 1929.

point to the role of the USA's Smoot–Hawley Tariff Act, which in 1930 raised US tariffs on numerous imports. This was intended to protect the USA's farmers and manufacturers against foreign competition. In the event it set in motion a chain reaction of countries putting up barriers to trade, which meant that everyone traded less and everyone was worse off. Some historians argue that raising tariffs prolonged the worldwide recession. Whatever caused it, the Great Depression that followed was the longest, deepest and most widespread of the 20th century.

The economic impact of the Depression

This severe economic downturn affected almost every country in the world, especially those that depended on heavy industry or on exports. It lasted for most of the 1930s and only came to an end when rearmament towards the outbreak of conflict in 1939 created an increase in demand, thus increasing sales and employment. World trade in 1930 slumped by more than 60% as almost all countries were hit by recession. These effects could be patchy, with quite striking regional variations. Worldwide GDP, the total wealth of nations, fell by 15% from 1929 to 1932. Unemployment soared around the world. In Germany it went up at a frightening rate, doubling during 1928, doubling again from 1929 to 1930 – and then unbelievably doubling a third time from 1930 to 1933:

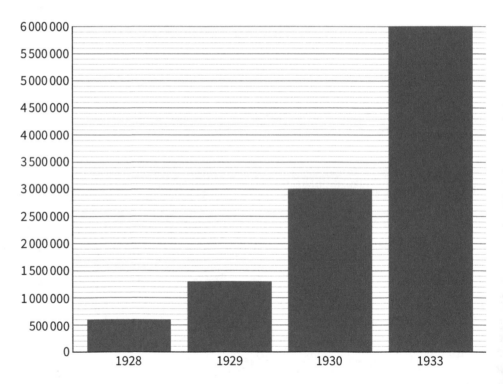

Figure 3.1: The unemployment rate in Germany doubled three times over in five years. (Figure 3.1).

These figures hide strong regional variations. Depressed industrial areas such as Thuringia had even worse statistics. Cities suffered most but even in rural areas things were bad, with crop prices falling by 60% as poverty undermined demand.

Weimar Germany was caught in a difficult situation in three ways. First, the German economy had achieved only modest growth during the 1920s, so it didnot enter the crisis in a good state. Second, after October 1929 the Smoot–Hawley Tariff Act denied Germany access to markets in the USA. This was a disaster for Germany because the USA was its major export market. Third, Germany lost US financial support in the form of huge loans negotiated in the Dawes Plan of 1924 and the Young Plan of 1929. These loans were withdrawn as the USA itself struggled. German banks could not fill the gap and German industrialists were unable to obtain credit from elsewhere. So, production and wages were lower, unemployment was higher. (See Figure 3.2 for an overview.) There was some financial support, but it was of necessity not generous. The tight rein kept by Chancellor Heinrich Brüning's government after 1930 meant that social welfare payments were limited and could do little to soften the blow.

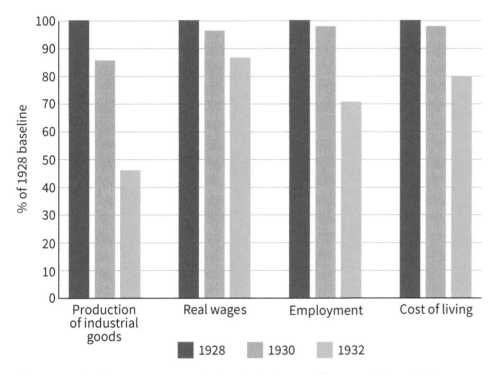

Figure 3.2: The deteriorating economic situation in Germany between 1928 and 1932.

It was by no means easy for the government of Weimar Germany to cope with all this economic turmoil. As the percentage of the working population without work went up from around 7% in mid-1928 to around 15% by mid-1930 and on upwards, so the number of people claiming social welfare payments went up, while the number of people in work and paying taxes went down, which meant government expenses went up while government income fell. Significant increases in government expenditure, often through major programmes of public works, would have been a brave though risky economic approach: it would have created employment but pushed up borrowing. The Brüning government decided this was not a realistic economic policy option. For one thing, Germany, without US bank loans and still with reparations payments to be met, was not in a position to raise the huge sums necessary for such a major economic boost. (In fact, 90% of the reparations debt was later cancelled, but that was not until 1932.) The international financial markets were in turmoil and the German government, like German manufacturers, looked in vain for sources of adequate loans.

ACTIVITY 3.1

What did Stresemann mean in his quote from Voices from the past? Explain:

1.   the surface
2.   short-term credits
3.   volcano.

To what extent do you think this source helps us to understand the economic situation in Germany? Remember to take account of the time at which Stresemann made these comments.

The government knew that a sharp increase in government expenditure often leads to inflation, and memories of disastrous hyperinflation were still raw. The Weimar Republic had lost the support and trust of the middle class (*Mittelstand*), which had been especially badly hit in that earlier economic crisis.

Germany had suffered from a vast trade deficit of 2.9 billion Reichsmarks in 1928. By 1931, this has been turned into almost its mirror opposite, a trade surplus of 2.8 billion Reichsmarks. This means that it exported more than it imported, which sounds like good news. However, Adam Tooze argued that the surplus was the result of domestic demand for foreign imports falling.[1] The Depression caused rising poverty, and households and businesses could not afford to buy much.

Germany had to import raw materials of all kinds, even food. Germany's main export was manufactured goods made from these imported raw materials. Huge industrial companies and corporations like Siemens, AEG, IG Farben and the Vereinigte Stahlwerke were the backbone of the German export economy. But even these industrial giants were not safe from the world economic downturn. The Vereinigte Stahlwerke (Combined Steelworks) was a large conglomerate that brought together some of the biggest steel makers in Germany, most of them concentrated in the Ruhr valley. Its creation in 1926 pulled into one company some of the best-known industrialists of the period, including Fritz Thyssen, who became the group's chairman. (The group did not include Krupp, as it did not itself manufacture steel.) When this group was set up, prices had already begun to slip and sales to drop off. After the Great Depression struck, the company was part-nationalised in 1932 to avoid bankruptcy, with the Weimar government buying stock in a deal that sparked controversy. The controversy only deepened when Chancellor Heinrich Brüning claimed the company had then donated 500 000 Reichsmarks to the NSDAP to support its campaign in the 1932 elections.

Below these large companies were hundreds of smaller mass-producers, making and exporting everything from bolts to binoculars. As Adam Tooze makes clear, light industry in central and eastern Germany, heavy industry in the Rhine valley, and the ports of the Baltic and the North Sea had one thing in common: they depended on foreign trade. With the world in recession, there were not enough individuals and companies able to buy their manufactured goods.

 Voices from the past

Gustav Stresemann

Shortly before his death in early November 1929, when the effects of the Wall Street Crash had only just begun, Gustav Stresemann had already said:

The economic position is only flourishing on the surface. Germany is in fact dancing on a volcano. If the short-term credits are called in, a large section of our economy would collapse.[2]

The social impact of the Depression

For millions of German workers wages had to be earned to put food on the table and clothes in the wardrobe, to pay rent, to buy school books. For that to be possible, jobs had to exist. Steelworkers in the Ruhr area, bank clerks in Berlin or labourers on Hanover building sites all depended on the good health of an export-led economy. The economic downturn meant that more and more people who had been in work, able to earn money and make plans, found themselves without work, without money and with little hope for the future. Whenever a large business was hit by the consequences of the Great Depression, the results fanned out through a huge number of other employers. The first impact might be on the hundreds of thousands of workers at these huge industrial concerns, but it always spread to those with jobs in the smaller manufacturers who were their suppliers, the dock workers who loaded their manufactured goods onto ships for export, and then the shops where all of these people and their families were customers.

Betty Scholem was more fortunate than some other victims of the economic downturn because she had some savings to fall back on. However, as a shopkeeper she depended for survival on the banks which, by 1931, were in severe difficulty. A similar pattern of poverty and unemployment was to be found all over Germany in the early 1930s, especially in former mining areas (shown in Figure 3.3, for example).

Figure 3.3: Families of unemployed miners in the Ruhr Valley search for winter fuel in the remains of a slag-heap, 1931.

The effect of all this economic turmoil on the lives of ordinary families in Germany cannot be overestimated. Many families continued to enjoy a degree of prosperity.

However, even they will have felt the menace of poverty and homelessness all around them. People of all sorts – children, parents, families, old and young – were all affected. Prices for goods including food were declining sharply, so for those in secure work, things might actually have improved. But for those without a job, there was a daily struggle to afford food and fuel while the economic news became ever worse.

The political impact of the Depression

The Great Depression had a major effect on German politics. Many neoconservative and right-wing groups had never felt any sort of commitment to the liberal and democratic ideals of the Weimar Republic. The social elites were, in

 Hidden voices

Betty Scholem

Betty Scholem, whose shop in Zemsdorf, a village in north-east Germany, sold price tags and similar goods, wrote to her daughter in the summer of 1931:

My dear child,

Your letter of the twenty-second arrived on the thirtieth. Meanwhile, you should already have received two letters from me describing the terrible situation. Technically, I'm in no position to give you a complete picture of the collapse, which you'd need in order to really understand what's happening. The year 1930 was still a good one. We were a bit in the red; but given more or less normal business, we still hoped to make it up eventually. We never would have taken such a long trip if we'd had an inkling that such a crisis lay ahead!! It hit us like a catastrophe. An enormous fall in the demand for price tags caused our debts to swell. Just as all business came to a halt, the bank failed; so there was no one to speak to. The banks went into a government holding company, which showed no interest in the debts of 'customers'. All of this happened at once. It looks as if we'll lose everything. It's cold comfort to know that the entire commercial sector is in the same position and that more shops are going under than staying afloat. Since everywhere you look there's desert, you see no chance to plant anything new. The situation is desperate. […]

I cannot continue to maintain my own house and household – this much seems certain. A pity, isn't it? My mama, hardly a wealthy woman, at least died in her own apartment. Of all the possible alternatives left to me, moving in with Erich seems the best. […] As long as we can still keep the house, I want to stay in my own apartment. For now, the rent of

170 marks is still easy to come up with. Martha helps with the cleaning, and for lunch I go upstairs. I make my own breakfast, and evenings I'm mostly out. As an innocent victim of Germany's crisis, I will have to place my existence upon the famous 'other basis' and enjoy the last good thirty years of my life like a fine-tasting stew.

Even though at the moment things aren't so bad that I have to give up the household, they could reach that point at any time. I'll ask you now if you could use anything, because it takes two to three weeks to get a letter back. Selling things amounts to giving them away. I'll let Werner have what he can take; other things can be stored in the attic of the Fregehaus. It's impossible to send furniture to Palestine, isn't it? Shipping and taxes are expensive, and who can pay them? You must bear in mind that we have nothing. […]

With kisses, Mum[3]

Discussion points

1. What was the situation of Betty Scholem's business before the crash?
2. How did the Depression affect the business?
3. Describe briefly the situation that Betty Scholem foresaw for herself and her family.
4. What social class would you see the Scholems belonging to and what political party do you think they saw as their representatives?
5. To which ethnic or religious group do you think the Scholems belonged and what evidence do you have for this in the text?

general, opposed to Weimar but had supported it when revolutionary Bolshevism on the Russian model had seemed all too likely in Germany after 1919. This support faded. The middle class, so badly hit in the hyperinflation of 1923, would never trust the Republic again. Much working-class support went to the extreme political parties of the left, especially to the KPD.

Political extremism on the right was growing as the economic crisis in Germany deepened in the early 1930s. The DNVP, the second largest party in the 1928 federal elections, had lost support to the NSDAP. The latter, led by Adolf Hitler, had emerged as the standard bearer of the extreme right, offering apparent solutions that in more normal times might have been rejected by the electorate out of hand.

There are clear signs of political instability in the last years of the Weimar Republic. There were four national elections between 1928 and 1933, with two of them in 1932 alone. Also in 1932, President Hindenburg appointed no fewer than four chancellors. Voters began to abandon the parties of the political centre ground and move their support to the extreme parties of both right and left. This made the creation of coalitions harder. For a political system that the electorate had only known for a decade or so, this was bound to undermine confidence.

The Müller government

When the SPD won the May 1928 elections, the Wall Street Crash was still a year and a half in the future. After a period of negotiation, Hermann Müller became chancellor in June, leading a coalition in which his own Social Democrats were joined by the Centre Party, the moderate DDP and Stresemann's DVP. Müller and Stresemann got on well, but the coalition was under continual strain. Among other conflicts, the DVP would not support the SPD in providing financial assistance to the 200 000 or more employees of the Ruhr iron and steel industry whom the employers had locked out during their bitter 1928 strike.

Agreeing the 1929 budget and the external liabilities of the Reich was a huge problem, and the partners put their hopes in renegotiating the conditions set by the Allies. As the Depression began to take effect in Germany, all issues concerning the budget became of ever greater importance until disagreements within the coalition proved fatal. Müller was unwell and unable to manage affairs as effectively as was necessary in the job of chancellor in an argumentative coalition. As unemployment climbed, the cost of welfare payments rose and the parties were unable to reach a compromise on how to fund this. In October, Stresemann, whose diplomatic skills had helped keep the coalition together, died. When President Hindenburg refused to support Müller's government by using the Article 48 emergency powers, Müller had no choice but to resign on 27 March 1930. Müller himself had only a year to live, and his resignation constituted the end of the normal democratic process in Germany.

The 1930 federal election

The Social Democrats had declared the Weimar Republic in 1918. They had established it with a constitution and elections in 1919 on social democratic principles. They had been a dominating presence through the first decade of its existence. By 1932 they had lost considerable support. From nearly 30% of the vote in May 1928 their share slumped to just over 10% by November 1932. The

---

ACTIVITY 3.2

Betty Scholem relates her own circumstances to the wider picture of the German economy and society. Write a paragraph taking note of what she says and develop this contextualisation yourself, drawing on your answers to the discussion points and commenting on the way this source throws light on the economic situation in Germany.

ACTIVITY 3.3

1. Review the period of hyperinflation in Germany 1921–1924. Reread your notes on its key social effects and the groups in society it affected, or make new ones.

2. Now make similar notes regarding the economic situation 1929–1933, with high unemployment. Find out more about the social effects and the groups in society it affected.

conservative and Roman Catholic Centre Party, which had helped write the 1919 constitution, kept a steady proportion of the vote in federal elections 1928–1932 of around 15%. But its socially conservative right wing (which communicated most naturally with parties like the DVP) had become more influential in decision-making than its social-justice left (which could reach agreement with the DDP and SPD). During this period the Centre was in alliance with the equally conservative and Roman Catholic Bavarian People's Party (BVP), which had begun as a Centre party breakaway in 1919, and had been marked by monarchism and a tendency to support Bavarian independence from Berlin. 'Zentrum' had been successful in the coalition politics of recent years. However, although it proved capable of maintaining its percentage in election results, Germany had a substantial majority of Protestants, so the party was incapable of reaching out beyond its core vote to become a majority force in politics.

It was instead to the political parties of the extreme right and extreme left that many voters turned for a solution to Germany's problems. The federal election to the Reichstag of May 1928 had seen the NSDAP gaining just 2.6% of the votes cast, getting them 12 seats, slightly down from their 1924 achievement and dwarfed by the DNVP. However, in the federal elections of September 1930 they gained 18.3% of the vote and 107 seats, while the DNVP lost some of its support. It was a breakthrough election for the Nazis: for the first time they were a major player in the political game. For years the DDP, DVP and Centre had been in government with less support and fewer seats than this.

In the two and a half years between these two elections, politics in the Weimar Republic had become more and more unstable as successive governments struggled to cope with the economic crisis of the Depression. The Social Democrats, traditionally the strongest party in the Weimar Republic, gained nearly 30% of the vote and 153 seats in the Reichstag in 1928. But they slipped to 24.5% and 143 seats in the 1930 election. Their loss in these two and a half years was one of the symptoms of the movement of voters to the Nazis and to a lesser extent to the Communists (KPD), whose share of the vote increased from 10.6% in 1928 to 13.1% in 1930.

The Brüning government

Following the departure of Müller, Heinrich Brüning, leader of the Centre Party, was immediately appointed Chancellor by the President. During his career in the Prussian parliament and the Reichstag, Brüning had built up a reputation for economic management. He had come to the President's attention in part when he led the Centre Party in supporting the Young Plan and insisted it be paid for it through tax increases and budget cuts. This reputation for financial caution was reinforced by his own private life, which was also modest and without luxury. As a result, he was considered well qualified to confront the economic crisis of the times. Brüning's greatest fear was inflation, and his economic policies – sharp cuts in government spending, tight control over money supply – did lead to sharp deflation of the German economy. This in turn led to a severe rise in unemployment, but some economic historians argue that this was an attempt to convince the Allies that reparations payments by Germany were no longer appropriate.

Brüning was a complex character. He had volunteered for service in the First World War, despite being short-sighted and not physically robust; he had been decorated for bravery. Like the great majority of Germans he loathed reparations and thought them deeply unfair. When younger, he had been involved in organising the passive resistance to the Ruhr occupation and seemed to favour political parties of a nationalistic, conservative sort. Lacking a majority in the Reichstag, he couldn't always force through the legislation he wanted, and so relied on President Hindenburg to push his economic policies through by decree. This was an option that was available to him in times of emergency under the Weimar Constitution, and one that was used far more than the writers of the 1919 Constitution could have foreseen.

As unemployment continued to climb, 1932 proved a year of rising political street violence. Brüning was not a man to tolerate this kind of thing. He banned both the Nazi *Sturmabteilung* (storm division, SA) and the communist *Roter Frontkämpferbund* (Red Front Fighters League).

Like all other Weimar leaders, he also depended on support from the Reichswehr and other conservatives. He seemed to left-wing critics to be overeager to keep the right happy. However, his career as chancellor was an undoubted balancing act. The army and many leading German industrialists were initially in favour of his appointment as chancellor, believing him to be a conservative who would take the Weimar government to the right. But as company profits declined and bankruptcies increased he became less popular with these powerful groups. He forced down prices, wages, salaries and rents, and many complained. In negotiations with France and Britain, his government succeeded in obtaining a moratorium on payment of reparations since the hostile economic climate was making it impossible for Germany to maintain these. Brüning's policy of distributing land to unemployed workers earned the anger of landowners, including the wealthy aristocratic Prussian Junkers. Hindenburg, a Junker himself, ended his support for Brüning simply by ceasing to sign emergency decrees. Having lost the confidence of President Hindenburg, Brüning resigned in April 1932.

The 1932 presidential election

In 1932 Hindenburg was 84 years old. He had already been recalled from retirement twice (in 1914 and again in 1925) and had only intended to serve one term as president, yet he was persuaded to stand for re-election. The key reason for this was that the candidate of the right was the NSDAP's Adolf Hitler. At first, Brüning plotted to have the Reichstag extend Hindenburg's term of office; this had, after all, happened once before, with Ebert at Stresemann's urging following the assassination of Rathenau. The chancellor made conciliatory moves towards the NSDAP and DNVP, but both Hitler and Hugenberg (the DNVP leader) rejected them. The surge in support for the NSDAP in the federal elections of 1930 made Hitler feel that he had the basis of a presidential campaign. Remembering the 1925 presidential campaign, the SPD and others decided that they didn't want to split the centre and left of centre vote. Moreover, faced with a choice between Hitler and Hindenburg, they backed the known incumbent against the unknown extremist. After all, while Hindenburg was no centrist or moderate, in his first term

Key term

SA: abbreviation of *Sturmabteilung*, German word meaning `storm division'; the NSDAP paramilitary wing.

in office he had shown he knew how to play by the rules and remain loyal to the presidential oath.

Canvassing by Brüning led most of the left and centre parties of German politics – DVP, DDP, SPD and his own Centre – to support the Hindenburg candidacy, even though the SPD's left wing initially opposed this move. While the NSDAP put up Hitler, the DNVP proposed *Stahlhelm* leader Theodore Duesterberg as its candidate. This far-right split destroyed the attempted unity of the **Harzburg Front** (a topic to which we shall return).

The left-wing vote split much as it had done in 1925. The KPD again put forward Thälmann, hopeful that SPD voters who could not face supporting Hindenburg would swing behind the only left-wing candidate on offer. The first round of voting took place in March 1932. Winning 49.6% left Hindenburg just short of the figure he needed for election victory; under the constitution he needed a simple majority. The coalition of parties supporting him was clearly working, though: he was winning votes from areas with a history of supporting the SPD or Centre in elections.

The Communists did not have a major breakthrough. Although their support was considerably up on the first presidential election of 1925, it was on a par with the 1930 federal elections, so they had obviously not won over additional disaffected Social Democrats. Duesterberg was the clear loser and dropped out of the race, leaving Hindenburg, Hitler and Thälmann to enter the second round of voting. This time the *Landbund* advised members to support Hitler. The DNVP and *Stahlhelm* offered no advice to their supporters, but the second-round numbers show that Duesterberg's supporters voted as a block for Hitler in the second round. Hindenburg was duly elected president with 53% of the vote, but Hitler's 30% was a respectable showing.

There was more to consider. Despite being a Protestant noble and Prussian officer, Hindenburg was returned to office only because of the support of Catholics and the left wing. He seems to have found this fact a personal embarrassment and to have taken steps to distance himself from his own supporters. In May he dropped Brüning, the man who had brought about his election.

Papen as chancellor

Franz von Papen was a Catholic aristocrat and Centre Party politician who came to be one of President Paul von Hindenburg's closest advisers. He replaced Heinrich Brüning as chancellor in June 1932. This promotion from what had been an influential but essentially backstage role owed a lot to General Kurt von Schleicher, another conservative who was part of President Hindenburg's inner circle of advisers and acted as effective head of the Reichswehr. Papen had already made himself unpopular with some in his party when he supported Hindenburg in the 1925 presidential election rather than the party's own Wilhelm Marx. In accepting the post of chancellor he made more enemies, since in doing so he was replacing the Centre Party's Brüning. Furthermore, only the day before he had assured the Centre Party's chairman that he would not accept an appointment. Papen, knowing he would be expelled from the party for this second piece of disloyalty, resigned his membership two days after his appointment as chancellor.

Key term

Harzburg Front: a campaigning group including several right-wing groups and parties.

ACTIVITY 3.4

Reread your notes on the 1925 presidential elections. Compare the range of candidates standing in 1932 with those in 1925, and the votes that they received. What do the differences tell you about changes in German politics and society over the intervening seven years?

Schleicher remained an important figure in the new government. He became defence minister. In addition, he, not Papen, chose the cabinet. Papen had little support in the Reichstag, which left him reliant on the president. Even among the right-wing parties only the conservative DNVP was willing to back him. In the hope of bringing the Nazis onto his side, he repealed Brüning's ban on the SA. In Berlin, Communists and the SA fought pitched battles in that gang-warfare extension of party politics into street life so characteristic of the period. Papen seized control of the situation and moved against the city authorities, for Berlin lay within the state of Prussia and the disorders gave him an excuse to arrest its leftist politicians on the grounds that they were supporting the Communists. An emergency decree from Hindenburg declared Papen commander of the area: one more democratic institution had been subverted.

It is important to remember that even with all the politicking, government and diplomacy was continuing. For example, during the Papen administration, German representatives met those of Britain and France in Lausanne, Switzerland, in June–July 1932. The Lausanne Conference agreed to suspend Germany's payment of reparations. This built on the preceding achievements of Gustav Stresemann from 1924 to 1929, and on the moratorium agreed the previous year. Also in July 1932, Papen called a federal election, vainly hoping it would give him the Reichstag majority and thus the legitimacy he lacked. He only succeeded in strengthening the Nazis' hand as they were the main winner, becoming the largest party.

Seeing the results, Papen asked Hindenburg to decree the dissolution of the Reichstag. He then held in reserve what he assumed was a trump card, watching to see how the first session of the newly elected Reichstag played out. The Communists were bound to table a motion of **no confidence:** surely the right-wing parties wouldn't want to be seen supporting them? In the event, the expected opposition to the Communists did not occur. Papen accordingly decided to read the dissolution decree. However, to do this he needed the permission of the new president of the Reichstag. This was now the Nazi Hermann Göring and the latter ignored him pointedly. The Nazis supported the Communist motion, the vote of no confidence went through and another election was automatically triggered.

Four months after their triumph in July, the NSDAP again emerged as the largest party, but again without an absolute majority of Reichstag seats. Rather than prop up the Papen government, Hitler tried to form a Nazi government with himself as chancellor and Nazis taking the key ministerial positions in the cabinet. Papen refused to cooperate, but was no more able to form a government than Hitler was. A meeting between the president and Hitler failed to produce an agreement. Some voices in the NSDAP leadership wanted a negotiated solution to the standoff. That was not Hitler's style. He was, as his biographer Ian Kershaw said in *The 'Hitler Myth',* a gambler.

The July and November 1932 federal elections

By the time of the July 1932 elections, the economic situation had worsened. The NSDAP was now acting like a major party. It was drawing on a strong party organisation, making use of effective propaganda and backed with adequate funding. In addition, its political message now appealed to more voters. In July 1932, 37% of the voting electorate supported the NSDAP and it won 230 seats in

Key term

No confidence: In politics, a leader or government that lacks the confidence of parliament is no longer trusted by a majority of that parliament and is unable to govern. After a vote of no confidence, the government is obliged to resign.

ACTIVITY 3.5

Make notes briefly comparing Brüning's response to the economic crisis with Schleicher's. You might find the best way to do this is to divide a piece of paper in half vertically and putting one on each side of the dividing line. Review the comparison and briefly list what strike you as the major advantages and disadvantages of each approach.

Key term

Nationalism: a political point of view or tradition whereby one's country is prioritised above competing demands on one's time and resources; the belief that one's own country is special – this can take the form of believing it is always best, always right or both.

the Reichstag. It had doubled its representation in the Reichstag. This was easily the largest vote for any party, well over 10% greater than the second-placed Social Democrats. This was a historic moment, the first time that the SPD had not occupied the top spot in a federal election since the founding of the Republic. The SPD lost a few seats; the KPD celebrated a modest increase in support. Proportionally the bigger losses were sustained by the three small parties of the centre ground: the DVP lost 23 of its 30 seats; the renamed DDP (now the German State party) lost 16 of its 20 seats; the WP (the *Mittelstand* party) lost 21 of its 23 seats.

This change in voting patterns has been much analysed by historians, and it has been shown to reflect different things for different social classes and groups. But the fact that the NSDAP was able to take account of voter discontent so much more effectively than the KPD is striking. It suggests that in supporting the NSDAP, voters had decided that class- and social-group solidarity was trumped by **nationalism** and national solidarity.

The option of blaming other Germans for the crisis, which the KPD offered, did not appeal as much as that of blaming non-Germans – the Treaty-of-Versailles-foreigners outside Germany, and Jews and other minority groups within Germany. Within months another election became necessary, and the situation was largely repeated. In November the NSDAP were again the largest party, though their vote slipped back a little to 33% and 196 seats, in part as a consequence of Hitler having turned down the post of vice-chancellor – but they were still by far the largest party in the Reichstag. The SDP vote slipped a little further; the KPD strengthened a little, perhaps at the expense of the SDP. Even so, as the total number of Reichstag deputies was 584, the Nazis and other right-wing extremist parties could have no absolute majority without the removal of Social Democrats and Communists. It was becoming impossible to marginalise the NSDAP: they were redefining the middle ground in German politics and would have to be brought into government.

The Schleicher government

General Kurt von Schleicher was a soldier who was active in civilian politics. It was he who had proposed Papen to Hindenburg for chancellor in June 1932, he who chose the cabinet and he who only served as minister of defence from June to November 1932. On Papen's losing both the 1932 elections, he agreed to become chancellor himself. In common with almost all senior Reichswehr officers, he bitterly resented the Treaty of Versailles of 1919 and its military restrictions and spent a good deal of time and energy in seeking to evade them. Schleicher was an advocate of 'total war', which means involving the entire population in the war effort and implies mass conscription and mobilisation of the civilian population, and might involve strategic bombing, blockade, unrestricted submarine warfare and even the use of civilians and prisoners of war as forced labour. Total war needed authoritarian government of the type promised by Hitler and the Nazis, rather than the more complicated processes of the democratic Weimar Republic, with all its compromises and delays in decision-making, and its argumentative Reichstag. This made his attitude towards the authoritarian NSDAP relatively favourable.

Schleicher made a decisive intervention in the field of economic policy, reversing the Brüning years of austerity and big cuts in government spending. He initiated a major public-works programme for Germany in January 1933. Given time, this might have brought him popularity and thus political security. Unfortunately for Schleicher, he was not in office for long enough to reap the rewards of this economic policy in terms of a fall in unemployment. Schleicher's downfall came in the area of agriculture. In his plans to respond to the economic crisis, he managed to offend the Agricultural League (*Landbund*). He had promised to introduce protectionist tariffs on food imports and had not done so: the agriculture minister had demanded them, the economics minister had opposed them and the chancellor had not taken a lead on the issue, so nothing was done. The powerful agricultural lobby complained bitterly to Hindenburg. Because of his background, the President was naturally close to landowners, and as letters and telegrams from the Junkers started arriving on Hindenburg's desk, demanding Schleicher's dismissal, he summoned the chancellor to a meeting.

The appeal of Nazism and communism

The tactics and fortunes of the extremist parties

The political mood in Germany had become tense after 1929. The political legitimacy of the Weimar Republic had been based on the factors illustrated in Figure 3.4, but the situation was now changed.

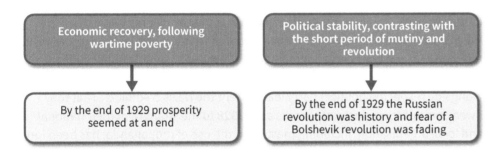

Figure 3.4: The basis of legitimacy of the Weimar Republic.

The 'Liberty Law' (*Freiheitsgesetz*) campaign

The various right-wing groups in Germany, influential in many of Germany's most powerful institutions, began again to agitate against the liberal democracy of the Republic. An early example was the campaign for a 'Liberty Law' (*Freiheitsgesetz*). In response to the Young Plan, a coalition was formed to lobby for the implementation of this law, which had three aims:

1. to put an end to reparations payments and make it a criminal offence for any civil servant to collect any
2. to repudiate the presence of foreign troops on German soil
3. to reject absolutely the war-guilt clause (Clause 231) of the Treaty of Versailles.

This coalition was formed by the DNVP leader, the vehemently anti-Semitic and nationalist politician and businessman Alfred Hugenberg, and comprised a number of conservative groups including the NSDAP, the *Stahlhelm* and the anti-Semitic, anti-Polish Pan-German League, as well as the DNVP itself.

Hugenberg had been Chairman of the Board of Krupp before 1914 and had supervised their financial operations with great success. After 1918 he had bought up many local newspapers and controlling shares in a number of national media outlets. He used these to keep up a relentless attack on the Weimar Republic. He also took over the UFA film studios near Berlin. A long-time monarchist and ultra-conservative, Hugenberg's political activity in the late 1920s was concentrated on his leadership of the DNVP. He appointed himself to leadership of many of the right-wing pressure groups so prevalent in Weimar Germany.

Under the terms of the Weimar Constitution, if 10% of the electorate signed a petition on an issue, it had to be put to a vote in the Reichstag. The coalition held mass rallies and set about gathering signatures. In this, they succeeded, and the measure was accordingly put to a vote in the Reichstag in 1929, where 18% voted for it, not enough for it to become law; the centrist parties all opposed it and for now they were powerful enough to defeat it. The campaign then moved, under the terms of the constitution, to a referendum in December 1929, where it again failed to garner enough votes. Almost all those who turned out to vote did support the campaign, but the voters were the minority; the majority did not vote at all and that fact was what defeated the campaign.

Even though it failed, the fact that the campaign got as far as it did was a measure of the growing strength of the right in German politics. The campaign contributed to the improved standing of the Nazis. This was the sort of political activity that Hitler's party relished: it played to their strengths in the world of **propaganda**. The referendum campaign had granted the Nazi Party considerable publicity through Hugenberg's newspapers, giving Hitler nationwide prominence. Appearing alongside respected political party leaders lent the Nazis credibility. That they owed some of their electoral success after 1928 to the strength of their national and local organisation, including mastery in the use of propaganda, has been long recognised. But they owed a great deal too to Hugenberg's financial and media support.

The Harzburg Front and the Iron Front

Two years later, the Nazis engaged in a second campaign with Hugenberg, though of a different kind. Hugenberg was the driving force behind the founding of the Harzburg Front in October 1931. The Harzburg Front brought together a number of political and paramilitary parties and groups of the right. As with the *Freiheitsgesetz* campaign, these included the NSDAP, the *Stahlhelm*, the Pan-German League and Hugenberg's own DNVP. They were joined by the Agricultural League, which had a history of voting with the DNVP in the Reichstag.

The NSDAP was not going to be led by established, elderly politicians like Hugenberg. They were willing to join the Harzburg Front, but it was only a temporary measure. Adolf Hitler had already been in discussions about the future with President Hindenburg. It was typical of the politics of the unsettled years 1928–1933 that the parties of the left reacted to the establishment of the Harzburg Front in October 1931 with the formation of the **Iron Front** a few months later.

Key terms

Propaganda: Publicity or communications material that is deliberately aimed at pushing a particular political (and often simplified) message onto its audience in an appealing and convincing way in order to affect their views and behaviour.

Iron Front: a left-wing campaigning group including several left-wing groups and parties.

This included the **Reichsbanner**, the SPD and other groups on the democratic left of Weimar politics. It excluded what they regarded as the extremist KPD. The *Reichsbanner* was a paramilitary organisation, largely of former soldiers, dedicated to the protection of the Weimar Republic and parliamentary democracy from extremist conservative groups on the right and communists on the left. Its banner was the black, red and gold of the Republic. It was formed in 1924 from members of the SPD, the Centre Party and the DDP, but came increasingly to be seen as the militant arm of the first of these. It protected SPD meetings, marches and rallies and fought Red Front communist and Nazi SA members in the streets and in halls. This was street politics; it was also gang warfare. Both Harzburg and Iron fronts quickly fell apart and were ineffective, mainly due to internal rivalries.

Key term

Reichsbanner: a paramilitary group dedicated to the protection of the Weimar Republic and parliamentary democracy.

Thälmann and the tactics of the KPD

In times of increasing desperation, voters tend to turn to political parties on the extremes. The most spectacular gains in votes between 1928 and 1932 were made by the Nazis, but the Communists too won more votes, from 10.6% in the federal election of 1928 to 16.9% in November 1932. Led by Ernst Thälmann (Figure 3.5), they relied on the paramilitary Red Front Fighters League for protection at meetings and rallies, and had solid support in working-class areas such as Wedding in Berlin.

Figure 3.5: Ernst Thälmann (centre with raised fist) marches at the head of the Red Front through Berlin-Wedding, 1927.

Thälmann had been a member of the SPD before leaving to join the USPD in 1917 and then the KPD in 1920. Within months he had been elected to the KPD's Central Committee. In 1921 he travelled to Moscow and met the Russian Bolshevik leader Lenin. A nationalist grenade attack on his home the following year failed as he was

Figure 3.6: A Communist Party election poster from 1932, 'Schluss mit diesem System' (Enough of this System).

out at the time. In 1925 he became chairman of the Red Front and then the party's chairman. That year he ran for president against Hindenburg and the Centre Party's Wilhelm Marx. Like the NSDAP, the Communists appealed to people's frustration with the political system. A 1932 poster (Figure 3.6) contrasts a huge, strong, working man with the small plutocrats of the government.

For Thälmann, the principal enemy was the SPD, and he was responsible for a policy of conflict with the Social Democrats, both in political debate and in street fighting. Under direct instructions from Communist Moscow, this remained the policy until 1935, by which time the KPD and SPD were both banned, Thälmann himself in prison and Nazi power already unassailable. In the March 1932 presidential elections, Thälmann again ran as the KPD candidate. His campaign slogan lumped the two other candidates together as militarists:

'A vote for Hindenburg is a vote for Hitler; a vote for Hitler is a vote for war'.

The failure of the campaign was also the failure of that slogan and all it implies. In 1918, one of the widely supported revolutionary demands was the immediate end of the First World War. In 1932, an anti-war policy was not capable of rallying sufficient support. In the first round Thälmann gained 4 983 000 votes (13.2%) and the second round 3 707 000 (10.2%), suggesting that some of his supporters had voted tactically for Hindenburg to keep Hitler out.

The role of propaganda

Nazi use of propaganda

Hitler himself had been clear about the role of propaganda in *Mein Kampf*. He makes clear that political parties need to communicate with ordinary people:

 Voices from the past

Gregor Strasser

In January 1928 Gregor Strasser was put in charge of the Nazi Party national organisation. He became a leading figure in the Nazi hierarchy, a fine organiser but branded too sympathetic to the socialist roots of the NSDAP by Hitler. He was later executed on the personal orders of the Führer in June 1934 as a part of the violent suppression of the *Röhm Putsch* (the 'Night of the Long Knives').

In May 1932 Strasser made a major speech in the Reichstag, of which he was an elected member. This was later published as a pamphlet, 'Work and Bread'.

The necessities of life come from work: food, accommodation, clothing, light, and heat. The wealth of a nation lies in labour not capital and that is the point. And so when it is dealing with the question of wealth

creation the State must never ask 'Have I got the money for it?' But rather there is only one question: 'What should I use the money for?'[4]

Here was an approach to the economic problems of the country which contrasted strongly with that of the government. It was an anti-austerity message, designed to challenge Brüning's approach to the economic crisis. It helps put into perspective the concept of 'national socialism'.

Discussion points

1. Are there ways in which the political programmes and messages of the NSDAP and the KPD were similar?
2. Do you think that some voters were not choosing between the KPD and the SPD, but between the KPD and the NSDAP?

The broad masses of the people are not made up of diplomats or professors of public jurisprudence nor simply of persons who are able to form reasoned judgment in given cases, but a vacillating crowd of human children who are constantly wavering between one idea and another.

As a result, he says, a party cannot put forward evidence, analysis and argument in a political campaign. It must offer propaganda that appeals to the emotions:

Propaganda must not investigate the truth objectively and, in so far as it is favourable to the other side, present it according to the theoretical rules of justice; yet it must present only that aspect of the truth which is favourable to its own side.

Finally, the party needs to keep repeating its simple message:

The receptive powers of the masses are very restricted, and their understanding is feeble. On the other hand, they quickly forget. Such being the case, all effective propaganda must be confined to a few bare essentials and those must be expressed as far as possible in stereotyped formulas. These slogans should be persistently repeated until the very last individual has come to grasp the idea that has been put forward.

This was the basis of Nazi communication through its newspaper the *Völkischer Beobachter*, beginning in 1920, and from 1927 by Goebbels' *Der Angriff*. An experienced journalist, Joseph Goebbels knew his business. He did not limit his activities to publishing articles. He also organised demonstrations to disrupt the American film of the German novel about the horrors of the First World War, *All Quiet on the Western Front*.

Following the March 1933 election, Goebbels became minister of propaganda with the task of defining the regime's foreign and domestic enemies. High on the list of enemies were Jews. Jews were attacked in Nazi newspapers and later films such as *The Eternal Jew* (1940), which depicted them both as ill and as an illness in the German population. As well as Jews, topics for repeated attack included the Treaty of Versailles and the Communist threat. At the same time other topics were being supported: eugenics and nationalism. One of the most famous Nazi propaganda vehicles before the NSDAP came to power was an aeroplane. In the 1932 presidential elections, Hitler flew to numerous places to speak in a campaign called *Hitler über Deutschland* (Hitler over Germany). This allowed him to be seen and heard by a lot of people, but the novelty of the flight was news in itself and made Hitler seem new, modern and energetic.

Ever since its founding in 1921, the NSDAP had, in common with other nationalist and monarchist political parties and groups, been loudly critical of the Weimar Republic and all the Republic stood for. The German army had not been defeated in 1918, they declared, but had been 'stabbed in the back' (*Dolchstoss*) by cowardly civilian politicians – socialists, Bolsheviks and especially Jews, groups which the right wing tended to lump together. These were 'the November criminals' who had signed the November 1918 armistice and then gone on to sign the humiliating and unjust 1919 Treaty of Versailles. Reparations payments arising from 'war guilt' put an intolerable burden on Germany, and, it was felt by parties such as the NSDAP,

Draw a spider diagram showing:

1. how the elements in Nazi propaganda were related to one another
2. whom the propaganda was intended to affect.

Among the campaigns in which Münzenberg was involved were:

- humanitarian relief during the 1921 Russian famine
- protests against the prosecution and then execution of two American anarchists, Sacco and Vanzetti
- the World Congress Against War (held in Amsterdam in 1932)
- the World Committee against War and Fascism
- the League Against Imperialism
- the Hollywood Anti-Nazi League
- the World Society for the Relief of the Victims of German Fascism
- the International Brigades in the Spanish Civil War.

1. List the features that these different campaigns and organisations have in common.
2. Write notes commenting on the strengths and weaknesses of using these as a vehicle for the KPD message.
3. Write a short paragraph contrasting KPD propaganda with NSDAP propaganda.

the restrictions imposed on its armed forces were unacceptable to a warlike nation.

These deceitful allegations had been so often repeated by the Nazis and others that by the end of the 1920s they had acquired a large measure of public acceptance. They offered a message that was received ever more readily as the Weimar Republic struggled to cope with the third major economic crisis in the 15 years of its life. Having put the failed Munich Putsch behind him, Hitler had led the NSDAP on the long road through election campaigns. His was now a constitutional party, but he looked to exploit any weakness in the Weimar Constitution for his own ends. Weimar democracy was just not strong enough after 1929 to resist the growing political power of the right in German politics. Many right-wing groups began to coalesce around the Nazi party, which had proved itself to be well organised and ruthless, equally effective in the Reichstag and on the streets – and with an unbeatable propaganda machine.

Communist use of propaganda

The KPD head of propaganda was Willi Münzenberg. Münzenberg had a background in trade unions and the SPD, which he left, with the USPD, over how to respond to the outbreak of the First World War. He knew Lenin even before the Russian revolution, helped to create the KPD, and was a KPD deputy in the Reichstag. As the KPD was tightly linked to the Soviet Union, Münzenberg knew he had to increase Soviet influence and raise its standing. To do this, he created various organisations to act in specific campaigns, wherever possible uncontroversial ones. This would bring together communists and non-member sympathisers on the left of politics. The intention was that the experience of these single-issue campaigns would move liberals and socialists from working together with communists (against militarism, against imperialism, for peace or for famine relief) to supporting communism at elections and joining the party as activists. In addition, he built up a portfolio of newspapers, publishing houses, cinemas and theatres in Germany and in other countries, for this was an international campaign.

Münzenberg sent speakers to different countries and toured himself. In 1934 he went round the USA in the company of, among others, Welsh Labour politician Aneurin Bevan, who would later join the British government. Eventually he became disillusioned with Stalin's leadership and was expelled from the KPD. He died in France in 1940, though whether as a result of suicide, or murdered by Nazi Gestapo agents or Soviet NKVD agents, is still unclear.

Münzenberg was a great advocate for the use of film. He wrote that earlier, people on the left had been suspicious of cinema and even advised boycotting it and advising the working class to do so as well. The problem was funding, he admitted, but argued that with Soviet Russia, leftist films with an anti-bourgeois message could be made to offset the effect of pro-bourgeois commercial cinema. In the words of the title of one of his publications, the left had to 'Conquer Film'.

The *Volksfilmverband für Filmkunst* (People's Film Association, VFV) was founded in 1928. It published a magazine, *Film und Volk* (Film and People). This published articles encouraging people to make films, though few of them did, and attacking the influence of conservative and **reactionary** thinking on commercial films. The VFV also helped produce one feature film and several documentaries. *Ums tägliche Brot* (For Our Daily Bread; it is also known under other titles) was a 1929 silent film about poverty and hardship among the coal miners of Silesia. Initially Social Democrats and Communists worked side by side in the VFV, but eventually the SPD decided it was a communist front organisation and some, but not all, Social Democrats pulled out.

Hindenburg, Hitler and the path to the chancellery

Rule by presidential decree undermined democracy because it avoided the need for approval by the elected Reichstag. This meant that the central concept of representative, accountable government had been sidelined. Government had effectively become a constitutional dictatorship, a step towards tyranny. Under the Weimar Constitution, a president could rule in this way only under conditions of a national emergency. As soon as the president declared a state of emergency, rule by presidential decree became possible, bypassing the normal democratic procedure. Those who designed the Weimar Constitution in 1919 included this mechanism (Article 48) assuming that it would be used only in unusual situations, but in fact all four of the Weimar Republic's chancellors between 1930 and 1933 (Brüning, Papen, Schleicher, Hitler) ruled in this way. Presidents also had the power under the Constitution to appoint and dismiss any chancellor regardless of their support in the Reichstag. This combination meant that Paul von Hindenburg was a central figure in the political process.

President Hindenburg's refusal to appoint Hitler chancellor in August 1932 resulted in even fiercer Nazi opposition to the government led by Papen. It might have seemed a serious setback to Nazi ambitions, but the situation continued to be changeable, and Hitler was watching for the chance not to share power but to take power.

When he became chancellor, Schleicher had the same problem as Papen: a democratic deficit. He did not have support in the Reichstag. His response was to plot with the Nazi leader in Prussia, Gregor Strasser, offering to put him in charge of a new Prussian government, restored after Papen's shutting it down, as well as being vice-chancellor at the federal level. He hoped that as a result either the Nazi party would split or Hitler would be forced to support him to avoid such a split. This would then allow him to put together a coalition of Nazis and other conservatives such as the Centre Party and thus begin to win votes and pass legislation without endlessly resorting to presidential decrees. Strasser lobbied for his colleagues to follow him in supporting Schleicher. Hitler vigorously opposed this, arguing that the Nazis should stick to their campaign for Hitler to be chancellor and settle for nothing less. Hitler won the argument.

Hitler's appointment as chancellor

Article 54 of the Weimar Constitution was clear on the nature of the appointment by the Reich president of the Reich chancellor:

Key term

Reactionary: of a right-wing point of view created in reaction to a left-wing expression or course of action; conservative; wishing to re-establish a set of circumstances which have been changed.

The Reich chancellor and the Reich ministers, in order to exercise their mandates, require the confidence of the Reichstag. Any one of them has to resign, if the Reichstag votes by explicit decision to withdraw its confidence.

In plain language, the President should only appoint a chancellor who had a majority in the Reichstag or at least a sufficient number of allies to vote with the chancellor in order to pass proposals. Hindenburg was no enthusiast for the Weimar Republic, but he had taken a solemn oath (Article 42): *I swear to devote my energy to the welfare of the German people, to increase its prosperity, to prevent damage, to uphold the Reich constitution ...*; and, as a soldier, he knew all about performing his duty. Hitler was the leader of the single largest party in the Reichstag and the president was bound to consider him for the post of chancellor.

There was a small group around President Hindenburg known as the **Camarilla**, composed of Papen, Schleicher, Meissner and the President's son Oskar. This was an informal but powerful group whose advice the President considered carefully.

Of these, Meissner was regarded as Hindenburg's right-hand man. He certainly knew how things worked in the civil service. No records were kept of the discussions among the *Camarilla*. Nevertheless, Papen is usually credited with persuading President Hindenburg to choose Hitler as chancellor of Germany in January 1933. Papen seems to have argued that it was better to have Hitler inside government than outside. A cabinet including Nazis but without a Nazi majority, and with Papen effectively acting as vice-chancellor, should be enough to control Hitler, Papen thought.

Schleicher was still in the *Camarilla*, although out of favour over agricultural tariffs and his failure to achieve a majority in the Reichstag. He too tended to favour Hitler as an authoritarian figure, but also because his priority was control of the army: he concluded that he stood a better chance of being made minster of defence under Hitler than in a new Papen administration. In addition, senior officers of the Reichswehr were now lobbying for Hitler and the Nazis.

Eric Weitz puts the responsibility for the collapse of the Weimar Republic firmly on backstairs intrigue among these close personal advisers of the president and on the traditional social elites in Germany. There was, argues Weitz, nothing inevitable about the appointment. The NSDAP itself did not manage to pull the nation behind it. Their entry into government depended on 'the support of elite officers, businessmen, civil servants and nobles'.[5] Many historians take the view that when they plotted together, Hindenburg, Papen, Schleicher and the rest underestimated Hitler. But what reason did they have to be afraid of him? Papen was confident that Hitler would be his employee, willing to do what he was told. When told that in supporting Hitler to be chancellor he had made a critical error, he replied cheerfully,

'You're wrong: we've hired him.'[6]

Perhaps this misplaced confidence was the result of differences in social class. It is sometimes said that the noble Prussian Field Marshall Hindenburg struggled to imagine the lower-middle-class Austrian corporal Adolf Hitler as German chancellor. An indication of the lack of respect is the old man's habit of referring

Key term

Camarilla: President Hindenburg's group of advisers.

to him as a 'Bohemian', rather than Austrian. In the period from 1930 to 1933, Hindenburg had three times appointed as chancellor people (Brüning and Papen from the Centre Party, and Schleicher) who did not meet the constitutional test of having 'the confidence of the Reichstag'. This meant that all three had to rule by presidential decree under Article 48 of the Weimar Constitution as they did not have the support they needed in the Reichstag. This arrangement could not continue indefinitely. On 30 January 1933 President Hindenburg accordingly installed Adolf Hitler as chancellor of Germany.

Political developments of Hitler's early power

The first Hitler government

The government that Adolf Hitler formed in January 1933 was a coalition. Several posts went to NSDAP members. Hitler himself was chancellor. Wilhelm Frick, a veteran of the Munich Putsch, was minister of the interior (a post he would hold for the next 10 years). Hermann Göring was appointed interior minister of Prussia, giving him control of the largest state with the largest police force in Germany. There were non-party politicians: Papen (who had left the Centre Party the previous year) was rewarded for his support of Hitler and made vice-chancellor. However, Schleicher was to be disappointed: responsibility for the army was given to Werner von Blomberg, a fellow soldier but a man he personally detested. The wealthy Hugenberg took the Economics Ministry as one of the government's DNVP members; he was to hold it for only six months before rapidly losing political influence. Franz Seldte, the son of a factory owner, co-founder of the *Stahlhelm* and also DNVP, had supported Hitler's candidacy for the chancellorship: he became minister of labour. In April the *Stahlhelm* merged with the SA and Seldte joined the NSDAP.

Even though Papen was vice-chancellor and a majority of the January 1933 cabinet were not Nazis, in theory allowing Hitler to be outvoted, he and his conservative allies were marginalised until Hitler's cabinet was reshuffled following the March 1933 election, which was dominated by the Nazi party.

The Reichstag fire

On 27 February 1933, just six days before polling day for the March elections, there was a serious arson attack on the Reichstag building in Berlin. A young Dutch communist, Marinus van der Lubbe, was caught at the scene and later confessed to starting the fire. The Nazis used this event as evidence of a communist conspiracy against the government of Germany. Hitler urged President Hindenburg to declare a state of emergency, suspending a number of civil liberties and allowing him to govern by presidential decree as provided for in the Weimar Constitution.

The emergency decree was approved by Hindenburg and in the next few weeks there were mass arrests of KPD members, including Reichstag deputies. Thousands of left-wing activists were arrested. Among them Ernst Thälmann, the KPD leader, was arrested on 3 March 1933 and spent 11 years in solitary confinement before being executed in Buchenwald **concentration camp** in August

Key term

Concentration camp: a prison created by a barbed-wire fence and containing huts; a more temporary structure than a traditional prison; built to hold large numbers of prisoners chosen for their membership of specific groups rather than in response to their own specific (criminal) actions.

Voices from the past

Figure 3.7: President Hindenburg appoints Adolf Hitler chancellor, January 1933.

Adolf Hitler

Hitler lost no time. His first radio address as chancellor of Germany was delivered on the evening of 31 January 1933. This 'Appeal to the German People' was in effect the opening of the Nazi election campaign. Largely written by Hitler himself, it was also distributed using posters and newspapers.

Over fourteen years have passed since that unhappy day when the German people, blinded by promises made by those at home and abroad, forgot the highest values of our past, of the Reich, of its honour and its freedom, and thereby lost everything. Since those days of treason, the Almighty has withdrawn his blessing from our nation. Discord and hatred have moved in. Filled with the deepest distress, millions of the best German men and women from all walks of life see the unity of the nation disintegrating in a welter of egoistical political opinions, economic interests, and ideological conflicts.

As so often in our history, Germany, since the day the revolution broke out, presents a picture of heart-breaking disunity. We did not receive the equality and fraternity which was promised us; instead we lost our freedom. The breakdown of the unity of mind and will of our nation at home was followed by the collapse of its political position abroad.

We have a burning conviction that the German people in 1914 went into the great battle without any thought of personal guilt and weighed down only by the burden of having to defend the Reich from attack, to defend the freedom and material existence of the German people. In the appalling fate that has dogged us since November 1918 we see only the consequence of our inward collapse. But the rest of the world is no less shaken by great crises. The historical balance of power, which at one time contributed not a little to the understanding of the necessity for solidarity among the nations, with all the economic advantages resulting therefrom, has been destroyed.

The delusion that some are the conquerors and others the conquered destroys the trust between nations and thereby also destroys the world economy. But the misery of our people is terrible! The starving industrial proletariat have become unemployed in their millions, while the whole middle and artisan class have been made paupers. If the German farmer also is involved in this collapse we shall be faced with a catastrophe of vast proportions. For in that case, there will collapse not only a Reich, but also a 2,000-year-old inheritance of the highest works of human culture and civilization.

All around us are symptoms portending this breakdown. With an unparalleled effort of will and of brute force the Communist method of madness is trying as a last resort to poison and undermine an inwardly shaken and uprooted nation. They seek to drive it towards an epoch which would correspond even less to the promises of the Communist speakers of today than did the epoch now drawing to a close to the promises of the same emissaries in November 1918. …

It is an appalling inheritance which we are taking over.[7]

Discussion points

1. What is Hitler referring to in his opening sentence about 'fourteen years'?
2. What are the virtues and vices that Hitler cites (for example, honour and discord)?
3. What is Hitler implying when he refers to 'the Communist method of madness'?
4. What groups and social classes does Hitler refer to in his speech? Now comment on this source, putting it into the context of German politics in 1933.

1944. Otto Wels, the SPD leader, fled from Germany in June 1933 after the SPD was banned.

With KPD deputies gone, the Reichstag was smaller and the Nazis now had an absolute majority and could force through any measure they chose. The Reichstag met for several months in the Kroll Opera House nearby. Three leading communists were also arrested in connection with the fire. All were Bulgarians and one (Georgi Dimitrov) was a senior Comintern official responsible for all international activities of the Soviet Union in Western Europe.

At the trial, held in Leipzig in July 1933, van der Lubbe was found guilty but the others acquitted because evidence of their involvement in a criminal conspiracy was lacking. Van der Lubbe, who always maintained that he had acted alone, was executed in January 1934. Despite van der Lubbe's confession, some have argued that the Nazis were behind the fire. One theory is that the SA deliberately set fire to the building, entering the Reichstag through a tunnel and sprinkling flammable liquid inside. However, the evidence for this is thin. The debate about who was responsible nevertheless persists, because the fire occurred just a few days before the election and the Nazis benefited greatly from it, as it allowed them to discredit and eliminate the KPD and any other political opponents.

The March 1933 federal election

By 5 March 1933 and the federal election, other parties as well as the KPD had felt the effects of the Reichstag fire and the presidential decree. The Social Democrats and the Centre Party (both former members of the *Reichsbanner*) had also been harassed and some issues of the newspapers they controlled banned. The DVP, the party Stresemann had led in government, was harassed to the point where it ceased to operate in March 1933. Papen and his conservative allies in the cabinet made no protest about President Hindenburg's emergency decree, with its suspension of certain civil rights. After all, these emergency powers were provided for in the Weimar Constitution and had been used a number of times since 1919. Besides, Hitler had been chosen as an authoritarian by people who believed in authoritarian government.

The second Hitler government

Few voting in the elections held in March 1933 could have guessed that this would be the last multi-party election held in Germany until after the defeat of the Nazis, and Germany, in another world war. Once again the NSDAP gained victory, but once again they took fewer than half the votes, so again Hitler had not gained a majority in the Reichstag. It was a victory for the right wing, but other parties shared that victory.

Party	Vote / 39.3 million valid	%	Reichstag seats / 647 total
NSDAP	17.3 million	43.9	288
SPD	7.2 million	18.3	120
KPD	4.8 million	12.3	81

Party	Vote / 39.3 million valid	%	Reichstag seats / 647 total
Centre	4.4 million	11.3	73
DNVP	3.1 million	8.0	52
DDP	0.3 million	0.9	5
BVP	1.1 million	2.7	19
Other parties	1.1 million	2.7	9

Table 3.1: Results of the March 1933 federal election.

It should not go unnoticed that despite all that the Nazis and their allies had done, 12 million people chose to vote for political parties that had already been made more or less illegal: almost a third of the voting electorate. You might see this a tribute to their courage and determination as individuals, but it also says something about the continuing strength of democratic institutions in the Weimar Republic.

Even though the NSDAP still did not take a majority of Reichstag seats, the arrests and harassment quickly allowed Hitler to move from coalition government to a one-party state. Political opponents in the Reichstag had been banned since January 1933. Many were arrested and placed in concentration camps, others were on the run. Nazi officials entered the ministries in Berlin to begin what they regarded as their social revolution.

On 12 March 1933 President Hindenburg banned the flag of the Weimar Republic and ordered that the flags of Imperial Germany and the NSDAP be flown side by side instead. On 15 March, Chancellor Adolf Hitler proclaimed the Third Empire (*das Dritte Reich*). The expression used in English, the **Third Reich**, is a curious partial translation of *Dritte Reich*.

The German expression was coined to show Nazi rule as the successor to the Holy Roman Empire (which began in the early Middle Ages and lasted until 1806) and the Kaiserreich, Imperial Germany (1871–1918). Despite Hitler's proclamation – itself a propaganda move – the German state under Nazi rule largely continued to refer to itself simply as *Deutsches Reich* (German Empire), just as it had done before March 1933. Meanwhile the construction of the persecuting state progressed. On 20 March, Dachau concentration camp about 20 km east of Munich, was completed; it opened two days later.

The Enabling Act and the end of democracy

On 23 March 1933, Chancellor Hitler presented to the Reichstag an amendment to the Weimar constitution called the *Ermächtigungsgesetz*. Known in English as the **Enabling Act**, its full name was the *Gesetz zur Behebung der Not von Volk und Reich* (Law to Remedy the Distress of the People and the Empire). Far from being presented as a piece of law that would allow Adolf Hitler dictatorial powers in ruling Germany, it was proposed in moral terms as an act of 'cleansing' and indeed a remedy for distress as the law's name stated. Hitler presented it to the Reichstag in these terms:[8]

Key terms

Third Reich: partial translation of Dritte Reich (Third Empire), an expression coined to show Nazi rule as the third stage of German imperial success, following the Holy Roman Empire (which began in the early Middle Ages and ran until the beginning of the 19th century) and the Kaiserreich (1871 -1918), a German state dominated by Prussia and ruled by Prussia's king as Emperor.

Enabling Act: 1933 Nazi law abolishing political parties and democratic process.

By its decision to carry out the political and moral cleansing of our public life, the Government is creating and securing the conditions for a really deep and inner religious life. …

In this speech Hitler went on to say:

The Government will treat all other denominations with objective and impartial justice. It cannot, however, tolerate allowing membership of a certain denomination or of a certain race being used as a release from all common legal obligations or as a blank cheque for unpunishable behaviour, or for the toleration of crimes.

Hitler went on to reassure the main Christian churches, both Protestant and Catholic, that he wanted full and cordial relations with them. However, the warning to 'a certain denomination' or 'a certain race' would have been well understood by his audience as a reference to Judaism and Jewish people. Only Otto Wels, the SPD leader, spoke against the Enabling Act in the Reichstag (meeting in the Kroll Opera House following the fire the previous month). Wels declared:

At this historic hour, we German Social Democrats pledge ourselves to the principles of humanity and justice, of freedom and socialism. No Enabling Law can give you the power to destroy ideas which are eternal and indestructible. … From this new persecution too German Social Democracy can draw new strength. We send greetings to the persecuted and oppressed. We greet our friends in the Reich. Their steadfastness and loyalty deserve admiration. The courage with which they maintain their convictions and their unbroken confidence guarantee a brighter future. … You can take our lives and our freedom, but you cannot take our honour. We are defenceless but not honourless.

Three months later Wels fled the country.

The SPD presence had been reduced: some deputies had already fled or been arrested. The 81 SPD deputies then in the chamber voted against the Enabling Act, but they were heavily outnumbered. The KPD, who might have voted with them, had been banned. The other parties, perhaps not realising they were effectively voting to abolish themselves and the Republic, all voted with the Nazis, and with the necessary two-thirds majority, the constitution was amended.

The state of Germany by March 1933

Hitler had come to power in a state that had weakened its own constitution time and again. It did have an elected president and an elected national assembly, but the elections had proved less and less able to produce unified, effective governments. During periods of prosperity, vigorous political disagreements are likely to be viewed by an electorate as necessary or at least as tolerable. During crises, such as when over 6 million people are without work, they are likely to seem an unaffordable luxury.

By the time that Hitler became chancellor, the process of bypassing the Reichstag by the use of presidential decrees was an established political method. His resort to it would not shock or even surprise. Other governments had a record of regarding the eastern borders established in 1919 as merely temporary, and other politicians had openly discussed Poland's very existence as an obstacle to be overcome, rather than a diplomatic fact to be lived with. Hitler's published views on this matter would thus surprise no one. The Nazis' anti-Semitism was also well known. But it too was a view widely shared across German society. The move to arrest SPD and KPD members might have shocked Social Democrats and Communists themselves, but as many people viewed them as to blame for much of what was wrong, this too would have had a good deal of support. Despite (or perhaps because of) the fact that the Nazis themselves had participated vigorously in the gang warfare that passed for an extension of political debate, Hitler was seen as the man who could end this kind of violent disorder.

Historical interpretations not merely of this period but of 19th and 20th century German history as a whole are often framed by the desire of historians (and the wider public) to account for how the Nazis came to power. For those who focus on the period immediately before Hitler's appointment, the roles of individuals at the centre of power are examined. There is no doubt that the period 1928–1933 is dominated by infighting among the coalition partners of different governments, disagreement about how to respond to the economic crisis, and at the end, by political intrigue among the President's closest advisers. However, others analyse a much longer period of German history. The US historian William Shirer believed that an unbroken line existed between Luther in the 16th and Hitler in the 20th centuries. His influential 1960 book *The Rise and Fall of the Third Reich* argues that the Third Reich was the product of the 'German' national character (even though Germany was not a single country until unification in 1871). Shirer treats the Weimar Republic as a failure specifically because it did not prevent the rise of Hitler and the Nazis.

Hans-Ulrich Wehler is a prominent member of the 'Bielefeld school' of historians. In the 1960s he and others advanced the so-called Special Path or *Sonderweg* theory. They focused on Germany after 1871 until 1914, the period of Imperial Germany, and suggested that Germany had followed a special path on its journey from monarchic **autocracy** to democracy, one unlike that followed by any other nation.

The survival of autocratic institutions in Germany and a relatively rigid social structure at a time of rapid **industrialisation** were much studied. Wehler's five-volume *Deutsche Gesellschaftgeschichte* (*German Social History*) of 1987 remains a highly influential work. Other historians who have looked at the bigger picture and located the rise of the Nazis in a long-term historical process include A.J.P. Taylor and Sir Lewis Namier. The whole idea of a *Sonderweg* was rejected by British Marxist historians David Blackbourn and Geoff Eley in their 1984 book *Peculiarities of German History*.

The equally distinguished German historian Heinrich Winkler, in his 2006 book *Germany: The Long Road West*, put the concept of a *Sonderweg* into context. Once, this supposed 'specialness' was assumed to be a positive, meaning that the country had a unique role in civilisation. Then after 1945 it was taken to mean something uniquely negative, that everything led up to Nazi rule. But as Winkler says, the fact that Germany's history is different in some ways from those of other

Key terms

Autocracy: a political system in which a single figure possesses unrestrained power.

Industrialisation: the development of industry and the increasing dependence of a country on industry as opposed to agriculture for income and employment.

countries doesn't actually tell us very much. After all, they are all different from one another; there is no such thing as a 'normal path', so the idea of a 'special path' is meaningless.

This way of reading the situation in Germany at this point in its history allows us to emphasise the ways in which the developments there resembled those in several other countries. The Great Depression of the 1930s affected the economies of most countries in the world. In some, these political pressures led to the installation of ultra-conservative, monarchist or nationalist political regimes. The specific way in which these political developments occurred in each country reflected those countries' particular circumstances. When the politics and society of a country was resilient to such pressures, as in the UK, political parties of the extreme right grew in strength and influence but were unable to achieve the breakthrough they did in, for example, Germany.

According to this interpretation, Germany should be regarded as different from Spain, Italy, Romania and others only in ways that reflected its own recent history. These are complex matters regarding which we need not wait for a correct interpretation or hope to be able to give a single right answer.

Timeline

1928	
May	Federal elections
June	Marx's fourth cabinet ended; Müller became chancellor
August	Kellogg–Briand Pact signed
October	Hugenberg became head of DNVP
December	Kaas became head of Centre Party; farmers' demonstrations
1929	
June	Young Committee met and agreed a package of measures
October	Gustav Stresemann died of a stroke; Wall Street Crash in New York, USA; 'Liberty Law' (*Freiheitsgesetz*) campaign
December	Liberty Law referendum failed to reject Young Plan
1930	
January	Formal adoption of Young Committee proposals
March	Müller resigned as chancellor, replaced by Brüning
June	French troops left the Rhineland ahead of schedule
July	Brüning's budget passed using Article 48
September	Federal elections with NSDAP gains
1931	
October	Founding of the Harzburg Front
December	Founding of the Iron Front

1932	
April	Hindenburg re-elected president
May	Brüning resigned as chancellor
June	Papen became chancellor and formed government
June-July	Lausanne conference suspended reparation payments
July	Federal elections, NSDAP largest party
November	Federal elections, NSDAP lost votes but remained largest party; Papen resigned as chancellor
December	Schleicher became chancellor
1933	
January	Schleicher resigned as chancellor; Hindenburg appointed Hitler as Chancellor
February	Reichstag fire
March	Federal elections; Hjalmar Schacht appointed president of the Reichsbank; Hitler presented Enabling Act to the Reichstag
April	*Gesetz zur Wiederherstellung des Berufsbeamtentums*, Law for the Restoration of the Professional Civil Service

Practice essay questions

1. 'Germans turned to Hitler out of desperation rather than out of a deep commitment to Nazi ideology.' Assess the validity of this view.
2. 'It was the old elites who still controlled access to political power in Germany between 1930 and 1933.' Assess the validity of this view.
3. To what extent was the Nazi rise to power based on violence and the threat of violence?
4. With reference to the sources below and your understanding of the historical context, assess the value of the three sources to a historian studying the causes of the collapse of democracy in the Weimar Republic.

Source A

A Nazi Party activist recounts a meeting of four hundred storm-troopers in Idar-Oberstein (in Merkl, P.H., *Political Violence Under the Swastika: 581 Early Nazis;* Peter H. Merkl, Princeton University Library)

One after the other, our four speakers had their say, interrupted by furious howling and catcalls. But when, in the ensuing discussion, an interlocutor was reprimanded for saying, "We don't want the brown plague in our beautiful town", tumult broke out. There followed a battle with beer steins, chairs, and the like, and in two minutes the hall was demolished and everyone cleared out. We had to take back seven heavily injured comrades that day and there were rocks thrown at us and occasional assaults in spite of the police protection.

Source B

From an interview with Hans Leidler, a former railroad worker and SPD member (in Allen, W.S., *The Nazi Seizure of Power*, Chicago: Quadrangle, 1965, and at yadvashem. org).

In the spring of 1932 the Nazis made their first attempt to organise the railroad workers. Nazism was already strong among the directory, control offices, bureau workers, etc. It started with the highest officials and worked downwards. From 1931 on, the officials saw to it that those workers who belonged to the Brownshirts got privileged treatment. … There were often excited arguments and even some fights. When I argued with workers against the Nazis I was ordered by the directors not to speak in working hours.

Source C

Manifesto of the Harzburg Front, 11 October 1931 (in Stackelberg, R. and Winkle, S.A., *The Nazi Germany Sourcebook: An Anthology of Texts*).

Determined to protect our country from the chaos of Bolshevism and to save our polity from the maelstrom of economic bankruptcy through effective self-help, thereby helping the world to achieve real peace, we declare: We are ready to take responsibility in governments led by nationally minded forces in the Reich and in Prussia. We will not spurn any hand offered to us in the spirit of truly honest collaboration. But we refuse to support in any way the preservation of a false system and the continuation of false policies in the present government…

Chapter summary

By the end of this chapter you should understand how the economic and political situation developed in Weimar Germany and how the Weimar Republic ceased to exist. You will understand the economic context of the Great Depression, the significance of the emergency provisions of the 1919 Constitution, the movement of electoral support away from parties of the centre, and the specific attractions of the NSDAP. You have also learned about individuals who plotted for what they thought was right for Germany and for their own political advantage. You have learned about:

* how the Wall Street Crash began the Great Depression; unemployment in Germany rose and Müller's government found its social and economic intentions unaffordable; Brüning's austerity programme worked in its own terms, but unemployment remained high and deflation slowed down the economy

* the way that voters started to abandon moderate parties; the KPD slowly increased its vote, but the NSDAP quickly went from being a minor party to the largest in the Reichstag

* the way in which the Communists were hampered by their internationalist agenda and Moscow's control, while the Nazis were free to use propaganda to promote their extreme nationalist programme

* the plotting by the president and his advisers to appoint a government that would act authoritatively, and how after a couple of short-term solutions the president appointed Hitler chancellor

* the fire at the Reichstag building during the 1933 election campaign; how the Communists were blamed; the sweeping arrests and the banning of left-wing parties authorised by the Nazi-led government, so that the NSDAP dominated the Reichstag and closed down left-wing and moderate parties until Germany was a one-party state.

End notes

1   Tooze, A. *The Wages of Destruction*.
2   In Tooze, A. *The Wages of Destruction*.
3   Scholem, G., *A Life in Letters*.
4   In Longerich, P., *Goebbels*.
5   Weitz, W.D., *Weimar Germany*.
6   In, for example, Shirer, W., *The Rise and Fall of the Third Reich*.
7   Translation from Noakes, J. and Pridham, G., eds., *Nazism 1919–1945, Volume 1*.
8   Law to Remedy the Distress of the People and the Empire.

4 Nazi rule, 1933–1939

In this section, we will look at how the Nazis extended their power, creating a one-party state in which the people of Germany were drawn into involuntary or voluntary membership of the NSDAP where they were expected to give personal loyalty to Hitler. Throughout the 1930s the Nazis introduced laws on race, the economy and political resistance, and Hitler unpicked the terms of the Treaty of Versailles piece by piece, resulting in the outbreak of war in 1939. We will look into:

- Hitler's consolidation of power from March 1933 to 1934: governmental and administrative change and the establishment of the one-party state; the Night of the Long Knives and the impact of the death of President Hindenburg

- the 'Terror State': the police, including the SS and Gestapo; the courts; extent, effectiveness and limitations of opposition and non-conformity; propaganda: aims, methods and impact; extent of totalitarianism

- economic policies and the degree of economic recovery; Schacht; Göring; the industrial elites

- social policies: young people; women; workers; the churches; the degree of *Volksgemeinschaft*; benefits and drawbacks of Nazi rule.

Hitler's consolidation of power, 1933–1934

In March 1933, the Enabling Act had removed Hitler's rivals to power from the German political system. In the weeks that followed various political parties were shut down, harassed or monitored closely. In particular, the main opposition party in the Reichstag, the SDP, was effectively neutralised. This left a clear field for the NSDAP, with the help of the smaller numbers of Centre and DNVP members, to pass Nazi proposals. This situation was greatly assisted by the facts that the President of the Reichstag was Herman Göring, and the Kroll Opera House, to which the legislators had to move after the Reichstag fire, was much smaller, allowing the mood of Nazi intimidation to be that much more frightening.

Gradually, opposition parties ceased to exist in any effective form. The enemies of the NSDAP might have thought that the Nazis had now achieved what they wanted. In fact, the process of creating a Nazi state had only just begun.

The Nazi state

The establishment of the one-party state

The structure of the Third Reich was complicated. Much of the state machinery of the Weimar Republic remained, as did institutions that dated back to the creation of Imperial Germany in the late nineteenth century. The Weimar Republic had all of the structures of a modern state, with a developed civil service and court system at both national and regional levels. Trade unions and other groups – particularly the Catholic Church – exercised considerable power in lobbying government. It was onto this existing system that the new Nazi state was built.

It is vital in making sense of the Nazi state to understand the way in which the Nazi party grafted its own organisations on top of existing structures. The German Labour Front (*Deutsche Arbeitsfront*, DAF), for example, took control of both the trade unions and the Nazis' own National Socialist Factory Cell Organisation. Led by Robert Ley, the DAF's purpose was to allow employers and employees to discuss pay and working conditions. Ley was on the 'socialist' wing of the NSDAP, and when the DAF set wages, it was deliberately generous, ensuring that the Nazi state had employees' loyal support.

The Reich Ministry of Public Enlightenment and Propaganda (*Reichsministerium für Volksaufklärung und Propaganda*, RMVP or more simply *Propagandaministerium*) was set up in March 1933. Headed by Reich Propaganda Minister Joseph Goebbels, it controlled all printed and broadcast media: the news organisations and the arts and entertainment industries. Within the RMVP was a department dedicated to anti-Soviet propaganda; it characterised the threat as being from as 'Jewish Bolshevism'.

The **Gestapo** (*Geheime Staatspolizei*, Secret State Police) was created in April 1933 by Hermann Göring, minister-president of Prussia. It brought together two existing Prussian departments for intelligence and political police work. He then moved NSDAP members into the new office, abolishing the distinction between working for the state and working for the party. The NSDAP's regional organisers, or **Gauleiter**, became important figures in regional government.

Key terms

Gestapo: contraction of Geheime Staatspolizei, German expression meaning 'secret state police'.

Gauleiter: German word meaning 'District Leader'.

As chancellor in a one-party state, Hitler could demand oversight of (or direct control over) any policy matter. In practice, he could only consider a tiny fraction of the considerable number of issues arising every day from this form of personal rule. Furthermore, he did not enjoy paperwork and had never liked Berlin, preferring to spend most of his time at Berchtesgaden, his mountain retreat in Bavaria. It was those in his immediate circle, regardless of their official rank within the NSDAP or the state, who selected the papers Hitler actually looked at and who delivered the **Führer's** judgements.

Wilhelm Frick, for example, served in Hitler's cabinet from 1933 to 1943 as minister of the interior but seldom even saw the Führer and had very little influence. By contrast, Hitler's personal car drivers were given a rank equivalent to that of a general and had many opportunities to influence his decisions. The army, the navy and the air force all made sure they had representatives permanently living at Berchtesgaden, knowing that decision-making power was in the hands of those who could be close to Hitler.

Avoiding paperwork and committee meetings (especially discussions), Hitler announced many of his decisions in one-to-one interviews in which no official record was made of what was said. This makes it difficult to track or validate pronouncements coming from the Reich Chancellery (*Reichskanzlei*), meaning the Führer and his officials. Unsurprisingly, there was often tension between the NSDAP and the civil service. Many Nazis had been used to the pre-1933 struggle, a sort of crusade to combat what they viewed as corrupting influences that might pollute the German **Volk**. These Nazis were often intolerant, if not openly contemptuous, of civil service concern for legal restrictions and bureaucratic rules.

The 'Night of the Long Knives'

During the period when the NSDAP were political outsiders, the SA (*Sturmabteilung*) led by Ernst Röhm had provided security at meetings and rallies, and had been the party's street-fighters. Now that the party was in government, responsible for maintaining order and in charge of the police, the courts and

Key terms

Führer: German word meaning 'leader' or 'guide'; a party leader in Weimar Germany; Hitler.

Volk: German word meaning 'nation', 'people'.

Voices from the past

Otto Dietrich

Hitler took little notice of the fight between Party and civil service. He considered himself above such things.

Otto Dietrich was an SS-*Obergruppenführer*, Nazi Party Press Secretary and a member of Hitler's inner circle. Imprisoned at the post-war Nuremberg Trials, he wrote his memoirs, *The Hitler I Knew*. In them he commented on the nature of Nazi rule:

In the twelve years of his rule in Germany Hitler produced the biggest confusion in government that has ever existed in a civilised state. During his period of government, he removed from the organisation of the state all clarity of leadership and produced a completely opaque network of competencies.[1]

Dietrich went on to say that he believed Hitler had done so as a means of strengthening his personal authority.

Discussion points

1. What led to the confusion in government that Dietrich described?
2. How can creating confusion have strengthened Hitler's authority, as Dietrich claims?

ACTIVITY 4.1

1. List some of the principal targets of the 'Night of the Long Knives'.

2. In each case, note down what made them a target. You might need to include more than one reason.

3. Now write a paragraph explaining what you think was the main intention of the violence of 30 June and 2 July 1934, and explaining why you think that.

Key term

SS: abbreviation of Schutzstaffel, German word meaning 'protection squadron'.

Figure 4.1: President of Germany Paul von Hindenburg, after 1925.

the army, the SA was increasingly an embarrassment. Hitler realised that the electorate wanted to see an end to street violence. In addition, the powerful men who owned German industry disliked Röhm's talk of a 'second revolution' to redistribute wealth and to fulfil the socialist goals of the NSDAP. Furthermore, and crucially, the Reichswehr (the armed forces) was hostile to the SA. Röhm had demanded that the Reichswehr be absorbed into the SA and he be made minister of defence. The generals made it clear to Hitler that the SA had to be curbed. Hitler wanted the full support of the Reichswehr in order to consolidate his position, much as all previous Weimar chancellors had.

The answer was short and brutal: to the astonishment of almost everyone, Hitler used one branch of the NSDAP to attack another. Between 30 June and 2 July 1934 a large number of political assassinations were carried out. Ernst Röhm and many other SA leaders were murdered, mostly by **SS** (*Schutzstaffel*, protection squadron) and Gestapo (*Geheime Staatspolizei*, secret state police) units. In addition to removing the SA (and Röhm's threat to his personal authority), Hitler also took the opportunity to eliminate other potential opposition, including Gregor Strasser. In addition, unsympathetic conservatives including former general and chancellor Kurt von Schleicher were killed. Former chancellor Brüning was luckier than the others: tipped off that he was to be arrested, he fled abroad.

One person who escaped with his life was Franz von Papen. Earlier in June 1934, the vice-chancellor, with the president's support, had given a speech at the University of Marburg, criticising the role of terror in politics, including the activities of the SA. Hitler had been outraged by this disloyalty, but Goebbels' suppression of reports was ineffective: the *Frankfurter Zeitung* printed part of the speech and its author had released copies to the foreign press. At the time, Papen defended himself by pointing to Hindenburg's support for the speech and offering his resignation from Hitler's cabinet, pointing out that he would inform Hindenburg of the suppression of his speech. Göring sent the SS to arrest Vice-Chancellor Papen in his office. Accompanying Gestapo officers shot his secretary on the spot. They arrested Edgar Jung, the man who had written the speech; he too was later shot. Papen himself was released on Hitler's orders; for the rest of the period of Nazi rule he occupied minor jobs and never again spoke out.

The impact of the death of President Hindenburg

In August 1934 President Hindenburg died. His status within Germany as a hero of the First World War (as military leader and victor of the Battle of Tannenberg in August 1914) had ensured his election in 1925 and then again in 1932 as president. Although initially he had been reluctant to enter politics, he was persuaded by the DNVP's Admiral Alfred von Tirpitz to stand as an independent candidate. He was a non-party candidate, but his politics – conservative, nationalistic, authoritarian, monarchist and against the Treaty of Versailles – were those of the DNVP and other right-wing parties. For many Germans he was a figure of continuity when so much had changed, including the whirlwind comings and goings of chancellors and governments.

With Hindenburg dead, Hitler declared that he had taken over the post of president in addition to that of chancellor. This was an unconstitutional move, since he was not first in line to do so under the Enabling Act. In addition, removing the distinction between head of state and head of government made a nonsense of the constitutional structures of the Republic. However, with Hindenburg dead, the opposition parties broken and the Reichstag sidelined, there was nobody to oppose Hitler. He went on to abolish the *Reichsrat*, the Upper House that represented the individual states of Germany. These two steps are enough to show that the government no longer regarded itself as bound by the 1919 Constitution.

When Hitler took over as President of Germany on the death of Hindenburg in August 1934 he automatically became Commander-in-Chief of the Reichswehr. All soldiers who volunteered took an oath of personal loyalty to the **Führer** (leader). This was an example of what Hitler could achieve as head of state that he could not do as chancellor, that is, head of government. Hitler was now chancellor and president of Germany and leader of the NSDAP in what was now a one-party state. All of these positions were combined into Hitler's new role as *der Führer*.

Hans Frank, the head of the Nazi Association of Lawyers and of the Academy of German Law, summed up in 1938 what it meant to be Führer:[2]

1. *At the head of the Reich stands the leader of the NSDAP as leader of the German Reich for life.*

2. *He is Head of State and chief of the Government in one person. He is Commander-in-Chief of all the armed forces of the Reich.*

3. *The Führer and Reich chancellor is the delegate of the German people.*

4. *The Führer is the supreme judge of the nation.*

Adolf Hitler possessed absolute power. There were no restraints on him except those he chose to accept.

Practice essay question

> How far do you agree that the death of President Hindenburg in August 1934 was a defining moment in Hitler's rise to absolute power in Germany?

The Terror State

The police, the SS and the Gestapo

A number of prominent Nazi party leaders were given key positions in the Nazi state and set about their work after March 1933 without delay. One such was Heinrich Himmler. He was a Catholic from a middle-class Bavarian background. He had studied agronomy at the Technical University in Munich before joining the Nazi party in August 1923. He rejected Christianity and became passionately anti-Semitic soon after this. He held various posts under Gregor Strasser, organising the Nazi party in Lower Bavaria. Himmler joined the *Schutzstaffel* (Protection Squadron, SS) in 1925, the SS being at that stage a unit of the SA with responsibilities for defending Nazi meetings and officials. The SS was also initially intended as Hitler's bodyguard, following his release from Landsberg am Lech prison. Himmler became SS Gauleiter in Lower Bavaria in 1926.

Heinrich Himmler and the SS

Himmler so impressed Adolf Hitler with his idea of turning the SS into a totally loyal, racially pure, elite unit that he was appointed to lead the unit as *Reichsführer SS* in 1929. Under his leadership the SS grew in size tenfold. His appointment to the police and security role was a priority of the party leadership. He effectively became the enforcer of the Nazi party and government, and is usually credited with the central place in the creation of the police state. His role as *Reichsführer SS* brought him police powers previously in the hands of officials at the Ministry of the Interior. (This was another example of the tension between Nazi party officials and the civil service.) By stages he effectively became security chief in Nazi Germany, taking control of all the police forces in Germany as well as of the SS. He also had control of the secret police. He set up the first concentration camp in Germany at Dachau, near Munich, as early as March 1933. Initially this camp housed political opponents of the Nazis, but later it also took all those considered by the Nazis as 'socially undesirable', especially Jews.

Despite beginning as a branch of the SA, the SS played a central role in the Night of the Long Knives.

 Thematic link: one-party state

The police

In the Weimar Republic (and before), responsibility for the police was in the hands of the states (*Länder*). Accordingly, when Göring became minister-president of Prussia in April 1933, he took charge of the biggest police force in Germany. A year later, in April 1934, Hitler put Himmler in charge of all the police forces outside Göring's Prussia. The police were firmly under Nazi control by this time, and they took no action during the Night of the Long Knives.

Formal distinctions remained between the different branches of uniformed and plainclothes police and their work:

- the *Ordnungspolizei* (Order Police) were uniformed and largely engaged in conventional law enforcement
- the *Kriminalpolizei* (Criminal Police) were plainclothes police and concerned with investigation of crimes.

Then in 1936, Hitler ordered that all the separate *Länder* police should be merged into a nationwide force. Himmler was now head of a unified German police force. As Wilhelm Frick was interior minister, this should have meant that Frick was Himmler's superior. However, Hitler's decree in fact partially removed the police from the Interior Ministry, making them subordinate instead to, and in some ways a branch of, the SS. Himmler answered to Hitler only. The *Sicherheitspolizei* (Security Police) was the term used for the police created by combining the *Kriminalpolizei* with the Gestapo.

The Gestapo

Many of the police forces in the different *Länder* already had political departments under the Weimar Republic (and indeed under the Imperial rule that preceded it). These political police were accustomed to monitoring the activities of left-wing parties and organisations. As minister-president of Prussia, Göring set up the *Geheime Staatspolizei* (Secret State Police, Gestapo) by merging two existing departments, detaching the result from the normal channels of police control, and introducing into it a number of NSDAP members. Initially an organisation within the large state of Prussia, it became nationwide and was led from 1934 by Reinhard Heydrich. Control was passed to Himmler and the SS two years later in 1936. As previously noted, although the Gestapo was set up within the existing structures of the police as servants of the state, the introduction of NSDAP members erased the line between the state and the party. Nevertheless, large numbers of the membership of the Gestapo continued to be former members of the police forces that had existed under the Weimar Republic.

The Gestapo's brief was to investigate treason, spying and sabotage, attacks both on the state and on the NSDAP, another example of the merging of those two concepts. The general heading of 'treason' covered all opposition to Nazi rule, whether open or secret. This meant that the Gestapo carefully monitored individuals and networks from which opposition might come, including priests, aristocrats, students, and former members of other political parties. The Gestapo's authority lay in the support of Hitler and the Nazi leadership. It operated without reference to any other police authority or indeed to the courts and the law. The Gestapo was able to send people to concentration camps without any right of appeal even though they had been found not guilty by the courts, an example of a Nazi agency acting without state (civil service) input. Although Gestapo members did infiltrate suspected groups and networks, the Gestapo depended heavily on denunciations rather than investigation. Part of their success in preventing the growth and effectiveness of opposition was due simply to the fear that they generated, and the resulting tendency of opposition groups to overestimate how much the Gestapo knew.

The courts

Franz Gürtner was a DNVP member and had served as justice minister in Papen's and Schleicher's 1932 cabinets. He retained this post following Hitler's appointment as chancellor. Despite speaking out against some Nazi actions, he joined the NSDAP himself in 1936 and continued as minister until his death in 1941. Gürtner's contribution to **Gleichschaltung** ('coordination', the policy of bringing all German institutions into line with the NSDAP's aims) was to oversee the nazification of the ministry, the judiciary and the German legal profession.

To do this, he carried through a merger of the associations of German judges and lawyers with the new National Socialist Lawyers Association. All judges, lawyers, and legal staff who were Jews or of suspect politics were dismissed. Nazi flags were hung in all courts of law and police stations. Nazi ideological notions were also introduced into the body of German law. Despite his legal training and previous career, Gürtner presided over the change from the administration of law under the constitution to the application of a state of emergency in which

Key term

Gleichschaltung: German word meaning 'coordination' or 'making equal', the policy of bringing all German institutions into line with the NSDAP's aims.

Hitler's word (and even his presumed wishes) had the force of law. In addition, the Gestapo and SS acted without reference to other agencies of law, such as the courts of justice.

The normal processes of police work and law courts did continue, but alongside this special courts quickly sprang up. For example, when the trial of the accused in the Reichstag fire ended with three acquittals and only one conviction, Hitler ordered the establishment of a so-called *Volksgerichtshof* (People's Court). The presiding judge was initially Roland Freisler and later Otto Georg Thierack, both NSDAP members. Operating outside the framework of the German legal system, it specialised in crimes against the NSDAP and against Nazi **ideology**.

Key term

Ideology: set of ideas and ideals that underpins and gives shape to e.g. a policy or political programme.

Defendants thus included oppositionists, including those who plotted against Hitler's life in 1944. Trials were quick and defendants were barely allowed to speak. Little defence was offered. The judge sided with the prosecution and shouted at the accused. Most trials ended in convictions and the courts issued frequent death sentences. The Weimar Constitution of 1919 had abolished separate military courts, but these courts martial were reintroduced by the NSDAP. The *Reichskriegsgericht* (Imperial War Court) had jurisdiction not only over the military but crimes that took place in territory where the military were still active. Charges included treason, subversion and conscientious objection. It was responsible for large numbers of executions.

Even as early as 1934, it was noticeable that the law courts took no action in response to the extra judicial killings of the Night of the Long Knives. The judiciary chose instead to support Hitler's drive for absolute power in Germany. With Hitler's assumption of the post of president on the death of Hindenburg in July 1934, with the courts compliant even in the face of extrajudicial political murders, with the marginalisation of the Reichstag and the Nazis as the only legal political party in Germany, Hitler's drive to consolidate his personal position was complete.

Key terms

Labour camps: Camps in which prisoners were forced to work and held in harsh and sometimes fatal conditions.

Transit camps: Camps in which prisoners were held while waiting to be moved elsewhere.

Internment camps: Prisons built as a series of huts surrounded by a barbed-wire fence, rather than as a high-walled building. These were places where anyone considered an enemy or threat of any kind could be sent and held.

Thematic link: Totalitarian state

Concentration camps

The rapid growth of the police state meant that the regime needed to have space in which to intern those who were arrested and removed from society; its principal method was the concentration camp. There were Nazi concentration camps in 70 locations. However, it is important to distinguish between different kinds of camp. Some were **labour camps**, where forced labour was exploited; others were **transit camps** or **internment camps**, hastily built prisons for moving or holding prisoners.

The camp at Oranienburg in Germany was opened in March 1933. Some 4500 prisoners were sent there until its closure in 1936. Many were political opponents of the Nazi state, which wasted no time in getting them out of the way. KPD members from the Berlin region and SPD people were imprisoned there by the SA, as were some male homosexuals. The camp was on a main road not far from Berlin, so was easily visible by the local population. These initial camps were not a secret. The creation of the Dachau camp, also in March 1933, was announced in a press release. It would hold, the press were told, 5000 KPD, *Reichsbanner* and SPD members. The purpose was to take the pressure off the existing prison system. Thus advised, German newspapers reported on the movement of these enemies of the Nazi party (and in the case of the KPD of the state) to the camp.

Extent, effectiveness and limitations of opposition and non-conformity

Most Germans remained loyal to the Nazi state. Especially in the earlier years, they accepted Nazi rule with varying degrees of enthusiasm, willingness, indifference or fear. With the nazification of the police force and the creation and growth of the SS and the Gestapo, it was both difficult and dangerous to oppose the NSDAP 'terror state'. The most obvious potential leaders of such opposition would have been politicians from other parties, but beginning in January 1933, they had been arrested, had gone into hiding or had fled abroad. The Nazi network of spies and informers might have been less extensive than oppositionists tended to believe, but the Gestapo was nevertheless effective in the suppression of dissent. It is possible that around 77 000 German citizens were executed for resistance to Nazi rule. It is difficult to be sure what forms this resistance took: the various plots to assassinate Hitler involved small numbers. There was no coordinated large-scale resistance to the Nazi state as was found in occupied countries such as Yugoslavia and France. In Germany itself, there were individuals or small groups, but the Nazi destruction of many social and political groups and their infiltration or takeover of others meant that the organisations and networks open to resisters abroad had been largely neutralised at home.

Nevertheless, there was opposition, even if it never became a large-scale movement and only rarely, and briefly, posed a threat to Nazi rule. Sometimes it took the form of speaking out in private discussions or in public places, such as in church. Sometimes there were attacks and acts of sabotage. With the political parties and trade unions abolished or merged under *Gleichschaltung*, the army remained a source of potentially effective opposition. However, attempts to persuade the army to stage a coup against the Nazi state did not bear fruit until late in the war, by which time it had become obvious that Germany would lose.

Religious opposition to Nazi rule

One source of determined opposition was the churches. Of about 60 million Germans, perhaps 40 million were Protestant. The German Evangelical Church was the largest Protestant organisation, and was an institution in German society. Hitler sought to win the churches over by using the language of religious morality in his speeches, as when he introduced the Enabling Laws in 1933 in the Reichstag.

Within the Evangelical Church there was a long-running debate between those who wished to maintain the church's traditional loyalty to the state and who argued for the idea of German Christians (**Deutsche Christen**) and those of the Confessing Church (**Bekennende Kirche**) who opposed the Nazi state and argued that the allegiance of the Church should be to God and scripture, not to a worldly Führer.

Key terms

Deutsche Christen: German expression meaning 'German Christians', Protestant churches and church members who accepted or supported the Nazi regime.

Bekennende Kirche: German expression meaning 'Confessing Church', Protestant churches and church members who opposed the Nazi regime and argued that the allegiance of the Church should be to God and scripture, not to a worldly Führer.

Voices from the past

Michael von Faulhaber

An indication of at least one of the Catholic Church's reasons for signing this concordat, namely the fear of Bolshevism, is given by the German Cardinal Michael von Faulhaber, who visited Pope Pius XII in Rome on 12 March 1933 and reported on his return:

Let us meditate on the words of the Holy Father, who in a consistory, without mentioning his name, indicated before the whole world in Adolf Hitler the statesmen who first, after the Pope himself, has raised his voice against Bolshevism.[3]

Discussion point

Use your knowledge of the historical context to comment on this source. Remember, your topic is Germany 1918–1945, so don't be distracted into writing too much about the Roman Catholic Church as a whole.

A leading figure in the latter movement was Pastor Martin Niemöller, who spent seven years in concentration camps for his words and actions. Another leading member of this group was the Lutheran theologian and pastor Dietrich Bonhoeffer. His open opposition to the forced euthanasia programme and to Nazi anti-Semitic policies earned him the enmity of the authorities. He would later be arrested by the Gestapo in April 1943 and executed.

The Catholic Church, dominant in places such as the Rhineland, Bavaria and Austria, was overall about half the size of the Protestant Church. Hitler himself had been brought up in Austria by a Catholic mother (and an anti-clerical father). The 20 million or so Roman Catholics in Nazi Germany made up about a third of the population. Few of them voted for the NSDAP. Initially cooler towards Nazism than the Protestant churches and without a nationalist tradition, their political leaders were suspicious of the Nazis. This was especially the case as the Catholic Centre Party had been one of the main political props of the Weimar Republic, and had indeed been founded to defend Catholic interests, where necessary against the state. Before 1933 some Catholic bishops prohibited members of their flock from joining the Nazi party, but this ban was dropped after 1933. Centre Party Chancellor Heinrich Brüning had spoken out against the Enabling Act until the Centre was given reassurances by Hitler; Brüning agreed to withdraw his opposition under pressure from party colleagues.

Some brave individuals such as Bishop Galen preached against Nazi beliefs and acts, but the main Catholic tactic towards the Nazi government was one of cautious compromise and accommodation – much like the German Evangelical (Protestant) Church. In July 1933 the German government and the Vatican signed the *Reichskonkordat* (imperial concordat), a treaty between the Catholic Church and the Nazis. In exchange for certain guarantees for Catholic clergy, the *Reichskonkordat* specified that the appointment of Catholic Bishops be subject to the confirmation of the Nazi regime (Article 14) and that they must take an oath of loyalty and respect the government (Article 16). Another contentious article was Article 13, which subjected the Catholic Church's rights and prerogatives 'to legal regulation under civil law'. This article effectively allowed full control by the Nazi state over the Catholic Church.

The Catholic Church opposed the policy of *Gleichschaltung*, since the Nazis aimed to achieve control of Catholic schools, and all youth groups, workers' clubs and cultural groups. The Church also spoke out against some key Nazi policies, including that of the forced sterilisation of people judged to be suffering from a hereditary disease. When crucifixes were removed from schools and replaced with photographs of Adolf Hitler, there was widespread popular discontent. A prosecutor's account from 1937 describes how 30 to 40 villagers entered a school and, while not touching the newly introduced portrait of the Führer, restored the crucifix. The man who actually went up the ladder to do this was later imprisoned. Other police reports noted the increased attendance at Catholic events such as pilgrimages. As with protests about crucifixes, these were all conducted in an orderly manner and did not have the appearance of anti-government demonstrations. However, police reports suggested that these religious gatherings were nevertheless motivated by disapproval of Nazi measures and so should be categorised as political events.

Political opposition to Nazi rule

One might have expected left-wing opposition to Nazi rule. However, the Enabling Act of 1933 had allowed Hitler's regime to break both KPD and SPD structures, making both parties ineffective. In addition, the KPD had been ordered by the USSR's Communist Party to regard the SPD as the main enemy, not the NSDAP. The very organisational structures that had allowed the SPD and the KPD to become mass-membership parties with representatives being elected as Reichstag deputies made them vulnerable in a police state. Their records were seized and their membership hunted down. By contrast the far smaller *Internationaler Sozialistischer Kampfbund* (International Socialist Militant League, ISK) had the forethought to destroy its records. As a result to all intents and purposes it disappeared from view. This made it more able to participate in anti-Nazi activities. In secret it issued leaflets, helped political refugees leave the country, attempted to set up secret trade unions, and engaged in political graffiti, all at great danger to activists. Its great achievement came with the opening of the first *Autobahn* by Adolf Hitler in 1935. The night before, ISK members visited the route the Führer was to travel and wrote anti-war, anti-Nazi and anti-Hitler slogans on the road, the bridges and fly-overs. The event went ahead, with slogans masked as quickly as possible, bridges being repainted and sand being strewn over affected parts of the road. The news film had to be carefully edited before it was released.

In addition to disorganised left-wing hostility to Hitler, there remained conservative opponents. One such group was known as the **Kreisau Circle** after the estate in Kreisau where they met.

The estate belonged to Helmuth James Graf von Moltke, part of a family with a tradition of commanding the Prussian and German armies. The others in the group were largely from army and aristocratic backgrounds, and tended to be social conservatives, monarchists and Christians. They shared a vision of a Christian Germany under a restored monarchy with the individual federal states that made up Germany having much of their individual character and authority restored. Even before the war broke out, they agreed that Hitler's rule was a disaster for Germany. However, this was a debating society rather than a conspiracy: they made little attempt to plan the overthrow of Nazi rule.

 Key term

Kreisau Circle: group of opponents to the Nazi regime, especially from army and aristocratic backgrounds, largely social conservatives, monarchists, liberals and Christians.

Some members of the army had been opposed to Hitler and Nazi rule from the beginning. There were several planned assassinations hatched by army officers. These tended to be people whose anti-Nazi stance was based on conservative, Christian political views. They were German nationalists, but of a very different type from Hitler. However, the popularity of the initial successes against Czechoslovakia, Poland and France meant that they were reluctant to speak out. For both the army and the Kreisau Circle, the opportunity to act effectively only came when the war started to turn against the Nazi leadership. Even then Hitler's habit of making deliberate last-minute changes to his timetable meant that he more than once avoided secret attempts to kill him. The nearest they came to success was the July 1944 bomb plot, to which we shall turn in a later chapter.

Other forms of opposition to Nazi rule

Historians such as Detlev Peukert have shown that there was a significant degree of resistance to the Nazi regime expressed during the course of everyday life. This was often a response to dissatisfaction with the regime due to, for example, corruption among Nazi officials or the state of the economy.

The Edelweiss Pirates (**Edelweisspiraten**) were only in part a form of opposition; they were also an example of non-conformity.

This youth protest movement was started in the Rhineland in 1937. The Pirates were mainly-working class youths and their protest against the regime – or perhaps more specifically against the enforced uniformity of the Hitler Youth – included wearing Bohemian clothes and playing prohibited music such as jazz and blues. Some of them deliberately picked fights with Hitler Youth members and groups in a manner reminiscent of the party-political gang warfare of the 1920s. There were similar, more middle-class 'swing' groups that acted in a similar fashion. Initially regarded by the authorities as merely an irritant, after the outbreak of war in 1939 the Nazi state took a dimmer view of such youth groups and members were sometimes arrested, sent for short periods in prison camps and even executed.

Propaganda: aims, methods and impact

Political opponents were either in jail or in hiding. The Nazis controlled all police services. Social control was an important way of keeping any opposition to Nazi rule intimidated or invisible. In this context, one tool that was wielded expertly was the use of propaganda; the man behind it was Joseph Goebbels.

Goebbels was intelligent, well-educated and politically capable. After his academic research in German literature, in 1923 the nationalist campaigns against the French and Belgian occupation of the Ruhr district made him aware of the NSDAP. He joined the Nazi party in 1924 and rose swiftly in their ranks to become *Gauleiter* (District Leader) of Berlin just two years later in 1926. In his attempts to persuade a mainly working-class electorate to support the NSDAP he had to exploit his developing skill in the use of propaganda, because there was much opposition to the Nazis from the KPD and others. His work caught the eye of the party leadership. By 1930 he had risen to become one of the most senior members of the party and a close associate and avid admirer of Adolf Hitler. He was strongly anti-Semitic.

Key term

Edelweisspiraten: German expression meaning 'Edelweiss Pirates', groups of young Germans who imitated e.g. American clothes and played American music.

As Hitler himself had written in *Mein Kampf*, an important element of indoctrination is repetition. Since the foundation of the NSDAP in 1921, the Nazi propaganda machine had been hammering away with its message. They constantly repeated that the German army had not been defeated in 1918, but rather 'stabbed in the back' (*Dolchstoss*) by cowardly politicians back home. They argued that the same treacherous civilians had signed the grossly unfair Treaty of Versailles, and that Jews and communists continued to plot against Germany. Constant repetition does not make an argument true, but it can sometimes make it seem so, especially when no counter-argument is allowed anywhere. Much of the success of the Nazi party in the national elections between 1930 and 1933 has been attributed to their mastery of propaganda, and propaganda continued to play a vital role in the Nazi state after 1933.

Hitler and the Nazis believed that they were embarking on a social revolution in 1933, one that would embed the idea of **Volksgemeinschaft** ('nation community', an ideal community of all 'racially pure' Germans) deep in German minds.

Effective propaganda was vital to this task. One of the first acts of the Nazi government newly strengthened by the March 1933 elections, just six weeks after Hitler became Chancellor, was to establish a Ministry of Popular Enlightenment and Propaganda. It would be headed by Goebbels, who had led the Nazi propaganda section since 1930. As the full name of the new ministry suggests, this was to be 'popular enlightenment' as much as 'propaganda'. Goebbels himself wanted to drop the word 'propaganda' in favour of 'culture' but he was overruled.

Key term

Volksgemeinschaft: German word meaning 'nation community'; an ideal community of Germans regardless of social status and based on race.

Thematic link: propaganda

A constant, omnipresent barrage of images of Nazi power and triumphalism flooded the nation. Goebbels swiftly gained controlling supervision over news media, the arts and information. At his first press conference after his appointment, on 15 March 1933, he declared that:

> I see in the setting up of the new Ministry of Popular Enlightenment and Propaganda by the Government a revolutionary act in so far as the new Government no longer intends to leave the people to their own devices. This government is in the truest sense of the word a people's government.[4]

Goebbels made full use of the technological developments of the times. The first was radio, which only came into commercial use in the late 1920s. He made available cheap radios subsidised by the Nazi party and he arranged that every district had its loudspeaker so that the speeches of Nazi leaders might have the widest possible audience. As before, the same few simple messages expressed in simple language were often repeated. The technological innovation exploited by Goebbels in 1932, the aeroplane, by means of which Hitler and other top Nazi leaders could travel widely around Germany campaigning, continued to be used. All outlets for 'popular enlightenment' were gradually brought under the propaganda ministry. These included newspapers and other publishing, film, theatre, opera and music. The use of bold, eye-catching political posters, at which the Nazis had always excelled, continued. One of the most enduring images of Nazi pomp and power is to be seen in *The Triumph of the Will (Triumph des Willens)*, a film made by Leni Riefenstahl about the 1934 Nazi Nuremberg Rally. The film opens by announcing that it was made on the Führer's orders and has a text prologue declaring '20 years after the outbreak of the world war, 16 years after the beginning of Germany's suffering, 19 months after the beginning of Germany's rebirth, Adolf Hitler flew to Nuremburg to review his gathered faithful followers.' A key element in the opening sequences – after drums and fanfares, a flight over the clouds and shots of the old city of Nuremburg – is the cutting between the flying plane and the columns of marching supporters, both sides heading towards the meeting point. It enacts the idea of a relationship between leader and led. Riefenstahl's innovative use of tracking shots and slow motion has caused many, including in recent years *The Economist* magazine, to call her 'the greatest female filmmaker of the 20th century'. She went on to make a film about the 1936 Berlin Olympics.

Propaganda in education and schools

The Nazi leadership recognised the difficulty of indoctrinating an older generation whose values had been formed earlier during the culture of Imperial rule (1871–1918) or the democracy of the Weimar Republic (1919–1933). A key element in their propaganda was the focus on youth. As Hans Schemm, leader of the Nazi Teachers' League and chess enthusiast put it, 'Those who have youth on their side control the future.' Education was thus a key Nazi target for control. The anti-Semitic legislation of 1933 had led to the removal from schools and universities of all Jewish teachers, professors and administrators. Bernhard Rust, appointed minister of education in June 1934, had already been active in Prussia. He had insisted that all students and teachers should greet each other in schools using the Nazi salute. Indoctrination in Nazi ideas was made compulsory in January 1934. The primary and secondary curriculum focused on 'racial biology', population policy, geography and physical fitness. Military education became the major component of the last of these. There were even exam questions that pushed Nazi ideas about society, such as:

To keep a mentally ill person costs approximately 4 marks a day. There are 300 000 mentally ill people in care. How much do these people cost to keep in total? How many marriage loans of 1000 marks could be granted with this money?

(The Nazis made loans to couples planning to get married in order to encourage new German families.)

Book-burning as propaganda

One of Joseph Goebbels first acts as minister of propaganda was to organise a public burnings of what he deemed as 'degenerate' books. This took place throughout Germany in May 1933 (see Figure 4.2). The books included:

- *the works of traitors, emigrants and authors from foreign countries who believe they can attack and denigrate the new Germany*
- *the literature of Marxism, Communism and Bolshevism*
- *pornography and explicit literature by Jewish authors*
- *literature by Jewish authors, regardless of the field*

- *literature with liberal, democratic tendencies and attitudes, and writings supporting the Weimar Republic*
- *all historical writings whose purpose is to denigrate the origin, the spirit and the culture of the German Volk.*

The list is of interest in many ways, not least because it blames Jewish authors for *all* 'pornography and explicit literature'. Also note the complete rejection of the values of the Weimar Republic. The book burning was carried out by students and members of the SA, who whooped with delight as they broke into nearby premises and private houses to ransack libraries.

Voices from the past

As part of the indoctrination of the young, the study of history was of great importance. Here, a writer from the Nazi Ministry of Education addresses the question of what kind of history should be taught.

The German nation in its essence and greatness, in its fateful struggle for internal and external identity is the subject of the teaching of history. It is based on the natural bond of the child with his nation and, by interpreting history as the fateful struggle for existence between the nations, has the particular task of educating young people to respect the great German past and to have faith in the mission and future of their own nation and to respect the right of existence of other nations. The teaching of history must bring the past alive for the young German in such a way that it enables him to understand the present, makes him feel the responsibility of every individual for the nation as a whole and gives him encouragement for his own political activity. It will thereby awaken in the younger generation that sense of responsibility towards ancestors and grandchildren which will enable it to let its life be subsumed in eternal Germany.

A new understanding of the German past has emerged from the faith of the National Socialist movement in the future of the German people. The teaching of history must come from this vital faith, it must fill young people with the awareness that they belong to a nation which of all the European nations had the longest and most difficult path to its unification but now, at the beginning of a new epoch, can look forward to what is coming full of confidence.

The certainty of a great national existence is for us based at the same time on the clear recognition of the basic racial forces of the German nation which are always active and indestructibly enduring. Insight into the permanence of the hereditary characteristics and the merely contingent significance of environment facilitates a new and deep understanding of historical personalities and context.

The course of history must not appear to our young people as a chronicle which strings events together indiscriminately, but, as in a play, only the important events, those which have a major impact on life, should be portrayed in history lessons. It is not only the successful figures who are important and have an impact on life, but also the tragic figures and periods, not only the victories, but also the defeats. But it must always show greatness because in greatness, even when it intimidates, the eternal law is visible. Only a sentient grasp of great deeds is the precondition for an understanding of historical contexts; the powerless and insignificant have no history.[5]

Discussion points

1. What are the ideas underlying this outline of the history that should be taught in schools?
2. How important do you think propaganda in education was to the Nazis' project of changing German society?

Figure 4.2: Book burning in Berlin, May 1933.

Among others the burned books included those by important thinkers such as Sigmund Freud and Albert Einstein (both Jewish), as well as Bertolt Brecht and George Grosz (both left-wing). Of those who wrote in English, books by H.G. Wells, D.H. Lawrence and Aldous Huxley, among others, were also burned. The 19th-century German poet Heinrich Heine's books were put into the fire; he was Jewish. He had written in 1821 that 'where they burn books they will in the end also burn people'. This book-burning was another means of preventing people from making any sort of critical decision about values. It was not very successful in a practical way, but it was effective as political theatre and as a means of getting across the Nazi message yet again.

The Olympic Games as propaganda

When we think about propaganda, we tend to think about the written word and the printed image. Certainly newspaper articles, posters and cartoons were important elements in the work of Goebbels and the RMVP. However, Goebbels also understood the importance of the propaganda event. During the April 1932 election, the 'Hitler over Germany' campaign had Hitler flying from place to place giving speeches. It gave him the attractive appearance of an energetic, modern man.

In 1936 Germany staged the summer Olympics. The arrangement for the Olympics to take place in Berlin had been made two years before the Nazis came to power by the Brüning government. New arenas were built. Berlin's Gypsies were arrested and moved to a concentration camp. Anti-Semitic notices were taken down. The whole thing was filmed by Leni Riefenstahl and released as *Olympia* in 1938 in

German but also in English and French. The film dramatised human achievements in the competitive events, but also German achievements in putting on the event.

The establishment and extent of the totalitarian regime

Nazi Germany was a totalitarian state in which Adolf Hitler achieved total power over the three branches of government: the executive, the legislature and the judiciary. Hitler exercised executive power as head of government and could appoint and fire people from positions of power and authority without reference to anyone else. As Germany became a one-party state, the powers of the legislative branch of government, the Reichstag, were reduced: the Enabling Act had banned some parties, and other parties folded under pressure. By the end of 1934, the Reichstag had no power, authority or influence. The nazification of the judiciary ensured that there would be no opposition to Hitler in the courts. In addition, he had merged the roles of head of state (president) and head of government (chancellor) so that the armed forces swore a personal oath of loyalty to him. This alone gave him an authority no Weimar chancellor had ever held. Germany had become a one-party dictatorship.

Not content with taking over all branches of government, and then of the state, the NSDAP had taken power over the agencies of civil society. As a result, there was almost no association which people could join or activity in which they could engage that was not a branch of the NSDAP or in some way sponsored by, administered by or monitored by Nazis. Taking authority over the mass media meant that in addition, all forms of printed and broadcast communication were either controlled by the Nazi state or at least vulnerable to interference and censorship. As a result information was provided only according to what the Nazis considered advantageous to them. This meant by extension that all political and moral debate took place within limits set by the government. Newspapers, newsreels in cinemas and radio broadcasts were carefully created to enforce the Nazis' ideology and continually assure people they were being well governed. It was this control of German civil society that makes Nazi Germany a totalitarian regime.

Economic policies and the degree of economic recovery

The economy of Nazi Germany from 1933 was above all based on the need to prepare for war: *Wehrwirtschaft*, a 'fighting economy', intended to prepare for war. Adolf Hitler and the Nazi leadership always regarded economic policy as secondary to a political programme. The NSDAP had been slow to develop an economic policy, but by the early 1930s it had found a group of economists ('the Reformers') such as Heinrich Dräger, whose radical economic ideas seemed a good fit with Nazi political and military aims.

The main Nazi domestic economic policy was to launch a large programme of public works. This had already been discussed by Strasser in 1932, and had been initiated by the Schleicher government. The policy reflected the influence of British economist J.M. Keynes. It meant a much higher level of government intervention in the management of the economy and what was called 'deficit financing' where government expenditure significantly outweighed government revenue. The argument for this was that government spending on building

ACTIVITY 4.2

The creation of a totalitarian state consisted of a series of steps and several interrelated processes over time. To make sure you have this aspect of Nazi Germany clear in your own mind:

1. Create a spider diagram showing how the Nazis achieved such a high level of control over German society and the German state

2. Write out a timeline listing the different things that happened in this process and putting in short notes explaining both what happened and what its significance was in each case.

When you have studied a little further in this subject, back and consider the following question:

3. To what extent do you think that the Nazis succeeded in their goal of achieving total control over Germany, 1933–1945?

roads, railways, dams and flood defences would eventually bring more revenue to the regime by bringing down unemployment, stimulating manufacturing and increasing public spending, all of which would result in greater tax receipts for the government. Not the least of the appeal to the Nazis of these ideas was that they represented a sharp break with what they saw as the failed economic policies of the Weimar Republic, notably the austerity of the Brüning governments. The risk of such an approach was inflation. Memories of the 1923 hyperinflation were still strong in Germany, and the Nazi state thus had to find ways of funding public works without putting large quantities of freshly-printed money into circulation.

The other main Nazi economic policy was the policy of autarky or self-sufficiency. This meant both protecting German production from cheaper foreign imports by raising tariffs or import duties on overseas goods and boosting production within Germany, especially agricultural output. Germany was not self-sufficient in a number of essentials and raw materials. Given the German experience of economic blockade in the First World War, and the impact of the Depression in peacetime, the drive for autarky is perhaps understandable.

The degree of government control over industry and business in achieving this had a mixed reception from German business leaders, especially those whose businesses were dependent on exports. However, the Nazis could argue that world trade had already been affected by other countries, notably the USA, putting up protective tariffs since the Wall Street Crash in October 1929 and the following Depression. There were limits, however, to how far a government could impose a war economy in peacetime. The population had to be kept adequately supplied with goods and foodstuffs. Smaller businesses could not be alienated by the inevitable distortions of their operations. Lastly, for the time being, Germany was dependent on the international supply of many industrial raw materials and foodstuffs. The economic developments of the 1933–1939 period reflect these conflicting priorities.

Hjalmar Schacht as president of the Reichsbank

On 16 March 1933, Hitler appointed Hjalmar Schacht president of the Reichsbank. It was one of the most important decisions made immediately after that month's elections and it greatly strengthened his position. Many businessmen, economists and the general public were likely to be made nervous by news of deficit spending. In that context, Schacht was a reassuring presence at the head of Germany's central bank. By reputation cool and competent, he was best known for his steady monetary management in the difficult inflationary days of 1923 and 1929.

As soon as he was appointed President of the Reichsbank, Schacht began to develop methods of deficit financing. Normally a government that wants to spend money it does not have will borrow this money from the international money markets, offering a high interest-rate in order to encourage investors to lend money to the state. Germany had already, however, reached a legal maximum on what it was able to offer in terms of interest rates, and this meant that it was not possible to go to the international money markets for loans. Another option is that a government can simply print more money, but this had gone disastrously wrong in 1923. Instead, Schacht began an internal model that allowed the Germany government to purchase goods on 'credit' from large businesses. The basis of this was the '**mefo**' bill.

These were promises by the government to pay in the future for work carried out right away. They ran initially for six months but could be extended and even discounted. Some ran on for four years. They were accepted by a consortium of four major armaments manufacturers (the *Metallurgische Forschungsgesellschaft*, hence 'mefo') and enabled Schacht to finance the massive rearmament programme called for by the Nazi government. This was an important way of funding public spending without having to print new currency.

In recognition of his success, Hitler appointed Schacht minister of economics in August 1934, a post he held until November 1937. Until 1938, German rearmament was still secret, being a flagrant breach of the Treaty of Versailles, but after this time it came out into the open and the use of mefo bills was discontinued, when a total of 12 billion marks was outstanding. This gives some idea of the massive scale of these financial operations. The success of Schacht's economic policy was remarkable. Annual gross domestic product (GDP), the total wealth produced in a year, rose by 8–10% each year for the five years from Hitler's appointment as chancellor in January 1933. Of more interest to ordinary Germans, inflation fell from around 3% in 1933 to 0% in 1938, while unemployment, which had peaked at 6 million in January 1933, was reduced to 320 000 by January 1939. On the other hand, the country now had price controls and rationing of many everyday items, including foodstuffs: the economy was gearing up for war.

Schacht was bold in the sense that he adopted Keynesian economic principles at a time when they were not common. This involved a much greater degree of government intervention in the control of the economy than had existed in the recent German past. It also shifted the main focus of the economy from the supply side (the people who made things) to the demand side (the people who buy things). He was also quite lucky, as the German economy was entering a recovery phase in 1933 from the depths of 1930. September 1934 saw Schacht taking steps to deal with the foreign exchange crisis afflicting Germany. He suspended reparations payments and in his 'New Plan' introduced import restrictions and exchange controls. Although the steps taken were not new, they were implemented in a comprehensive way and with a speed and determination that were.

However, the new policies brought their own problems. True, employment had risen. But military spending was far larger than in most other countries, leaving civilian spending lagging behind. Imports outgrew exports, so the balance of payments – the balance left after payment for imports had been deducted from income from exports – slipped over into the red. This meant that the country was rapidly running out of the raw materials its manufacturing (including armaments) industries needed. This 1936 economic crisis had, so Schacht and his Reichsbank deputy Carl Goerdeler thought, been caused by too rapid rearmament. Military spending in Germany reached 10% of GDP in 1936. The distortions to the civilian economy in terms of the availability of non-military goods became severe. A growing group, headed by Schacht and Goerdeler and including several leading German industrialists, made the case for a 'free-market' approach that would redirect the economy away from huge military expenditure. Their view was supported by many smaller businessmen whose commercial operations depended on exports. Goerdeler's leadership of this group was significant, because as Reich commissioner for prices his task was to control the inflation arising from greatly increased military expenditure.

During the economic crisis of 1936–1937 Schacht helped to lead the free-market faction in the Nazi government, arguing against **protectionist** measures for German goods. He also drew attention to the inflationary threat of the huge increases in the rearmament budget. This faction was made up of the economists, businessmen and technocrats. Schacht was opposed by a faction around Göring, whose economic thinking was dominated by political and military considerations. Schacht's message was not one that Hitler wished to hear from his top economic advisers. He was determined above all to rearm Germany and to put the nation on a war footing without delay. Göring's appointment as 'plenipotentiary of the **Four-Year Plan**' in 1936 clearly showed that the economics minister's influence was waning.

Goerdeler resigned his post at the Reichsbank in March 1937. Schacht, out of favour since the summer of 1936, hung on as minister of economics until November 1937, when he was replaced by Göring.

Tackling unemployment

Tackling unemployment was one of the key promises made by the party in the elections of the early 1930s, and unemployment had to be eliminated once the Nazis were in power. Large numbers of unemployed men were a continual threat to social order, and potential supporters for revolutionary parties. In the eyes of many of their supporters, the NSDAP were in government to restore order. Because of the Great Depression, the unemployment rate was running at over 26% in 1933, meaning about 6 million people without work. The government took several steps to resolve this. It introduced compulsory job-creation schemes through the *Reichsarbeitsdienst* (Imperial Labour Service, RAD). Unemployed men had to join these schemes or face a prison sentence. Breaking the terms of the Treaty of Versailles, Hitler ordered the army to triple in size, and in 1935 he introduced conscription: by 1939, there were 1.4 million men in uniform, and this **remilitarisation** helped to ease the unemployment figures. Jews were dismissed from state employment and their posts were filled by Germans ('**Aryans**'). Women were excluded from the unemployment statistics, making the situation look better than it was.

Hermann Göring and the Four-Year Plan

In August 1936 Hitler decided to launch the Four-Year Plan for the development of the German economy. He put Göring in charge of it in October 1936, convinced that Schacht's 'New Plan' would never solve the problem of providing sufficient raw materials to sustain the rearmament drive at the same time as providing the population with adequate levels of consumption. Göring was, in practice, the most powerful figure in the NDSAP after Adolf Hitler. He had joined the Nazi party early, in 1922, and by 1923 had been put in charge of the SA. He had been a war hero in

Key terms

Protectionism: an economic approach designed to protect the producers in one country against the important of competing produce from any other country, usually through imposing tariffs

Four-Year Plan: project for the development of the German economy in readiness for war, with specific production targets; led by Göring

Remilitarisation: put armed forces e.g. Army back into an area

Aryan: south-central Asian tribe which in pre-history is believed by some historians to have invaded both northern India and Europe; pseudo-scientific classification for pure German.

the First World War as a fighter pilot. Hitler valued him as a fellow First World War veteran but also as an organiser who could get things done:

> *I liked him. I made him the head of my SA. He is the only one of its heads that ran the SA properly. I gave him a dishevelled rabble. In a very short time he had organised a division of 11 000 men.*[6]

Göring became president of the Reichstag in August 1932 and minister-president of Prussia in April 1933. His social connections were of particular value to Hitler as he sought to gain the support of German elites, and Göring's first wife Carin often hosted parties for the Führer; the fact that Hitler had no wife left a marked gap which she sought to fill. Göring was vain, pompous and flamboyant. He was also humorous and charismatic, and (crucially) he was personally close to Hitler.

1936 was a watershed year in Nazi economic development. Business interests were increasingly excluded from decision-making, and the drive for rearmament became even more pronounced. The object of the Four-Year Plan was to boost the output within Germany of raw materials crucial to any war effort. The Four-Year Plan was designed to be in effect until 1940, although by then the office of the Plan had become such a familiar part of the Nazi economic planning landscape and so influential that in effect it remained until 1945.

The plan had its successes and failures. Brown coal and explosives were success stories. Other items fell short of targets: mineral oil (including synthetic petrol) production increased, but not by nearly as much as the plan intended. This general failure to achieve autarky left Germany still dependent on the import of crucial raw materials from other countries. In 1939, Germany was still importing about a third of the raw materials it needed. In time of war, this continuing dependence of the military effort on imports was a major weakness and just what Hitler had wanted to avoid.

It was true that the government's income had increased during the period 1933–1939, but government expenditure had increased even faster, so government debt had climbed sharply. Meanwhile the figures for the balance of trade were badly in the red. Unemployment coming down was a good news story, but there was plenty of bad economic news which the Nazi-run newspapers did not report.

The Four-Year Plan also sought to give a boost to the public works programme. It succeeded to some extent, and the German economy was much better prepared for war in 1939 than it had been in 1914. However, the Four-Year Plan was a task beyond the economic capacity of Germany. No country could have hoped to achieve self-sufficiency, rearm, undertake massive public building programmes and, at the same time, keep a large population supplied with food and consumer goods.

The industrial elites

An important factor in the downfall of the Weimar Republic in 1933 was the unrelenting hostility of the traditional elites in Germany. In 1919 the new Republic received enough support from these elites to survive, but at a price. When the chance came to destroy the Republic in 1933, these elites, who had for some time

ACTIVITY 4.3

What do you think that dropping Schacht and appointing Göring to run the economy tells us about:

1. Nazi government priorities
2. Nazi attitudes to the economy?

been sympathetic to nationalist, monarchist and authoritarian political groups, did not hesitate. Perhaps the most traditional and powerful of these elites was the military, whose officers were usually recruited from aristocratic landholding families, often from East Prussia or Pomerania. It was no coincidence that the Nazi vote in the election of March 1933 was at its strongest in these traditionalist areas.

Industrialists were not usually drawn from these ranks, although Gustav Krupp von Bohlen und Halbach was of that background and had been personally chosen by Kaiser Wilhelm II to marry the industrial heiress Bertha Krupp in 1909. Gustav and Bertha Krupp were typical among industrialists in that neither of them had been supporters of the Republic. They were less typical in opposing Hitler and the Nazi party; this contrasts with, for example, another Ruhr steelmaker, Fritz Thyssen. Bertha Krupp always avoided meeting Hitler. Gustav Krupp advised President Hindenburg against appointing Hitler chancellor in January 1933. He was, however, a strong nationalist and his armaments factories in Germany and elsewhere had worked in secret to rearm the German military despite the restrictions imposed by the Treaty of Versailles in 1919. Once Hitler was appointed Chancellor, Gustav Krupp became a Nazi supporter, helping to finance the NSDAP campaign for the March 1933 election and later becoming President of the *Reichsverband der Deutschen Industrie* (German Chamber of Commerce). To put his actions in context, he had always treated elected officials of the Republic, such as the president, with the respect their office demanded.

The attitude of big business generally towards the Nazi state, especially outside the coal and steel sector, was mixed. Fritz Thyssen might have been a Nazi enthusiast but many large firms were not, especially those that were dependent on exports. They disliked the increased state intervention, autarky and deficit spending that were built in to Nazi economic plans. The main national pressure group in this field, the Reich Association of German Industry (RDI), attempted to frustrate these plans but was swiftly brought to heel by the Nazi government. For some big industrialists in Germany, it was partly a business decision to back conservative and authoritarian political parties. The Nazis promised to bring the trade unions under control and were committed to a massive programme of rearmament. Both of these would appeal strongly to major arms manufacturers like Gustav Krupp, who could see great profits for the company. Most industrialists had never liked the Weimar Republic, not least because of its social welfare programmes and its perceived tendency to support trade unions during strikes such as the 1928 *Ruhreisenstreit* (Ruhr iron strike); they also remembered the hyperinflation of 1923. They much preferred a strong, authoritarian form of government that could bring order and stability back to Germany.

Another important industrial sector was the automobile industry. The market leader in Germany in the 1930s was Opel, since 1931 owned by the US company General Motors (which had a controlling share from 1929). Founded as a sewing-machine company in 1862 by Adam Opel in Rüsselsheim, Hesse, it made its first car in 1889, and in 1930 became the first car manufacturer in Germany to produce 100 000 vehicles. According to US Army reports, GM's Opel became the largest producer of trucks for the German army. In 1935, GM built a new plant close to Berlin to produce the *Blitz* (lightning) truck; these trucks would be driven by the German army into Poland, France and then the Soviet Union. In August 1938 a senior executive for General Motors received a medal, the Merit Cross of the German Eagle, First Class, for his 'distinguished service to the Reich'. Historian Henry Ashby Turner studied GM's role in Nazi Germany and described a struggle in which the company's American owners managed to ward off a Nazi plan to take control of Opel.[7]

Henry Ford was well known for his great success as a US businessman, but also for his strongly held anti-Semitic views. Ford had been the only American mentioned in *Mein Kampf*. Then in 1931, Hitler had told an American reporter that he regarded Henry Ford as his inspiration, and that he kept a large portrait of the American industrialist next to his desk. Ford Germany provided money to support the Nazi campaign for the March 1933 election. In July 1938, German diplomats awarded Ford the Grand Cross of the German Eagle, the highest German decoration for non-Germans.

Figure 4.3: Henry Ford at the ceremony in which he was awarded the Grand Cross of the German Eagle.

The most famous outcome of the Nazi interest in cars was the *Volkswagen* (people's car). In 1933, Hitler called for the production of an affordable car that could carry a family of two adults and three children at about 60 mph. He proposed a scheme to finance people's purchase of the car. The need for a cheap car was something that Hitler discussed with GM executives in 1934: the German car industry was focused on luxury cars and, despite some manufacturers taking an interest in the mass market, there was no equivalent of the low-cost, mass-selling Ford Model T. In the event, industrialists concluded that the sums did not add up. Even with Nazi support, they could not produce a car of the quality Hitler specified for the price he imposed.

Hitler moved from the private sector to the idea of a state-owned factory. Prototypes were produced from 1936, a company was founded in 1937 by the German Labour Front and a new factory was built in 1938. With the outbreak of war, the emphasis shifted from consumer to military vehicles. Large numbers of people paid in advance for a car. However, civilian production took second place to military orders, the project was overtaken by the outbreak of war and few cars were produced.

Social policies

Gleichschaltungsaktion

The effort to bring all the institutions of Germany into line in pursuit of a common set of goals was called *Gleichschaltungsaktion* (coordination action). *Gleichschaltung* (coordination) was an important Nazi concept, meaning that every aspect of state policy – economic, military, social, cultural – was coordinated to achieve agreed ends and carry an agreed message. This included the civil service, but extended to many other organisations. Following the establishment of the DAF, any trade union not officially recognised by the Nazi government was forced to disband and, in the face of any resistance, its leaders were arrested and imprisoned.

Education was a key area for the Nazis. When they came to power in 1933, Hitler first appointed NSDAP Reichstag deputy Bernhard Rust cultural minister for the state of Prussia, and then, in the summer of 1934, minister for education. He and the ministry he now led had their part to play in *Gleichschaltung*. It was their task to nazify education: Nazi ideology was introduced into the curriculum, teachers and pupils were required to greet one another with the Hitler salute, and Jews and communists were driven out of the teaching profession and replaced with Nazis, as was anyone else assessed as an enemy of the regime.

This same policy lay behind the takeover of other organisations or their merger with Nazi ones. These included all youth organisations being subsumed by the Nazis' own youth movements, the **Hitlerjugend** (HJ, Hitler Youth) and the **Bund Deutscher Mädel** (BDM, League of German Girls).

Again, there were protests, but these had no effect. The same happened to organisations for lawyers, doctors and other professionals. In each case, Jews, communists and those judged unreliable were driven out of the organisation, Nazis were moved into positions of authority, and the whole was placed under NSDAP central control. This process allowed the Nazi party to control directly not just the apparatus of the state, but also all aspects of civil society.

Key terms

Hitlerjugend: German word meaning 'Hitler Youth'; paramilitary youth movement, part of Nazi organisation.

Bund Deutscher Mädel: German expression meaning 'League of German Girls'; Nazi youth organisation for girls, part of the Hitlerjugend.

Thematic link: Social policies

Young people

There was a strong tradition of youth organisations in Germany before 1914 representing many and various different groups – churches, political parties and the Scout Association. Some 5 to 6 million young people, boys and girls, were members of various youth groups at the start of 1933. From 1934 the HJ was the only official youth organisation in Germany. It was based on the youth wing of the NSDAP, founded as early as 1922. It was paramilitary in character and before 1933 was often used to break up the meetings of church youth groups. Membership of the HJ was at first voluntary but from 1936 it became compulsory for all boys aged 10 to 21. Other youth organisations were closed down.

The HJ was organised at district level into corps under adult leaders and had strong links with the army and the German Labour Organisation. Ten-year-old boys went into the *Deutsches Jungvolk* (German Young People). The main active membership was of boys 14 to 18. At local level it was formed into small cells that met regularly. At these, Nazi doctrine was taught. Regional rallies and military-style field exercises were also held. HJ membership was well over 2 million by the end of 1933 and 5 million by the end of 1936, when membership had become compulsory. Parents who refused to allow their child to join were warned that the state could take their child into care. In 1936, HJ leader Baldur von Schirach set himself the goal of all ten-year-olds joining; 90% of German ten-year-olds had done so in time for a ceremony on Hitler's birthday, 20 April, with drums, fanfares and the swearing of a solemn oath of personal loyalty. The importance of membership, and of each stage of development, was underlined by the use of 'admission ceremonies' and 'graduation ceremonies'.

The purpose of the HJ was to ensure that boys grew up with the attitudes the NSDAP wanted to encourage. The outdoor life of camping, marching and military exercises prepared them for joining the armed services when they were older. Armed HJ units were formed and deployed in combat during the Second World War. In addition, members were educated in German folklore and Nazi ideas about race. Finally, the uniforms and discipline helped encourage an atmosphere of obedience, something the Nazis wanted to characterise German society, not just the armed forces. In addition, all members of the HJ had to take an oath of personal loyalty to Adolf Hitler.

Ten-year-old girls joined the *Jungmädelbund* (Young Girls' Association), and then at 14 they went into the Nazi youth organisation for girls, the *Bund Deutscher Mädel*. The BDM took part in similar activities to the HJ boys, with the uniforms and outdoor life (see Figure 4.4, for example), but with less paramilitary activity and fewer intensely competitive sports. Instead of being treated like little soldiers, girls were educated in the importance of motherhood, part of which included lessons in Nazi racial theory.

Figure 4.4: Girls of the Berlin BDM, haymaking, September 1939.

The outbreak of war in September 1939 added a further impetus to the way in which the Nazi regime managed education. Large maps appeared on classroom walls into which pupils stuck coloured pins to show the advance of the victorious German army. As the age for military conscription was 15, those with sufficiently high grades attending one of the elite *Gymnasien* (grammar schools) took the entrance exam for higher education, the *Abitur*, a year early. In addition, after 1933 the Nazi regime converted state boarding schools into National Political Institutes of Education (Napolas), which had a military character. In 1937 the *Adolf-Hitler-Schulen* (Adolf Hitler Schools, AHS) were established by DAF leader Ley and HJ leader Baldur von Schirach, perhaps as a response to the increasing influence of Himmler and the SS over the Napolas. They charged no fees, were linked to the HJ and took boys from age 12. Graduates of Nazi schools might go on to the *NS-Ordensburgen* (Castles of the NS Order, reminiscent of the old chivalrous orders). These really were based in castles and were for men once they had married to continue with or re-enter education. Their emphasis was on military studies (including live fire, from which there were sometimes fatalities), competitive sports, and the Nazi version of academic subjects such as geography and biology. The men who had attended these had a high opinion of themselves as the party's elite youth members.

 Thematic link: Nazi ideology

Women

On the surface, the Nazis believed in a return to patriarchal values and traditional gender roles in society. They had gained some political and electoral support from those Germans who deplored the social and cultural changes that had taken place since 1919. Even progressive Weimar governments had been troubled by such things as the declining birth rate and rising divorce rate, and these continued to be issues of concern for the Nazi government. The National Socialist Women's League (**NS-Frauenschaft**) was intended to reverse these developments by encouraging domesticity and teaching traditional, socially conservative values and rejecting arguments for **women's rights**.

The *NS-Frauenschaft* was founded as the women's wing of the Nazi party in 1931 under the leadership of Gertrud Scholtz-Klink. By 1938 its membership topped 2 million or 40% of the Party membership.

The Nazi pre-war policy of sending women home to look after their children and husband proved more successful than the wartime attempt to bring them back into the labour force. When the Nazi message to women changed and they sought to persuade women to go out to work in factories and so on to support the war effort by taking over the jobs left by men, the response was, from their point of view, disappointing.

Workers

The Nazi regime decided early on that trade unions had be to be eliminated. They possessed power, so they were a threat to the Nazi regime, and they were connected with the Social Democrats and Communists and as such offered an alternative political perspective.

Hitler did want to destroy the unions, but he did not want to be seen as an ally of big industrialists. That kind of identification had helped prevent Weimar's right-wing political parties from acquiring widespread support. The Nazis had never been a purely right-wing organisation, and Hitler needed to win support from the working classes who had traditionally supported the SPD or the KPD. In an attempt to win the support of both employers and workers, Hitler announced the creation of the *Deutscher Arbeitsfront* (German Labour Front, DAF). This arm of government took over the task of negotiating with employers all matters to do with pay, conditions and contracts. The aim was to increase what employers were allowed to demand workers did, removing Weimar restrictions, and to balance this by making sure workers had proper job security and social security programmes. Strikes had been a problem for the Weimar economy. The Nazis banned strikes, but also sought to make strikes unnecessary.

By 1936, unemployment was down to around 8%. By the outbreak of the Second World War, it had been eliminated almost entirely. Some of this achievement was because real people had been given real jobs, but some of it was through managing appearances more than managing the economy. DAF membership was voluntary, just as membership of the youth and women's organisations was. However, it was harder to get a job if you weren't a member. Workers were used to paying union dues, so paying the DAF fees wasn't a hardship, and for the

Key terms

NS-Frauenschaft: Nationalsozialistische Frauenschaft, German expression meaning 'National Socialist Women's League', Nazi women's association.

Women's rights: women's civil rights as citizens; usually discussed in the context in which it is argued that women ought to possess the same civil rights and the same status of citizenship as men, but don't.

government it was a welcome source of additional revenue: the millions of small sums regularly paid added up to 300 million marks in 1934.

In addition to pay and conditions of work, the DAF included an organisation called *Kraft durch Freude* (Strength through Joy). This provided access to sports and leisure facilities, and tickets for cultural events. It also organised cheap and in some cases free holidays to reward workers. At the same time Nazi associations took over existing clubs for cycling, Christians, air transport and numerous other leisure pursuits, pastimes and hobbies. Taken altogether, the various Nazi organisations, supported by the increasingly comprehensive propaganda effort headed by Goebbels, provided a platform for the indoctrination of the German people, especially of the young. When membership of various organisations became compulsory, backed by the considerable force at the disposal of the Nazi state, this platform became even stronger.

The churches

The churches were affected by Nazi cultural and political pressure, and some cooperated with the policy of *Gleichschaltung*. Within the Protestant churches, 'German Christians' (*Deutsche Christen*) adopted Nazi ideology, including anti-Semitism. These individuals and pressure groups tried to make the Protestant churches to which they belonged become part of the Nazi, nationalist German movement. Like wider society, Protestant churches had been affected by the revolution of 1918, specifically by the abdication of princes, since these had occupied a regional leadership role in the churches since the reformation. This led to a confused situation in which churches were disestablished (had ceased to be an official part of the state), were governed by church councils, but continued to receive subsidies from the state.

In this context, and with the rise of Nazism, the *Deutsche Christen* made it their business to make Christianity, and the churches where it was celebrated, more German and less Jewish. They promoted the revival of *völkisch* (folk) traditions and they played down the importance of the Old Testament (Jewish scripture) in theology and in services; some wanted its complete removal from the Bible. They preached the view that Christ had been killed by Jews and emphasised the importance of respect for government, something which had been important in the work of Luther, the founder of German Protestantism, and which had formerly been visible in the role played by the princes. They supported the idea of *Gleichschaltung* for the churches, which would lead to a single, centrally governed national church.

Before 1933, the *Deutsche Christen* were one pressure group among many within the churches, advancing ideas and trying to support the promotion of their own members. Following Hitler's appointment as chancellor in January 1933, the Protestant churches agreed to lay plans for a national church, the *Deutsche Evangelische Kirche* (German Evangelical Church, DEK). Following setbacks, including the rejection of their candidate for the leadership role, the new church agreed to remove clergy of Jewish descent and ban clergy marrying 'non-Aryans'. They were opposed by others in the churches, leading to a split in which the *Bekennende Kirche*, Confessing Church, was created. In addition, because of their official status as civil servants, Protestant ministers were required to swear an oath of allegiance to Hitler: 'I will be loyal and obedient to the Führer of the German Reich and Nation Adolf Hitler.' During the controversy, Martin Bormann, a close associate of Hitler, wrote to Nazi regional authorities warning them to keep out of the debate and leave it to the churches to argue through.

The renowned theologian Karl Barth refused to take the oath and lost his job at Bonn University. Others decided they could take the oath as it was simply one of good citizenship. Similarly at the outbreak of war, some Christians, and even ministers, decided it was legitimate to fight for Germany even if not for Hitler. This was making a distinction that the Nazi regime itself had done much to destroy. Victoria Barnett, in her study of this topic *For the Soul of the People*, points out that the Wehrmacht offered a place of safety for Confessing Church Christians, as the army could protect them against Gestapo investigations.

Having a spiritual head and organisation centre outside Germany meant that the situation of the Roman Catholic Church was different from that of the Protestant churches. It did not go through a process of division as clear as that of the Protestants, but it did go through the same internal debate over how far to cooperate with the government (which it saw as the legitimate secular authority) and how far to protest against or oppose any measures which it saw as un-Christian or anti-Christian. Catholic priests and Catholic Church members tended to be less nationalistic than Protestants; they had a history of supporting the Centre party, not the NSDAP, the DNVP or other right-wing parties. They had, as a result, been much more comfortable with the processes of the Weimar Republic, having been directly represented in government at every stage. Before 1933, Catholic bishops had advised church members against joining the NSDAP, though this ban was dropped during 1933. The government signed a concordat with the Roman Catholic central leadership in the Vatican in 1933. Under this *Reichskonkordat* Catholic bishops took an oath of loyalty to the German head of state, Catholic priests were banned from working for political parties and Catholic priests were limited to religious responsibilities only. In return, the German government agreed to protect Catholics' rights as citizens. The intention was clearly to keep the Church out of politics and end criticisms, at the price of keeping the NSDAP out of the Church and keeping Church members safe in a dangerous place.

The concordat did not have long-term success. The Nazis continued to interfere in Catholic schools, and youth groups were merged into the HJ. The Pope, Pius XI, eventually issued an official statement called an encyclical. Called *Mit brennender Sorge* (With Burning Concern), it was smuggled into Germany to avoid any interference or censorship, and read out from the pulpit in every Catholic Church in Germany on Palm Sunday, a day when the church could be confident of large numbers of people being present. It criticised the developing cult of 'race' in Germany and the way in which the rights of the state were outweighing the rights of the individual. It also criticised anti-Semitic policies, stressing the importance of the Old Testament and the fact that baptised Jews were as much Christians as anyone else. The document refers to the government but not individual people or parties; it doesn't name 'Hitler' or use the word 'Nazi' at any point. The following day, the Gestapo raided churches to seize all copies.

The *Volksgemeinschaft*

The idea that the Nazis were composed of self-interested elites and mindless thugs would be a serious misinterpretation. No doubt the Nazis had more than their fair share of racist thugs and psychopaths, but to caricature the entire NSDAP in this way would be a very superficial, two-dimensional view. There were also intellectuals, writers, lawyers and academics. Dr Joseph Goebbels and Dr Hans Lammers were only two among many in the Nazi leadership. The Nazis were driven not least by a set of ideals. Hitler regarded himself as a social revolutionary in the sense that he wanted above all to protect the purity of the German *Volk* from pollution, as he saw it, from other, inferior, races. This ideology was fundamental to many nationalist groups in Germany, which had helped the Nazis gather support for building and sustaining a Volksgemeinschaft.

The first part of this word – *Volk* – is a German word that is loaded with meaning and association. English translations of German words based on *Volk* have sometimes used the English word 'folk', giving us the not very satisfactory 'folk music' for *Volksmusik*, 'folk song' for *Volkslied* and folk dance' for *Volkstanz*. *Volksmärchen* has ended up as the even less happy 'fairy stories'. That the German word is intended to mean 'nation' and 'people' is made clear by its frequent use in naming during the Nazi period: the people's radio (*Volksempfänger*) and of course the people's car (*Volkswagen*). The second part of the word – *Gemeinschaft* – means 'society' but also 'community', a group which holds shared values and a shared history. The Nazi idea of a *Volksgemeinschaft* was thus a 'community of the race', or a 'people's society'. This meant including all Germans regardless of social class or job, and excluding other 'races' or, at worst, eliminating them.

Every policy of the Nazi state was geared to achieving this goal, a coordinated effort on many fronts. Robert Ley's instructions to organised labour or General Blomberg's memo to the *Wehrmacht* are thus more than exercises in *Gleichschaltung* as a matter of administrative ease or totalitarian control. An aspect of this (which could also be pointed to as an aspect of propaganda) was the *Winterhilfswerk*. Partly in imitation of the kind of charitable work done by churches, this had been introduced by Hitler and Goebbels in 1933 with slogans such as 'No One is Allowed to Starve and Freeze', and a poster featuring a man rowing to the rescue of someone drowning. The message was clear: under NSDAP, there would be social solidarity: those with spare funds and goods would be generous to those with less and the Nazis would be the organisers and motivators. Families were encouraged to eat one meal which only needed a single saucepan to cook it, and to give the money saved to the fund. Collectors went from door to door and church bells were rung to remind people (and no doubt to give the event an echo of church collections).

Benefits and drawbacks of Nazi rule

The benefits and drawbacks of Nazi rule depended on who you were. If you were a German without Jewish blood and without a left-wing background, the Nazi state did improve the economy in a general way. Taking advantage of the latest economic thinking pioneered by the economist J.M. Keynes and initially with the steady economic management of Hjalmar Schacht, plus conscription and some juggling of the figures, unemployment shrank dramatically. As the Nazi state rearmed in earnest, factories returned to near-full capacity. Germans who had felt that the Treaty of Versailles was humiliating and unfair for Germany could watch with pride the steps taken by the Nazis after March 1933 to overturn various aspects of the treaty. This was an exciting change from Stresemann's patient but perhaps dispiriting 'fulfilment'. The armed forces welcomed an authoritarian government that was able to take decisions without all the delays and compromises of a democratic system. They believed that the military concept of total war, a conflict involving among other things the active participation of the civilian population, required such an authoritarian government.

For many Germans, from property owners to clerks to manual labourers, social order was important, and the Nazis did ensure that. Order and stability were also important to businesses and industrialists, so they too were willing to support the Nazi regime, despite doubts about some aspects of economic policy and its implementation. Workers had much of the security and guarantees for pay that the unions had been able to achieve, but employers were rewarded by the disappearance of strikes. It is easy with hindsight to concentrate on the importance of the Enabling Law or the Nuremberg Laws, and there is no doubt that these are central to an understanding of what was done, and how and why it was done. But we should remember that many – most – people were largely unaffected by these developments. While some people lost their jobs or were persecuted, far larger numbers were given work and reassured about their personal importance and the importance of their country.

The drawbacks of Nazi rule were felt with full force by those groups who had been excluded from the concept of 'German' by Nazi ideology. These included most notably the substantial Jewish population, but also other ethnic and social minorities. After March 1933 Jewish and other minority academics, civil servants and businessmen were persecuted and were either dismissed from their jobs or left unprotected. Those who embraced liberal values, the democratic process and the rule of law were in despair. Those on the revolutionary left of politics were hunted down; they were executed, imprisoned, in hiding or in exile.

Timeline

1933	
January	Hindenburg appointed Adolf Hitler as chancellor
27 February	Reichstag fire
March	Federal election; Hjalmar Schacht appointed President of the Reichsbank; Dachau concentration camp opened
23 March	Hitler presented Enabling Act to the Reichstag
April	*Gesetz zur Wiederherstellung des Berufsbeamtentums* (Law for the Restoration of the Professional Civil Service); Göring created Gestapo
May	Book burning

15 July	Nazis became only legal political party in Germany
September	Foundation of the *Reichskulturkammer* (Reich Chamber of Culture)
1934	
March	Hitler announced increase in size of the armed forces
30 June–2 July	'Night of the Long Knives' (Röhm Putsch)
2 August	Hindenburg died; Hitler assumed the office of president
August	Schacht appointed minister of economics
1935	
February	Hitler ordered Göring to create Luftwaffe in breach of Treaty of Versailles
September	Nuremberg laws passed: Law for the Protection of German Blood and German Honour; Reich Citizenship Law
1936	
March	Remilitarisation of the Rhineland
August	Berlin Olympics; introduction of conscription: two-year military service
October	Four-Year Plan launched – Göring put in charge; Himmler established the 'Reich Central Office for the Suppression of the Gypsy Nuisance'
1937	
March	Goerdeler resigned his post at the Reichsbank
November	Schacht resigned as minister of economics – post went to Göring; exhibition of 'Degenerate art' and *Grosse deutsche Kunstausstellung* (Great German art exhibition) in Munich
1938	
March	Union (*Anschluss*) with Austria
9 November	*Kristallnacht*

Practice essay questions

1. 'It was religious organisations that provided the greatest resistance to Hitler's power between 1933 and 1939.' Assess the validity of this view.
2. 'The Nazi regime achieved an "economic miracle" in Germany between 1933 and 1939.' Assess the validity of this view.
3. Assess the validity of the view that Nazi rule made most people better off between 1933 and 1939.
4. With reference to the sources below and your understanding of the historical context, assess the value of the three sources to a historian studying the control the Nazi party had over the education system in Germany.

Source A

From the Guidelines for Teaching History, *Reichsministerium fur Wissenschaft, Erziehung und Volksbildung*, Wiedmann, Berlin 1938 (translated in Noakes, J. and Pridham, G., eds, *Nazism 1919–1945, Volume 2*).

A new understanding of the German past has emerged from the faith of the National Socialist movement in the future of the German people. The teaching of history must come from this vital faith, it must fill young people with the awareness that they belong to a nation which [...] had the longest and most difficult path to its unification but now, at the beginning of a new epoch, can look forward to what is coming full of confidence. [...] The certainty of a great national existence [...] is for us based [...] on the clear recognition of the basic racial forces of the German nation which are always active and indestructibly enduring. Insight into the permanence of the hereditary characteristics and the merely contingent significance of environment facilitates a new and deep understanding of historical personalities and contexts

Source B

Recollections of an anonymous woman who left school at the age of 16 in 1939, Leonard Nachlass (in typescript), Box 12, Folder *Englische Untersuchungen ubuer die Deutscen zu verscheidenen Fragen der Schulpolitik*, George Eckert Instit fur Schulbuchforschung, Braunschweig (in 'Six Years Education in Nazi Germany', in Evans, R.J., *The Third Reich in Power*).

[Teachers] had to pretend to be Nazis in order to remain in their posts, and most of the men teachers had families which depended on them. If somebody wanted to be promoted he had to show what a fine Nazi he was, whether he really believed what he was saying or not. In the last two years, it was very difficult for me to accept any teaching at all, because I never knew how much the teacher believed in or not.

Source C

Report of a branch of the National Socialist Teachers' League in Franconia in 1937 (in Evans, R.J., *The Third Reich in Power*).

Many school pupils believe that they can just sail through their school-leaving examinations by sitting tight for eight years even if they fall way below the required intellectual standard. In the Hitler Youth and Junior Hitler Youth units there is no kind of support for the school; on the contrary, it is precisely those pupils who serve in leading positions there who are noticeable for their disobedient behaviour and their laziness at school. It is necessary to report that school discipline is noticeably declining and to a worrying degree.

 Chapter summary

By the end of this chapter you should understand the way in which Hitler built on his appointment as chancellor, appointed himself president and extended Nazi rule through the criminal justice system but also through churches and social groups into every aspect of German society. You have learned about the economic success story and the social policies that the regime carried through and the reasoning behind these. You have also learned about the curious and perhaps calculated inefficiencies of Nazi rule. Briefly, you have studied how:

- with the death of President Hindenburg, Hitler was the leader of both the NSDAP and Germany, with little to limit his exercise of power
- the bureaucracy of the Nazi state was inefficient and full of rival groups
- tensions existed between Nazi party officials and existing civil servants
- the armed forces supported Hitler and he ordered their politicisation
- the German economy recovered, with a major public-works programme and development of a war economy
- the Nazis quickly built a 'terror state', using propaganda, taking control of every aspect of society and using the police, Gestapo and SS
- the Nazis set out to create a *Volksgemeinschaft*, a nation of shared ethnicity and purpose in which social class ceased to be a source of division, and non-Germans were driven out or eliminated.

End notes

[1]   *US Chief Counsel for the Prosecution of Axis Criminality, Volume 3* (Washington DC: US Government Printing Office, 1946).

[2]   Original German text: MGFA (Militärgeschichtliches Forschungsamt)/DZ: W01-5/185; reprinted in Müller, K.-J., *Das Heer und Hitler: Armee und Nationalsozialistisches Regime 1933–1940* (Stuttgart, 1969). English translation: Noakes, J. and Pridham, G., eds., *Nazism 1919–1945, Volume 3.*

[3]   Falconi, C. trans. Wall, B., *The Silence of Pius X* (Boston: Little, Brown, 1970).

[4]   Manvell, R. and Fraenkel, H., *Doctor Goebbels.*

[5]   Noakes, J. and Pridham, G., eds., *Nazism 1919–1945, Volume 2.*

[6]   Trevor-Roper, H.R. (intro), *Hitler's Table Talk 1941–1944*

[7]   Turner, H.A., *German Big Business and the Rise of Hitler*

5 The racial state, 1933–1941

In this section, we will look at how the Nazis in power put into practice their ideas about race and society. We will study how they persecuted non-German minorities inside Germany, as well as those who came under Nazi rule during the war, and worked to bring Germans outside Germany into the Reich. We will look into:

- the radicalisation of the state: Nazi racial ideology; policies towards the mentally ill, asocials, homosexuals, members of religious sects, the Roma and Sinti
- anti-Semitism: policies and actions towards the Jews, including the boycott of Jewish shops and the Nuremberg Laws
- the development of anti-Semitic policies and actions; the effect of the Anschluss; Reichskristallnacht; emigration; the impact of the war against Poland
- the treatment of Jews in the early years of war; the *Einsatzgruppen*; ghettos and deportations.

The radicalisation of the state

Nazi racial ideology

The Nazis' racial ideology was fundamental to their thinking. Almost every aspect of their policy had a racial element – their persecution of 'racial', social and religious minorities in particular, but also in education, scientific research, health, social welfare, family, employment and many other areas. This ideology was no secret. Their large and efficient propaganda machine churned out endless material based on 'race'. They had made their ideas on race clear since their foundation in 1921. In addition, they announced new racial laws at the huge Nuremberg party rally in 1935. *Gleichschaltung* (coordination) of policies across a wide policy range ensured that, in theory, all Nazi policy was aimed at the creation of the *Volksgemeinschaft*. This radical Nazi scheme was no less than the building of a community in Germany based on 'racial purity'. Hitler liked to think of himself as a social revolutionary, dedicated to the building of a *Volksgemeinschaft* by means of a coordinated (*Gleichschaltung*) programme of social policies.

Beside the political idea of 'the people', the word *Volk* also suggested to Germans at the time the curiously historical–biological idea of 'the tribe', with associations of Germany's mythical, tribal past. It was thus used to promote the supposed 'Aryan' type, imagined by Nazis as tall, blond-haired, blue-eyed, lean, active warriors.

'Aryan' is another word with a complicated history. Strictly, it is used to mean a south-central Asian tribe that is thought by some historians to have migrated in different directions in prehistory, moving into northern India and Europe. This theory remains controversial and historians continue to discuss it. Nazi propagandists adopted it and promoted the idea that Germans were the Aryans' pure descendants, and were also a conquering nation. This theoretical link with northern India was the reason why the Nazis adopted the Indian symbol of the swastika.

The *Volksgemeinschaft*, a mixture of history, mythology, politics and biology, was thus the Nazi idea of the German nation, with all 'impurities' (foreigners, traitors and the unwell) excluded. The belief was that in such a nation all divisive ideas of social class would drop away. The concept of a superior race and of building unity out of exclusion necessarily implies that inferior races exist and must be excluded. If the Germans were tall, fair and heroic, the excluded remainder must clearly be their opposites, short and swarthy, devious and cowardly. The Nazis followed this well-established *völkisch* nationalist tradition. The idea of a *Gemeinschaft* for the whole *Volk* based on these principles appealed strongly to them. After 1933 they required schools to teach 'racial biology' and population studies, with the aim of supporting the idea that the *Volk* needed to expel those who did not conform to the racial and moral code of the *Gemeinschaft*. Accordingly the Nazis in power persecuted and discriminated against ethnic minorities, notably Jews but also Roma and Sinti people ('Gypsies'), as well as other groups they believed were imperfect and weakened the *Volk*, including the physically and mentally disabled or ill, and homosexual men.

Key term

Swastika: The 'hooked cross' symbol of the NSDAP, adopted from Indian traditions to symbolise the Aryan origins of Germans.

Thematic link: radical ideology?

Nazi policies towards the mentally and physically ill

In July 1933, a 'Law for the Prevention of Offspring with Hereditary Diseases' was passed. This was one of the measures taken by the incoming Nazi government to maintain what they saw as the racial purity of the *Volk* and to prevent its dilution or pollution. People who were mentally or physically disabled were regarded by the Nazis as 'socially undesirable'. They were expensive to look after, so the argument ran, and did not contribute anything to society. The list of those conditions which the law grouped together included:

- mental disabilities
- mental illnesses, including schizophrenia and bipolar disorder
- physical conditions, including epilepsy, Huntington's chorea, blindness, deafness, physical deformity
- psychosocial conditions, including alcoholism.

The requirement was that the condition was believed at the time to be hereditary. The law was a first attempt to 'solve' this supposed problem by forced sterilisation: this would mean (ran the argument) that over time these conditions would disappear from society. About 400 000 people were forcibly sterilised under the programme.

This programme came from a belief in '**eugenics**'. Eugenicists argued that while human beings had worked hard to improve the quality of farm animals, we had neglected our own stock. A simplified version of the ideas of Charles Darwin on the subject of evolution, onto which beliefs about superiority and inferiority were grafted, had helped create the view that too many 'unfit' and 'unsuitable' people were surviving who would naturally die early, leaving no offspring, and this was undermining the health and prosperity of the entire community. Ideas of this kind were not limited to Nazi Germany: eugenics had its enthusiasts in many Western countries, including the UK and the USA, and other countries, such as Canada and Sweden, also experimented with sterilisation. It is worth noting that the Nazis, along with others, also extrapolated Darwin's ideas about the natural world to apply to society; they believed that it was both natural and morally correct that the 'strongest' human beings should survive at the expense of weaker, 'inferior' humans. This was known as **social Darwinism**.

The Nazis' second answer to the 'problem' was forced euthanasia for those considered incurable, sometimes called 'mercy killing'. This was carried out on an industrial scale after 1939. This programme is sometimes called Action (or *Aktion*) T4 after the house at Number 4 Tiergartenstrasse in the Berlin suburb of Tiergarten, which was the headquarters of the Charitable Foundation for Curative and Institutional Care (*Gemeinnützige Stiftung für Heil- und Anstaltspflege*). This organisation was under the direction of Philipp Bouhler, chief of Hitler's private chancellery, and Hitler's personal physician Dr Karl Brandt. The involvement of the Führer's personal staff in this way is a measure of both the importance and

ACTIVITY 5.1

Draw up a spider diagram for Nazi racial ideology, showing the key principles and the way in which they affect different areas of activity. Draw on your studies so far to do this, reviewing your notes. You might want to revisit this diagram as you progress further with this topic, adding some additional notes and links to it.

Key terms

Eugenics: The attempt to control the characteristics of human populations by controlling breeding

Social Darwinism: late 19th- and early 20th-century pseudoscience based on applying the scientific ideas and discoveries of Charles Darwin about the natural world to society; in particular, the idea that the strongest human beings would and should succeed and thrive where the weakest would fail and die.

Figure 5.1: The text on this Nazi poster from around 1938 says: 'This hereditarily ill man will cost the *Volksgemeinschaft* 60 000 marks over his lifetime. Fellow German, that's your money too.'

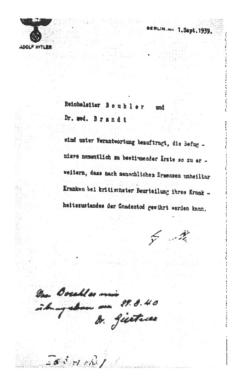

Figure 5.2: Hitler's order to establish the T4 Action, 1939.

the sensitivity of this programme. Between September 1939 and August 1941 some 70 000 mentally disabled people considered incurable were killed at various extermination centres located at psychiatric hospitals. A further 200 000 are estimated to have died as a direct result of the unofficial continuation of the T4 programme after August 1941 right through to the end of the war in 1945. Most were killed with gas, an experience in the techniques and technologies of mass murder that the Nazis were to use on other groups.

Physically disabled people classified as incurable (and as possessing a hereditary condition) fared no better. Some were included in the sterilisation programme; others were killed. Doctors played an active part in the decisions about who should die; they also supervised the killings and falsified medical records by listing false causes of death. One of the six extermination centres in Germany and Austria where these killings took place was Hadamar. The centre was located at a psychiatric hospital in the small town of Hadamar near Limburg in the state of Hesse, central Germany 1941-1945. Killings were by lethal injection or gas and the bodies of those killed were burned in crematoria. The forced euthanasia programme was kept secret, but it did get out eventually. This was an additional reason for the importance of Nazi propaganda posters (such as Figure 5.1) and public comments regarding the issue, to ensure a sufficient level of public support for the policy.

In English the order in Figure 5.2 reads:

Reichsführer Bouhler and Dr Brandt are charged with the responsibility of extending the authority of named physicians, so that patients who may reasonably be judged incurable, and after the most critical assessment of their condition, can be granted mercy death [Gnadentod].– Adolf Hitler

Nazi policies towards 'asocials'

The Nazis used the term *Arbeitsscheu* (workshy) to describe vagrants, tramps and beggars, people judged unproductive and so useless to society. These people who are at society's margins are sometimes called 'asocial' in English, in that they are judged not to be participating in mainstream social activities and groups. Beggars and others without homes or jobs could be sent to concentration camps, where they were identified by black triangle badges. Some Roma and Sinti people were classified as part of this group in the concentration camps.

In September 1933 coordinated police raids took place all over Germany. During what is known as 'Beggars' Week' 100 000 tramps and vagrants were taken into custody; most were later released. The persecution of 'asocials' became much worse in later years. They were registered and their movements recorded. In June 1938 the National Campaign against the Workshy resulted in the internment of some 11 000 people in concentration camps such as Buchenwald and Sachsenhausen, where they were forced to work. Although attempts were made to draft laws against asocials, nothing formal by way of legal restrictions emerged, but this did not stop their continued persecution through to 1945.

Nazi policies towards homosexuals

The Nazis believed that homosexuality was a disease, and a dangerous one as far as the *Volk* was concerned. Homosexuals, they believed, were weak and effeminate, not able to fight for the Reich or even become members of a healthy society. It was, perhaps, the tolerance of homosexuality in the Weimar Republic that had most persuaded the Nazis and other conservative groups of the 'degenerate' nature of Weimar society. What is more, the Nazis saw in homosexuals little chance of children, and a declining birth rate was again a threat to the *Volk*.

On 6 May 1933 a group of students led by SA stormtroopers broke into the Institute for Sexual Sciences in Berlin and confiscated its library of over 12 000 books and 35 000 photos. Four days later most of this collection was burned in the centre of Berlin in one of the notorious Nazi book-burnings taking place that evening in cities all over Germany. This was only the start of the Nazi campaign to eradicate homosexuality from German society. Local police had for some time been keeping lists of men in their area suspected of being homosexual – so-called 'pink lists' – and these were later used in police actions to detain such people. Gay clubs such as the Eldorado in Berlin were closed, and publications such as *Die Freundschaft* (Friendship) were banned.

Voices from the past

Law for the Prevention of Offspring with Hereditary Diseases (14 July 1933)

The Reich government has passed the following law, which is hereby promulgated:

1. Anyone suffering from a hereditary disease can be sterilised by a surgical operation if, according to the experience of medical science, there is a high probability that his offspring will suffer from serious physical or mental defects of a hereditary nature. Anyone suffering from any of the following diseases is considered hereditarily diseased under this law: 1. Congenital mental deficiency, 2. Schizophrenia, 3. Manic-depression, 4. Hereditary epilepsy, 5. Hereditary St. Vitus' Dance (Huntington's Chorea), 6. Hereditary blindness, 7. Hereditary deafness, 8. Serious hereditary physical deformity. Furthermore, anyone suffering from chronic alcoholism can be sterilised.

2. Applications for sterilisation can be made by the individual to be sterilised. If this person is legally incompetent, has been certified on account of mental deficiency, or is not yet 18, a legal representative has the right to make an application on this person's behalf but needs the consent of the court of guardians to do so. In other cases of limited competency, the application needs to be approved by the legal representative. […]

3. Sterilisation can also be requested by the following: 1. the state physician. 2. In the case of inmates of hospitals, nursing homes, and penal institutions, by the head thereof.

4. The application is to be made to the office of the Eugenics Court; it can either be made in writing or dictated to the court. The facts upon which the application is based should be supported by a medical certificate or confirmed in some other way. The office must inform the state physician of the application.

5. Responsibility for the decision rests with the Eugenics Court that has jurisdiction over the district in which the person to be sterilised officially resides.[1]

Discussion point

Put this source into the context of Nazi social policies. You should comment on the policy this refers to, how it was carried out, who was involved and what the reasons behind the decisions and actions were.

During the period of imperial rule, before the Weimar Republic, Paragraph 175 of the Criminal Code had already made homosexual acts illegal. However, this had been hard for the police to enforce. At the end of June 1935 the Ministry of Justice revised paragraph 175 to provide a legal basis for extending Nazi persecution of homosexuals in Germany. The revision meant that the term 'criminally indecent activities between men' could now be said to include simply being a homosexual. The courts further decided that just the intention or thought about such acts was sufficient for prosecution. In October 1936, Himmler formed within the security police the Reich Central Office for Combatting Abortion and Homosexuality, led by Josef Meisinger. The police now had the power to arrest and send to a concentration camp anyone they chose. Homosexuals recently released from prison were often rearrested if the police thought it likely that they would commit further homosexual acts and sent to a concentration camp where they had to wear a pink triangle on their prison uniform.

1937 to 1939 were the peak years of the Nazi persecution of homosexuals. Increasingly the police raided meetings, seized address books and created local networks of informers. Between 1933 and 1945 it is estimated that some 100 000 men suspected of being homosexuals were arrested. Most of the 50 000 or so who appeared before courts were sentenced to serve their time in regular prisons but up to 15 000 were sent to concentration camps. It is not known how many homosexuals died in the camps, but they were often ridiculed and beaten by the guards and given the most dangerous jobs. Because the Nazis believed that homosexuality was a disease, castration was offered and sometimes provided a way out of the camps for some homosexuals. Later, judges and SS camp officials might order castration without the homosexual prisoner's consent.

The Nazis did not regard lesbians as such a threat and they suffered considerably less persecution than did male homosexuals. They were rarely arrested for their sexuality (they might be sent to camps for other reasons, such as being Jewish) and in prison they did not wear the pink triangle.

Nazi policies towards religious groups

Members of certain religious (invariably Christian) sects were also subject to persecution and arrest. These were not members of the main Protestant and Catholic churches. Jehovah's Witnesses were considered to be potential opponents of National Socialism and the movement was banned in Germany in 1933 and actively persecuted. They believed that saluting national flags was a form of idolatry. Pacifists, they refused to perform military service, join Nazi organisations or swear allegiance to Adolf Hitler. Some 10 000, half of the total number of Witnesses in Germany at that time, were arrested. About 2000 of these were sent to concentration camps where an estimated 1200 died, 250 of whom were executed. Unlike the Roma and Sinti or Jews, they were not persecuted because of their ethnicity but because of their religious beliefs. Those few that were prepared to renounce their faith were released. Canadian historian Michael H. Kater has argued that the Jehovah's Witnesses' belief system was bound to collide with National Socialism because it too demanded complete commitment to an exclusive belief system.[2]

Christian Science was a small movement in Germany; among its members were Helmuth von Moltke's parents. The Christian Science Church was regarded with suspicion by the Nazis, especially after the USA joined World War Two, since its centre was in the USA. In 1941 the Church was banned, the Christian Science meeting places or 'Reading Rooms' were locked by the Gestapo and the Church's leaders taken for questioning.

Mormons made up a very small group indeed and that might partly explain why the regime took little interest in them. In addition, their social conservatism and practice of abstinence (from coffee, tea, alcohol and tobacco) were seen as compatible with Nazi policies for society. Helpfully for them, they had an institutional commitment to genealogical research and they were able to use this to prove members' German ('Aryan') ancestry.

Seventh Day Adventists attracted attention because of their practice of worshipping on Saturday, the Jewish Sabbath. To ensure that they were not seen as Jews, they agreed to various reforms of the kind recommended by the *Deutsche Christen*.

Nazi policies towards Roma and Sinti people

Roma and Sinti people, both groups probably originating in India, had over the centuries migrated to Europe. They have been called by different names, including 'Gypsy', which is based on the mistaken belief that they came from Egypt. Some settled in German lands from the 17th century or even earlier. They had a travelling lifestyle and were usually treated with prejudice, suspicion and hostility. From March 1933 they were actively persecuted. In some ways it was harder for the Nazis to classify Roma and Sinti people than it was in the case of Jewish people. As almost all were Christian, church records were of no use when attempting to classify this group. The bureaucrats turned to scientists to define a set of physical characteristics, taking advantage of the current research into the identification of ethnic origin through physical appearance. The science of the process has since been discredited, but it was taken seriously at the time and was useful for the Nazis.

Figure 5.3: Eva Justin of the Racial Hygiene and Demographic Biology Research Unit, a prominent Nazi anthropologist, with Roma Gypsies.

The key figure in Nazi Roma studies was Dr Robert Ritter, a child psychologist at the University of Tübingen. He specialised in 'criminal biology', the idea that criminal behaviour is genetically determined. In 1936 Ritter was appointed as Director of the Centre for Research on Racial Hygiene at the Ministry of Health. Here Ritter set about the study of the estimated 30 000 Roma and Sinti people then living in Germany (see Figure 5.3). Ritter announced that 90% of all Roma and Sinti peoples in Germany, although originally Aryan (because of originating in India), had become of mixed race through their long wanderings west into Europe and therefore posed a pollution danger to the German *Volk*. Ritter recommended that they be forcibly sterilised. The remaining 10% 'pure' Roma should be rounded up and placed on reservations for further study.

Also in 1936, Heinrich Himmler took centralised control of all police forces throughout Germany. He immediately established the Reich Central Office for the Suppression of the Gypsy Nuisance. That same year 'mixed' Roma were made subject to the racial, eugenicist and criminal laws:

- the Law for the Protection of German Blood and German Honour
- the Reich Citizenship Law (these two are known together as the 'Nuremberg Laws')
- the Law for the Prevention of Hereditarily Diseased Progeny
- the Law for Dangerous Habitual Criminals.

These could all be used against Roma and Sinti people. This in itself indicates the way the Nazis thought: Gypsies were seen as racially dangerous, ill and criminal. A short time before the Olympics in Berlin, 'mixed' Roma were rounded up, arrested and forcibly interned in a camp in a field outside Berlin called Marzhan, ringed with armed and uniformed police. The 600 or so Roma held here could leave to work during the day but had to return before nightfall.

Between 1935 and 1938, *Zigeunerlager* (internment camps for Gypsies) were set up by the Nazis all over Germany. These camps were just a preliminary stage on the road to genocide. The men in Marzahn were sent to Sachsenhausen concentration camp in 1938 and the women to Auschwitz extermination camp in 1943. In addition, many individual Roma were arrested because they were judged to be unemployed, homeless, beggars or habitual criminals, and sent to concentration camps. It has been calculated that altogether some 1.5 million Roma and Sinti were murdered by the Nazis between 1933 and 1945, although it is not possible to be precise about such things as most of the relevant records were destroyed. In the concentration camps, Roma had to wear a black triangle on their uniform if they had been classified as 'asocial' or green if 'habitual criminal'.

Anti-Semitism: policies and actions towards Jews

Anti-Semitism was certainly not invented by the Nazis. It had been a feature of European society for centuries. Political anti-Semitism was widespread at the end of the 19th century in Germany; Jews were barred from membership of established associations. As a result they founded their own organisations at a number of universities. Members of these new associations saw themselves as being loyal to Imperial Germany and also representing Jewish concerns. Yet great care needs to be taken in making judgements about the extent of anti-Semitism in Germany society before the Nazis came to power: it was certainly not the case that all Germans supported anti-Semitic rhetoric and policies from the Nazi party, as was shown by widespread apathy towards some early attempts at Jewish persecution.

Boycott of Jewish shops

As soon as the Nazis were in control of Germany after March 1933, they initiated a boycott of Jewish shops. Local SA groups were the first to take the initiative in an unplanned and unofficial way in March, standing outside Jewish-owned shops with placards apparently designed to warn prospective shoppers but also to intimidate them. The first official boycott action, called for by Propaganda Minister Joseph Goebbels, took place on 1 April 1933, when SA troops stood outside a large, chained-up department store in Berlin owned by the Tietz family. Their commercial empire had been founded in the previous century by Hermann Tietz and was now a huge commercial empire, with department stores all over Germany, a familiar sight to German shoppers. In the photograph by Heinrich Hoffman (Figure 5.4) one of the posters reads 'Defend yourselves against Jewish atrocity propaganda – buy only at German shops!' This slogan is in both German and in English, an indication of the Nazis' consciousness of international press photographers and journalists being in the country. They attempted to justify the boycott by saying that it was a response to negative overseas reports about the new Nazi regime in Germany, probably, they claimed, written by Jewish journalists. The boycott had only limited effect and seems to have irritated the German shopping public more than the Nazis expected. These boycotts were

ACTIVITY 5.2

Make a spider diagram about the groups that the Nazis persecuted. What did these groups have in common with one another? What does this tell you about Nazi views and policies?

dropped for a while but the Jewish community was persecuted in many other ways. Attacks on Jewish-owned shops in years to come meant that while there were some 50 000 Jewish small businesses in Germany in January 1933, by November 1938 barely a quarter of them remained.

Figure 5.4: A shop owned by Jews is closed – the main placard says 'Germans, defend yourselves! Don't buy from Jews!'

Berufsverbot Law

In April 1933 the new Nazi state lost no time in promulgating the *Gesetz zur Wiederherstellung des Berufsbeamtentums*. This is usually translated as the Law for the Restoration of the Professional Civil Service. It prevented 'non-Aryans', which in practice meant Jews, from working for the State, and allowed state employees to be dismissed for reasons of race or politics. This is why the law is also known as the *Berufsverbot* (professional ban). This and a follow-up law meant that Jews and political opponents could not work as civil servants. As well as people working in government ministries and local government, this included other public employees such as school teachers, university lecturers and doctors, and other professionals such as musicians and lawyers. At first the law included provision for certain exemptions at the insistence of Hindenburg: men who had fought in the First World War, those who had lost a father or son in that war, and those who had been working for the state continuously since 1 August 1914 (the start of the war). On Hindenburg's death, these exemptions were dropped.

Nuremberg Laws

In September 1935, two new laws were passed in the (now virtually powerless) Reichstag in Berlin. These were announced during the huge Nazi party rally (the seventh) of that year held, as usual, in the city of Nuremberg, and are thus known as the Nuremberg Laws. These laws provided the legal basis from this point for all anti-Semitic legislation and action in Nazi Germany.

- *The Law for the Protection of German Blood and German Honour* (sometimes called the 'Blood Protection Law') aimed to isolate Jewish people socially by prohibiting marriage or any sexual relations between Jews and non-Jews. Severe punishment awaited any Jewish person who disobeyed. Jews were also banned from flying the new Nazi swastika flag and from employing any Aryan woman under 45 in their home (for example as a servant).
- *The Reich Citizenship Law* that followed within a couple of months deprived Jews of all political rights.

Voices from the past

Victor Klemperer

The diary of Victor Klemperer from 1933 gives an eyewitness impression of events:

31 March, Friday evening

Ever more hopeless. The boycott begins tomorrow. Yellow placards, men on guard. Pressure to pay Christian employees two months' salary, to dismiss Jewish ones. No reply to the impressive letter of the Jews to the President of the Reich and to the government. No one dares make a move. The Dresden student body made a declaration today: United behind … and the honour of German students forbids them to come into contact with Jews. They are not allowed to enter the Student House. How much Jewish money went toward this Student House only a few years ago!

In Munich Jewish university teachers have already been prevented from setting foot in the university.

The proclamation and injunction of the boycott committee decrees "Religion is immaterial", only race matters. If, in the case of the owners of a business, the husband is Jewish, the wife Christian or the other way around, then the business counts as Jewish.

At Gusti Wieghardt's yesterday evening. The most depressed atmosphere. During the night at about three – Eva unable to sleep – Eva advised me to give notice on our apartment today, perhaps renting a part of it again. I gave notice today. The future is quite uncertain.

On Tuesday at the new Universum cinema on Prager Strasse. Beside me a soldier of the Reichswehr, a mere boy, and his not very attractive girl. It was the evening before the boycott announcement. Conversation during an Alsberg advertisement. He: "One really shouldn't go to a Jew to shop." She: "But it's so terribly cheap." He: "Then it's bad and doesn't last." She, reflective, quite matter-of-fact, without the least pathos: "No, really, it's just as good and lasts just as long, really just like in Christian shops – and so much cheaper." He falls silent. When Hitler, Hindenburg, etc. appeared, he clapped enthusiastically. Later, during the utterly American jazz band film, clearly with a touch of Yiddish at points, he clapped even more enthusiastically.

The events of March 21 were shown, including passages from speeches, Hindenburg's proclamation laborious, his breath short, the voice of a very old man who is physically near the end. Hitler declaiming like a pastor. Goebbels looks uncommonly Jewish. We saw a torchlight procession and a great deal of marching awakening Germany. Also Danzig with the swastika flag.[3]

Discussion point

What do you think the relatively unsuccessful boycott of Jewish-owned shops and department stores early in 1933 tells us about German society's attitude to Nazi racial policies?

ACTIVITY 5.3

Write a paragraph explaining how the Nuremberg Laws are connected to the Nazi concept of the *Volksgemeinschaft*.

Even though it was much easier to identify, define and trace Jews than it was Gypsies or homosexuals, there were still areas of confusion. The Reich Citizenship Law classified Jews according to their proportion of non-Jewish ancestry, or 'blood'. It used the term *Mischling* ('mixed breed' or 'mongrel') to describe racial mixing. Anyone with three or more Jewish grandparents counted as a Jew. Those with one Jewish grandparent did not. The definition of people with two Jewish grandparents was controversial. Eventually the ruling was that while those with three Jewish grandparents were Jews, those with two were only Jews if they followed Judaism or had married another Jew. Thus defined, Jews lost the right to vote, and those who two years earlier had been awarded an exemption from the Law for the Restoration of the Professional Civil Service were now dismissed from their jobs.

The development of anti-Semitic policies and actions

The Nazi leadership was acutely aware of the need to protect the reputation of the new regime at home and abroad. Attempts were therefore made to conceal the most radical Nazi ideas, particularly among their racial policies. However, they did not escape the attention of observers such as George Messersmith, the US Consul General in Berlin. He reported back to the US State Department in Washington on the current situation in Germany, noting the 'remarkable insincerity' of high-ranking Nazi officials. In May and June 1933 his reports described the developing persecution of racial minorities, especially of Jews, with the widespread dismissal from their posts of lawyers, doctors, university professors and so on.[4] By September, the situation had become even worse.

The effect of the *Anschluss*

German union with Austria, the **Anschluss**, was close to Hitler's heart as he had been born in upper Austria, gone to school in Linz and tried to study art in Vienna before 1914. Moreover, the union had long been an aim of German nationalists. This was the Greater Germany (*Grossdeutschland*) that many in Germany and Austria had long wished to see. In direct contravention of the Treaty of Versailles, which had specifically prohibited it, Germany annexed Austria in March 1938. There was little or no resistance in Austria itself and the international response presented no problems. Nazi propaganda was careful to publish photographs of cheering crowds, and there was indeed a vociferous and enthusiastic response to the *Anschluss* and to Hitler's arrival in Austria. The *Anschluss* was confirmed by a plebiscite the following month, April 1938.

Although there seems to have been genuine enthusiasm in the Austrian population, in the background Himmler and others had already arrived, and Jews, communists and social democrats were already being arrested. About 10% of the population had their civil rights removed and could thus not vote in the April plebiscite. Just one day after the annexation, the harassment of Jewish people in Vienna began. They were driven through the streets before jeering crowds and forced to scrub pavements. The Nuremberg Laws were applied in Austria from May 1938. All Jewish associations and organisations were banned.

Key term

Anschluss: The annexation of or union with Austria, from the German term meaning to join something together.

Reichskristallnacht

With rising anti-Semitism in Germany, the Polish government (itself anti-Semitic) began to fear that the 70 000 Polish Jews who were living in Germany would return to Poland. Accordingly, in March 1938 they announced that all Polish citizens living abroad who failed to renew their passports by the end of October that year would lose their citizenship. This decision had serious implications, as it would leave these people stateless. On the night of 28 October 1938, 17 000 Polish Jews were arrested by the SS in Germany and threatened with deportation back to Poland. Poland closed its borders a few days later and many of these 17 000 people were stranded between Germany and Poland for several harsh weeks.

In revenge for this and for the Nazi persecution of Jews generally, Herschel Grynszpan, the 17-year-old son of one Polish-Jewish couple caught up in this incident, entered the German Embassy in Paris, where he lived, early in November 1938 and shot Legation Secretory Ernst vom Rath, who died of his injuries a few days later. When Adolf Hitler was informed he authorised Goebbels to organise a series of violent and murderous attacks on synagogues and Jewish-owned shops, offices, factories, hospitals and homes across Germany and newly occupied Austria. This took place during the night of 9 November 1938 and in the days that followed was called **Kristallnacht** (the 'Night of Broken Glass').

Hundreds of Jews were killed (the exact number is not known) and around 30 000 were arrested and sent to concentration camps. The damage to Jewish property was extensive. Some allege that behind all this violence towards the German-Jewish community was the need of the SA and SS to increase their funds by eliminating commercial rivals, although there seems to be little or no evidence for this claim.

In Austria too Jewish-owned shops were looted and synagogues attacked. All synagogues in Vienna were destroyed except for the central *Stadttempel* that was located in a residential area. Thousands were arrested immediately, many of them sent to Dachau concentration camp. The Nazis presented the events of *Kristallnacht* to the world, and in particular the world's press, as a spontaneous outbreak of popular anger at the death of vom Rath in Paris. However, it was officially commanded, organised and administered.

Emigration

In Germany, following the Nazis coming to power in 1933, and in Austria following the *Anschluss*, many Jews who could do so **emigrated**.

An estimated 250 000 chose to leave, including many writers, academics, artists and scientists. Universities and research institutes were purged of their Jewish members, however distinguished. This was Germany's loss but a gain for the USA, Britain and other destinations. Among prominent physicists, for example, Albert Einstein went to the USA, Lise Meitner to Sweden and Max Born to the UK.

The impact of the war against Poland

When war was declared in early September 1939, anti-Semitism in Germany became even more blatant and ferocious than it had been before. The onset of

Key term

Kristallnacht: German word meaning 'crystal night' but often translated as 'Night of Broken Glass'; a night in 1938 when Jews were killed and arrested and their property seized and destroyed.

Key term

Emigration: movement of people out of a country to live in a different country.

war in effect removed any limitations on the Nazi regime's ability to implement its racial ideology using the most drastic of measures. Germany's Jewish community was perceived as 'the enemy within'. It was widely believed that, not being proper Germans, Jews could not be trusted to be patriots and support the war effort. Nazi propaganda encouraged the idea that because Jews were to be found in all European countries, they might use their family and faith connections to spy for their own advantage. Wartime thinking thus gave a green light to the further

Voices from the past

Samuel Honaker

The following eyewitness account is by US Consul Samuel Honaker:

American Consulate

Stuttgart, Germany

November 12, 1938

Subject: Anti-Semitic Persecution in the Stuttgart Consular District

To: The Honourable Hugh R. Wilson, American Ambassador, Berlin

Sir:

I have the honour to report that the Jews of Southwest Germany have suffered vicissitudes during the last three days which would seem unreal to one living in an enlightened country during the twentieth century if one had not actually been a witness of their dreadful experiences, or if one had not had them corroborated by more than one person of undoubted integrity. To the anguish of mind to which the Jews of this consular district have been subjected for some time, and which suddenly became accentuated on the morning and afternoon of the tenth of November, were added the horror of midnight arrests, of hurried departures in a half-dressed state from their homes in the company of police officers, of the wailing of wives and children suddenly left behind, of imprisonment in crowded cells, and the panic of fellow prisoners.

These wholesale arrests were the culmination of a day of suffering on the part of the Jews. The desecration and burning of synagogues started before daylight and should have proved a warning signal of what was to come during the course of the next few hours. At 10:30 A.M. about twenty-five leaders of the Jewish community were arrested by a

joint squad of policemen and plainclothes men. The arrested persons ranged from thirty-five to sixty-five years of age and were taken from their community officer (*Israelitischer Oberrat*) to the police station in two motor vehicles. As the victims passed from the building to the motor cars bystanders cursed and shouted at them.

Other arrests took place in various parts of Stuttgart. While this city was the scene of many anti-Semitic demonstrations during the course of the day, similar events were taking place all over Württemberg and Baden. Jews were attacked here and there. So great had become the panic of the Jewish people in the meantime that, when the consulate opened after Armistice Day, Jews from all sections of Germany thronged into the office until it was overflowing with humanity, begging for an immediate visa or some kind of letter in regard to immigration which might influence the police not to arrest or molest them. Women over sixty years of age pleaded on behalf of husbands imprisoned in some unknown place. American mothers of German sons invoked the sympathy of the Consulate. Jewish fathers and mothers with children in their arms were afraid to return to their homes without some document denoting their intention to immigrate at an early date. Men in whose homes old, rusty revolvers had been found during the last few days cried aloud that they did not dare ever again to return to their places of residence or business. In fact, it was a mass of seething, panic-stricken humanity.[5]

Discussion point

Discuss the issue of popular support for these Nazi social policies and their implementation, remembering that this is a controversial area about which historians have disagreed.

development of anti-Semitic persecution. The legal basis for this persecution was the Nuremberg Laws of 1935, but legality meant little to an SS stormtrooper considering ransacking a Jewish-owned shop or to a concentration-camp guard.

The German invasion of Poland from the west started on 1 September 1939, and the Soviet Union invaded from the east in a coordinated attack starting on 17 September. By 1 October 1939 the whole of Poland was occupied – the west of the country by Germany and the east by the Soviet Union. There was a substantial Polish-Jewish community at that time, the largest in Europe. The invasion meant that the Nazis' plans for Jews now had to accommodate 3.5 million more people. Some historians argue that this fact in itself might have helped change a policy of deportation and mistreatment into one of annihilation.

The treatment of Jews in the early years of war

Ghettos and deportations

In Occupied Poland, Jewish people were deported to **ghettos** by the Germans in hundreds of locations, many in cities such as Warsaw or Lvov.

Ghettos were areas of towns and cities in which only Jews were allowed to live, and they were not allowed to live anywhere else. This policy of deportation was made easier by the fact that ghettos has been established in earlier centuries. They had been abolished long since, but the areas had often continued to exist as 'Jewish quarters', places where most of the inhabitants were Jews.

The largest ghetto was in the Polish capital city, Warsaw. Created in October and November 1940, the ghetto held about 450 000 people. As such about 30% of the population of the city lived there, although it occupied only about 2.4% of the land area. Jews had been brought there from many other places and it was overcrowded. Food, water and electric power were all in short supply. Jews could be executed for leaving it without permission. Many died in this and other ghettos, such as those in Lubin, Lvov and Cracow, from disease, hunger or thirst. In addition, there were frequent executions. Their misery was only mitigated when Poles were able to smuggle in food and medicines. This was dangerous: Poles could be executed for helping Jews in any way – even giving them a lift or selling them food.

The Nazi revival of the ghettos was partly a matter of convenience, like concentration camps, making it easy to police a suspect social group. Later, holding Jews in ghettos eased administration, as from there they could be readily collected and moved on to **death camps**. To make the management of the ghettos and their vast populations easy, all the Jews were obliged to wear the six-pointed Star of David. In addition, the German authorities appointed a *Judenrat* (Jewish Council) to run local affairs and even a Jewish police force. The *Jüdische Ghetto-Polizei* (Jewish Ghetto Police) and *Jüdischer Ordnungsdienst* (Jewish Civil Police) were issued with armbands, badges and hats to identify them, and batons, though no firearms. Some of them were recruited from among the Jewish lawyers or police officers who had been deprived of their work by Nazi laws, but were accustomed to being part of the criminal justice system, and thus assumed to be

 Key terms

Ghettos: areas or district in which only members of a specified race live.

Death camps: Camps in which prisoners were deliberately and systematically killed in huge numbers.

willing to take police orders. Others had a background in crime, such as in the Jewish gangland, and were judged to be sufficiently ruthless.

Józef Andrzej Szeryński (born Josef Szynkman) had been a Polish police officer and joined the Ghetto Police. In the ghetto, he was caught smuggling black-market goods, but charges were dropped in exchange for his helping move people to Treblinka death camp. He survived two assassination attempts by the Jewish Combat Organisation, a resistance group, but then committed suicide.

Adam Czerniaków had been a politician. He was appointed head of the *Judenrat*, whose members had the responsibility for carrying out German orders. When the instructions came to organise the deportations of large numbers of people from the Warsaw ghetto to Treblinka death camp, he realised that the so-called 'resettlement in the east' meant execution. He requested that the children of an orphanage should be spared. His request having been turned down, he too committed suicide.

The deportation programme would not have been possible without the mass transport system provided by the railways and the railway employees. Both passenger and freight trains were used. The use of enclosed cattle trucks meant that fewer guards were needed. The numbers of people packed into the trucks were such that it was often difficult to sit or lie down. Transportation took place in all seasons. Food and water were not provided and many 'deportees' died in transit from suffocation and thirst.

A key figure in the deportation programme was Adolf Eichmann. He had been born in Germany but moved to Linz, Austria, with his family. He worked in a lot of different jobs during the economically unstable 1920s, and in 1932 joined the Austrian branch of the Nazi party and the SS. He spent part of the 1930s in the department tasked with monitoring Jewish organisations and negotiating with Zionist officials. From 1939 he was among the bureaucrats responsible for deporting large numbers of Jews from the land area then known as Great Germany to German-occupied Poland. He was transferred to the Gestapo, but his continued to be an office job concerned with transporting Jews, now to defined places of execution: death camps. He escaped at the end of the war, but was finally tried and executed in 1961–1962.

One of the more bizarre plans mooted by the Nazi regime was to forcibly relocate Jewish families to the island of Madagascar in the Indian Ocean. This idea had originally been considered by the Polish government, but in 1940 it became part of the Nazi plan to eliminate the Jews from Europe. Madagascar was a French colony and, with France close to defeat in the spring of 1940, Hitler planned to force the French to hand over Madagascar as part of the surrender terms. The failure to defeat the United Kingdom in the Battle of Britain, however, meant that Germany did not have access to the fleet of ships needed to make the plan work, and in any case the Madagascar Plan was eventually surpassed by the Final Solution in 1942.

Einsatzgruppen

Behind the German army invading Poland in 1939 came the **Einsatzgruppen**, SS paramilitary task forces that were effectively death squads.

Key term

Einsatzgruppen: German word meaning 'task forces'; specialist SS and SD units with the responsible for arresting and executing communist leaders and Jews in land taken by the German army on the Eastern Front during the Second World War; death squads.

They worked alongside *Ordnungspolizei* (civilian police) and were under the direction of *Reichsführer-SS* Heinrich Himmler. They were responsible for countless mass killings of Polish Jews as part of what became known as the Final Solution of the Jewish Question (*Die Endlösung der Judenfrage*). The people they killed were civilians, mostly by shooting. They were also ordered to kill Communists. Because of the role of civilian police, the *Einsatzgruppen* and their operations have been the focus of controversy, particularly around the question of how much popular support existed for the **Holocaust**.

A central book in this debate is Christopher Browning's 1992 book *Ordinary Men*. It tells the story of Reserve Police Battalion 10, a unit of *Ordnungspolizei* that was sent into Poland in 1942 and took part in the arrest and execution of large number of Jews. Browning argues that its members were ordinary, middle-aged, working-class men who were educated by their upbringing and police training to obey orders from people in authority and to cooperate with the group they belonged to. Not all the men involved were even Nazi party members. Even when their commander offered them the opportunity of not participating in an exercise, the men rarely took it. Daniel Goldhagen responded by writing *Hitler's Willing Executioners*, proposing the thesis that Germans had been extreme anti-Semites for centuries, and that the Holocaust was possible only because so many Germans supported the policy and took part in its implementation. Although Goldhagen's book has attracted a great deal of interest, other historians have adopted a more nuanced approach. Hitler's biographer Ian Kershaw has suggested that while a few people genuinely did hate Jews, more were simply indifferent to their fate.[6]

Key term

Holocaust: The organised mass murder of Jews by the Nazis.

Figure 5.5: Execution of Poles by *Einsatzgruppen*, October 1939.

Timeline

1933	
January	Hindenburg appointed Adolf Hitler as chancellor
27 February	Reichstag fire
March	Federal election; camps opened at Oranienburg and Dachau
16 March	Hjalmar Schacht appointed President of the Reichsbank
23 March	Hitler presented Enabling Act to the Reichstag
April	*Gesetz zur Wiederherstellung des Berufsbeamtentums* (Law for the Restoration of the Professional Civil Service); first official boycott of Jewish businesses
May	Students led by SA broke into Berlin Institute for Sexual Sciences and seizes its library; book burnings
June	Ministry of Justice revised paragraph 175
15 July	Nazis became only legal political party in Germany
July	Law for the Prevention of Offspring with Hereditary Diseases
September	Foundation of the *Reichskulturkammer* (Reich Chamber of Culture); coordinated police raids of Beggars' Week
1934	
30 June–2 July	'Night of the Long Knives' (Röhm Putsch)
2 August	Hindenburg's death; Hitler assumed the office of president
August	Schacht appointed Minister of Economics
1935	
September	Nuremberg Laws passed (Law for the Protection of German Blood and German Honour; Reich Citizenship Law)
1936	
March	Remilitarisation of the Rhineland
October	Himmler formed Reich Central Office for Combatting Abortion and Homosexuality; Four-Year Plan launched – Göring put in charge; Himmler established the Reich Central Office for the Suppression of the Gypsy Nuisance
1937	
March	Goerdeler resigned his post at the Reichsbank
November	Schacht resigned as Minister of Economics – replaced by Göring; exhibition of 'Degenerate art' and *Grosse deutsche Kunstausstellung* (Great German art exibition) in Munich

1938	
March	Union (*Anschluss*) with Austria
9 November	*Reichskristallnacht*
1939	
January	Schacht replaced as President of the Reichsbank
September	Germany invaded Poland

Practice essay questions

1. 'Between 1933 and 1939, Nazi racial policy was advanced primarily through the legal mechanisms of the state.' Assess the validity of this view.
2. 'Nazi racial policy was consistent and coherent from 1933 to 1939.' Assess the validity of this view.
3. To what extent did the onset of the Second World War change Nazi racial policy?
4. With reference to the sources below and your understanding of the historical context, assess the value of the three sources to a historian studying the development of anti-Semitic policy in Nazi Germany.

Source A

Decree from Goering relating to the payment of a fine by the Jews of German nationality, 12 November 1938 (http://www.nizkor.org/ftp.cgi?places/germany/kristallnacht/documents.007)

A later order permitted Jews to deduct these costs from their contributions towards the collective fine of one billion marks imposed on German Jews by another decree of Goring on the same day: The hostile attitude of Jewry towards the German people and Reich, which does not even shrink from committing cowardly murder, requires harsh atonement. Therefore, on the basis of the Decree for the Implementing of the Four-Year Plan of 18 October 1936, I make the following Order:

Section 1: The payment of a contribution of 1,000,000,000 Reichsmarks to the German Reich has been imposed on the Jews of German nationality as a whole. Section 2: Provisions for its enforcement will be issued by the Reich Minister of Finance in agreement with the Reich Ministers concerned

Source B

Speech by Hitler to the Reichstag, 30 January 1939 (in Baynes, N.H., *The Speeches of Adolf Hitler, Volume 1*, New York: Howard Fertig, 1969).

In the course of my life I have very often been a prophet, and have usually been ridiculed for it. … Today I will once more be a prophet: if the international Jewish financiers in

*and outside Europe should succeed in plunging the nations once more into a world war,
then the result will not be the Bolshevisation of the earth, and thus the victory of Jewry,
but the annihilation of the Jewish race in Europe!*

Source C

Order from Field Marshall Walter von Reichenau to the army on 10 October 1941,
NS-Archiv: *Dokumente zum Nationalsozialismus: Der 'Reichenau-Befehl': Verhalten der
Truppe im Ostraum* (from ns-archive.de).

*The most essential aim of war against the Jewish–Bolshevistic system is a complete
destruction of their means of power and the elimination of Asiatic influence from
the European culture. … The soldier in the Eastern territories is not merely a fighter
according to the rules of the art of war but also a bearer of ruthless national ideology
and the avenger of bestialities which have been inflicted upon German and racially
related nations. Therefore, the soldier must have full understanding of the necessity of a
severe but just revenge on the subhuman Jewry.*

Chapter summary

By the end of this chapter you should be aware of the ways in which the
Nazi regime made their racial policies an integral part of Germany society
and law, and of the police's work. You should have some insight into the
thinking behind their policies, and also understand the way in which
policies towards other specific groups reflected the same underlying
principles. In particular, you have learned that:

- the Nazis believed the German people needed protecting against
  various internal and external threats
- the Nazis felt that some threats came from racial groups, especially
  Jews but also Gypsies and Slavs, who were considered inferior and
  whose blood would therefore weaken the German nation wherever
  there was intermarriage or mixed-race children
- mentally or physically ill or handicapped people were also judged a
  threat, especially where the condition was believed to be hereditary
- homosexual men were considered both mentally ill and morally
  corrupt, as they were also assumed to be unable to participate in the
  nation as parents, which in itself made them an unhealthy element in
  society
- homeless and unemployed people, and members of certain minority
  Christian sects, were seen as a threat to social cohesion, health and
  prosperity
- laws were passed depriving members of these groups of civil rights,
  employment and citizenship, and they were increasingly subject to
  sterilisation, arrest and finally execution in increasingly large numbers.

End notes

1   Source of English translation: US Counsel for the Prosecution of Axis Criminality (Washington DC: US Government Printing Office, 1946).

2   In Grau, G., ed., *Hidden Holocaust?*.

3   Klemperer, V., *I Shall Bear Witness*.

4   Messersmith, G.S., *Papers* (University of Delaware Library, Newark, Delaware, USA, 1933).

5   US Department of State archive, reprinted in Mendelsohn, J., ed., *The Holocaust: Selected Documents* (New York: Garland, 1982).

6   Kershaw, I., *The 'Hitler Myth'*.

6 The impact of war, 1939–1945

In this section, we will look at how Nazi ideology shaped the conduct of the war. We will look at how the war affected everyday life, and its impact on society and the economy. We will study how the regime refused to conscript German women, but was willing to enslave prisoners of war and foreigners in occupied territories. We will also see how Nazi racial policies were turned into industrialised mass murder. We will look into:

- rationing, indoctrination, propaganda and morale; the changing impact of war on different sections of society including the elites, workers, women and youth

- the wartime economy and the work of Speer; the impact of bombing; the mobilisation of the labour force and prisoners of war

- policies towards the Jews and the 'Untermenschen' during wartime; the Wannsee Conference and the 'Final Solution'

- opposition and resistance in wartime including students, churchmen, the army and civilian critics; assassination attempts and the July Bomb Plot; overview of the Nazi state by 1945.

An overview of the war

A detailed account of the Second World War is beyond the scope of this book, but it is important to have some sense of how the war developed for Germany between 1939 and 1945 in order to make sense of what was happening inside Germany during this period. Hitler's great ideological enemy was, of course, Stalin's Soviet Union, but, in a surprise to the rest of the world, these two powers signed a non-aggression pact in August 1939. This pact provided that Nazi Germany and the Soviet Union would both invade Poland and divide the country between them, which they did in September 1939. It was the invasion of Poland that led Britain and France to declare war on Germany. Using *Blitzkrieg* tactics, involving motorised grounds troops, tanks and the **Luftwaffe**, Poland was quickly defeated. Open conflict did not break out between Germany, France and the UK in the autumn of 1939, the French and British preferring to take up defensive positions.

When this conflict came in the spring of 1940, it was a decisive victory for Hitler's Germany. It attacked France through the Ardennes, again using *Blitzkrieg* tactics; the French army collapsed and Hitler seized Paris. The British army was surrounded but managed to escape back to Britain, bringing with it troops from defeated countries, in the famous Dunkirk evacuations. Hitler had expected Britain to come to terms but, when it did not, he prepared to invade Britain, for which he needed mastery over the skies. The Battle of Britain in the summer of 1940 saw the Luftwaffe repeatedly attack the Royal Air Force and bomb the cities of Britain, but Germany was unable to achieve control, and by the autumn of 1940, Hitler had given up on invading Britain, preferring instead to wage a campaign against merchant ships in the Atlantic using Germany's submarines, the U-boats.

Hitler's attention now turned to the east. In 1941 he broke the Nazi–Soviet Pact and invaded the USSR. Again, the German *Blitzkrieg* advanced rapidly, reaching the major cities of Leningrad and Moscow by the end of the year. The USSR was able to hold off defeat, however, and throughout 1942 a bitter war was fought on the eastern front, culminating in the Battle of Stalingrad. Both sides suffered horrific casualties in the harsh winter of 1942 to 1943, but the Soviet Union was eventually victorious, defeating the German VIth Army. Germany suffered further setbacks in 1943, particularly in North Africa, where British troops were able to force the German army into retreat. Joined by the Americans, the Allies were able to advance up through Italy in 1944, diverting German troops away from the eastern front.

It was in the east, however, that the war was won. Over 1944 the Soviet Red Army advanced back across Eastern Europe before invading Germany itself, exacting terrible vengeance for German atrocities over the previous years. A western front was opened when American and British troops invaded across the English Channel, liberating France and advancing towards Germany's western border through the second half of 1944. In 1945 the Soviet Red Army invaded Germany from the east while the Americans and British invaded from the west. Berlin fell to the Red Army and Hitler committed suicide; Germany surrendered on 8 May 1945.

ACTIVITY 6.1

Create a timeline of Germany's involvement in the Second World War from 1939 to 1945. Identify key turning points in the conflict. You might wish to use further research to add additional details to your plan about the involvement of other countries, particularly the conflict between the USA and Japan.

Key term

Luftwaffe: German air force.

The changing effects of war on different parts of German society

Germany went from victory in 1940 to ruin in 1945, and the experiences of the German people between 1939 and 1945 went through distinct phases linked closely to the development of the war. On the one hand, Germany already had a militarised society in the late 1930s, meaning that the initial transition to war was not as starkly felt in Germany as in other countries. It was the case, however, that the German people increasingly felt the effects of war, particularly once the conflict turned against Germany in 1942 and 1943.

Rationing

The rationing system introduced in wartime Germany came into effect as soon as war was declared in September 1939. The failure of the Four-Year Plan to achieve autarky by the outbreak of war meant that Germany still had to rely on food imports to feed its population. Hitler himself was concerned that this would make the civilian population less willing to support the war effort. In his view, increasing shortages during the First World War had undermined national unity and support for the troops, creating an atmosphere in which the 1918 surrender became possible. Despite this, all civilians were issued with ration cards covering food such as meats, fats (such as margarine, oil and butter), and other items including tobacco products. These were distributed every other month. The cards were printed on heavy-duty paper, subdivided into many small sections called *Marken*, each printed with a value, such as 20 g of butter or 50 g of meat. These ration cards were also needed for meals in restaurants, which would cut out with scissors the required *Marken* for the particular dish ordered.

This rationing system needed a large number of bureaucrats to administer it and demanded careful calculation by civilians receiving these cards. There had been concern among the Nazi leadership about the possible negative civilian reaction to the introduction of a strict rationing system, as civilian morale was important in an age of total war, but these fears gradually subsided as the civilian population, at least for the first few years of the war, seemed on the whole reasonably content. The US journalist Howard K. Smith, based in Berlin with CBS from 1940 to 1942, later wrote that, given that they were engaged in what he called 'a life-and-death war', the German people in the early stages of that war 'ate amazingly well'. In the first years of the war the meat ration, for example, was 500 g per person per week. This was reduced to 400 g after the German invasion of Russia in June 1941 and then fell even further. After five months of fighting in Russia the home ration had been reduced by some 80%, so that by the time Smith left Berlin for the USA in December 1941, his assessment had changed, and he observed in *Last Train from Berlin*, published during the war, that now the Germans were undernourished. There were extra rations for men in heavy industries such as steelmaking or shipbuilding, while rations were lowered to starvation levels for Poles and Jews in occupied Poland. However, rations were not reduced in the same way for Poles brought to Germany to work in heavy industry.

There was even a scheme called the *Hungerplan* ('Hunger Plan'), designed by Herbert Backer and developed during the planning for the German invasion of the

Soviet Union in June 1941. The purposes of this plan were (1) to ensure that food supplies for the civilian population of Germany were prioritised over those of Poles and Russians in the occupied territories and (2) to provide a means of subjugation and control, even of starvation, for the peoples of the conquered territories. These two purposes, hunger for the conquered and food for the German civilians, were twinned consequences. A planned famine in the occupied territories was a means of mass murder.

Part of the reasoning behind the invasion of the Soviet Union in June 1941 was the acquisition of grain from the fertile Ukraine, then part of the Soviet Union. The grain was shipped in bulk back to Germany. Those who lived in the countryside, who could keep a few chickens for eggs and rabbits for meat, or even slaughter a pig from time to time, were better able to supplement their diet than were city dwellers. However, there were persistent complaints from farmers that at weekends townspeople would come and steal poultry and grain. There were also stories of various abuses of the ration system – from a market in stolen ration cards to wealthy people dining too well at restaurants.

Following the 1941 invasion of the USSR, rationing was extended to fruit and vegetables, including the vital staple the potato. The demands for *Winterhilfswerk* (Winter Aid), which had brought the NSDAP such praise initially, began to be resented as more people had less to spare.

 Thematic link: Society and the economy

Propaganda

Every midday on German wartime radio was to be heard a fanfare from Franz Liszt's symphonic poem *Les Préludes* followed by the words *Aus dem Führerhauptquartier, das Oberkommando der Wehrmacht gibt bekannt* (from the Leader's Headquarters, the Armed Forces High Command announces…). Reich Minister of Propaganda Goebbels and armed forces chief General Jodl regarded these broadcasts as vital for maintaining civilian morale. Although its role was to reassure and inspire, its tone changed as the news from the front changed. In the first months of the war the tone of propaganda was cautious before becoming triumphant after the fall of France in 1940 and early successes against the USSR in 1941. As the war turned against Germany between 1942 and 1944 the role of propaganda was to cover up and play down military defeats, while in the final months of the war the message was one of fighting on to the bitter end. By 1939, around 70% of German homes had a radio set, mostly subsidised by the Nazi Party. These radios deliberately only had a short range in order to prevent listeners from hearing foreign broadcasts. Radios were also positioned in public places and workplaces, and the broadcasts heard over loudspeakers.

The cinema gave Goebbels another powerful propaganda opportunity. The 1940 film *Der ewige Jude* (The Eternal Jew) was typical of the anti-Semitic material then made available. This film, a mixture of documentary footage and a feature film, purports to demonstrate the unchangeable racial characteristics of Jewish people and the inevitability of them becoming a wandering cultural parasite. Another main wartime propaganda vehicle in the cinema was *Die Deutsche Wochenschau* (German Weekly Review), a newsreel series on a variety of topics such as military and economic to mention a few.

Apart from film and radio, posters were a favourite propaganda medium. So too were the newspapers, of which the Nazi party newspaper *Völkischer Beobachter* (the Peoples' Observer) with a daily circulation by 1944 of 1.7 million, was a key propaganda platform and the official public face of the NSDAP the *Beobachter* only ever published good news, regardless of how bad the news really was. To leave the market free for NSDAP publications, other newspapers and magazines were banned. This included national and local papers. Even small newsletters, such as church pamphlets, could find themselves censored.

It is hard to be sure how effective any of this was. Some historians have argued that despite the enormous efforts of Goebbels and his ministry officials, most people were only marginally affected by the propaganda, did not believe all they heard or read, and tended to skip over articles which had clearly been published to tell them what to think. Similarly, although there was a large NSDAP membership, many of these people were only there for career reasons and a quiet life, and tended to avoid attending meetings.

Where propaganda succeeded best was where it reinforced existing beliefs, rather than attempted to change them. Thus Nazi propaganda was able to pick up the subject of colonial troops that had been such a right-wing concern during the Weimar Republic with the Ruhr occupation. Images of Africans menacing Germany were an aspect of propaganda in the later stages of the war and built on underlying racism. Similarly there was a genuine fear of the Red Army and the Russians, so successful propaganda about the threat to Germany posed by the USSR was not difficult to create. As a result, propaganda encouraging the population to support a policy of fighting on even when the tide had turned against Germany was successful. There was little or no organised opposition to the NSDAP regime and the population could see no other option but maintaining the fight and hoping for the best.

Morale

Civilian morale was of great concern to the Nazi leadership, and its careful (and secret) monitoring of it proceeded throughout the war. Various Party and police authorities were involved in monitoring the public mood, but their main source of information was the Security Police (*Sicherheitsdienst* or SD), the security unit of the SS, who reported direct to Reich Security Minister Heinrich Himmler. In the early, victorious, years of the war from September 1939 to 1943, civilian morale was high despite increasing food shortages, ration reductions, Allied bombing and disruption to travel with troop and military equipment moves eastward during the first part of 1941 as Germany prepared to invade the Soviet Union.

However, the news from the fronts, food shortages and the destruction created by Allied bombing all worsened. Daytime air raids by the US Air Force (USAF) from 1942 on top of the night raids of the Royal Air Force (RAF) were particularly hard to bear. Unsurprisingly, civilian morale sagged, despite Goebbels' propaganda machine attempting to present military reverses as victories or wise tactical retreats. From 1944 it had become obvious to many (though by no means everyone) that Germany was losing the war, with the Allies advancing from the west after the middle of June and the Red Army from the east. Civilian morale virtually collapsed, made even worse by disillusion when inflated claims of military successes proved groundless.

Social elite groups

German princely families had lost their political position, and much of their social status, during the revolutionary period of 1918. A few of them had supported the NSDAP, others had joined after the Nazi accession to power in 1933, as had members of many other social groups. This was a small social group, but its significance was not connected to its numbers. When individual princes joined the Nazi party, they legitimised it, helping change its appearance from that of a group of street-fighting ruffians and social upstarts into a more mainstream authoritarian party. Once the Nazis were in power, to be able to include the traditional ruling elite or aristocrats and members of royal houses in their social gatherings helped with fundraising, and also, curiously, helped with the Nazi message of taking Germany away from the old class system. Here was a government that could pull together people from many different backgrounds to work alongside one another. Many of the men from the social elites were conscripted into the *Wehrmacht*. However, they continued to enjoy a privileged position in society, unchallenged by the Nazis, even though the war did have a levelling effect.

This alliance was never a natural one, and the war put it under increasing strain. For as long as the Hitler government could show it was overcoming economic disasters and reversing the humiliation of Versailles, the princes and aristocrats were often happy to support it. Once the army started suffering defeats from 1942, this willingness weakened. The Nazi leaders knew this was the case. The fact that royalty and nobility are a European elite, not a specifically German one, brought them under suspicion. Jonathan Petropoulos gives the example of Prince Philipp von Hessen. He was a descendant of British and Prussian kings and a relative of the abdicated Kaiser. He had cooperated at first, joining the party in 1930; his brother was a member of the SS. He was sent to a concentration camp in 1943. His wife Princess Mafalda was the daughter of the Italian king. She was arrested by the Gestapo, interrogated and sent to Buchenwald concentration camp. She died following an Allied bombing raid, but Prince Philipp survived to face post-war questioning over his involvement in Nazi rule and the T4 programme.[1]

In the final stages of the war, the landowning nobility of East Prussia and other lands to the east of the river Elbe, who had been such a persistently dominant force in the officer class of the army through regal, imperial, republican and Nazi Germany, were to experience a catastrophic attack from the invading Red Army in 1944 resulting in the loss of their lands, the destruction of their mansions and often their arrest as 'capitalists'. Those who could, escaped to join the flood of German-speaking refugees driving, riding and walking westward.

Thematic link: Propaganda

Working men

The Nazi regime had spent its peacetime period in power by preparing for war, so the Second World War did not bring about sudden or unforeseen changes in people's lives. The German government did, however, begin to take a number of steps in order to ensure that the war was affordable and sustainable. Taxes were raised and wages lowered, with overtime payments removed completely. Workers were required to work longer hours for the same pay, and holiday arrangements were suspended. September 1939 also saw the publication of the *Kriegswirtschaftsordnung* (War Economy Decree). This reduced German workers' freedom of movement and made labour service compulsory. The Gestapo ran 'work education camps' for those judged not to be fulfilling their quota of work. With conscription in place, large numbers of working-age men entered the armed forces – particularly the army – meaning that the wartime workforce was increasingly composed of the old, those deemed unfit for military service and those who had been given an exemption from military service. Conscripted labour, particularly from prisoners of war and those placed in concentration camps, increasingly took the place of men drafted into the army. By the end of the war there were well over 4 million foreigners working as slave labour, around half of whom were Russians.

Working women

The impact of the war on women in Germany was considerable. The assumption had broadly been that women were home-makers, looking after their family. This social norm for women was by no means an invention of the Nazi state: it had been prevalent in Imperial Germany and, despite its progressive and liberal approach to social issues, in the Weimar Republic as well. The Nazi state reinforced this inherited ideal, which was particularly easily communicated in the more conservative areas such as rural Bavaria. Soon after the entry of Nazis into government, professional women started losing their jobs.

In the summer of 1939, the government signalled its support both for marriage and for the armed forces when it improved the support paid to soldiers' families. There was a rise in the number of marriages and 'war wives' leaving their jobs. By the outbreak of war in 1939, the number of women in full-time work had dropped considerably and the government had to backpedal somewhat from its social ideal of men who worked outside the home and women who did not. However, even in 1937 a law had been passed requiring women to undertake a compulsory year in a factory to help the economic recovery. Successful completion of this Duty Year was a qualification for marriage loans.

Unlike in Britain, women were not subject to military conscription, but increasingly women were drafted in to do jobs left vacant by men who had joined the Wehrmacht. The need for women to enter the workplace became acute in 1942 following heavy German casualties in Operation Barbarossa, requiring the regime to move men from formerly protected industries into the military. Around 1.5 million women were brought in to work in factories in 1943, and around 34% of women were involved in war work by the end of that year. In addition to working in munitions factories, they drove trams in Berlin, built ships in Hamburg and farmed in Baden.

Youth

The Nazi leadership believed that civilian morale could be maintained, despite military reverses, through the enduring loyalty of the Hitler Youth (*Hitlerjugend* or HJ). This organisation had been founded in 1922 as the youth wing of the Nazi party and was, between 1933 and 1945, the only official youth organisation in Germany. It had a distinct military flavour, especially in wartime after 1939. It was for boys aged 14 to 18, but it also had a junior branch (the *Deutches Jungvolk*) for boys of 10 to 14 and a girls' section, the League of German Girls (*Bund Deutscher Mädel* or BDM).

The coming of war in September 1939 gave the HJ an even more central role. Not only was it a fine preparation for military life but, as the conscription age was 16, the existing links between the Nazi party, the HJ and the Wehrmacht became even stronger. Bolstered by the activities of the HJ, National Socialism intruded into almost every aspect of the lives of young people in Germany. This was a powerful form of indoctrination and the hope was that in a few years a new, enthusiastic generation of Nazis would grow up to continue the work of the Nazi revolution. In some cases, however, it had the opposite effect. By underlining the authoritarian and coercive nature of the Nazi state it alienated some young people, generating cynicism and disillusion and even pushing them in the direction of resistance. The Nazi authorities were well aware of this danger and so monitored the youth situation carefully, using the Security Police (SD).

The wartime economy

The wartime economy of Germany was required, above all, to provide the Wehrmacht with the armaments and supplies it needed to fight successfully. It was, therefore, a crucial area for the Nazi leadership and needed to be managed efficiently. The economy was on a war footing, but only moved to what one might call a total war economy midway through the war. Initially, the desire to maintain high civilian morale had deterred the government from prioritising military needs and dismissing civilian ones; they had sought to maintain a balance.

The economy, foreign policy and war

After the outbreak of war in 1939, the German economy developed an even stronger focus on providing the military with supplies. The fact that Germany had not become self-sufficient proved an urgent strategic problem, most significantly in its dependence on oil imports: the German war machine, particularly the Luftwaffe and Panzer divisions, depended on a reliable source of fuel. Maintaining a food supply was also a problem, as was access to credit, for major financial organisations in the USA and the UK would not offer loans to the Nazi regime. Hitler had always had an ideologically driven aim of conquering Eastern Europe in

Key term

Lebensraum: German word meaning `living space'; territory claimed by Hitler's Germany in eastern Europe.

order to create **Lebensraum** (living space) for the German people: in 1939, gaining this land was also a matter of economic necessity.

An eye to the rich grain-producing areas of central and southern Poland and the USSR, and the oilfields of the Caucasus between the Black Sea and the Caspian Sea, had a significant influence on strategic military thinking during the war. The invasions of Poland in 1939 and the Soviet Union in 1941 were both in part designed to secure for Germany the grain and oil supplies that the country needed.

At the outset of the war, however, the emphasis was not on the east, but the west. The Nazi–Soviet pact of August 1939 created an uneasy peace between Nazi Germany and the USSR, but both sides capitalised on this in preparing for war. In return for German industrial supplies, the USSR provided Germany with large quantities of grain. Weak oil supplies were in part bolstered by imports

Voices from the past

Regular SD reports, such as the one below from August 1943, attempted to identify those who opposed the NSDAP or the HJ, and analysed their motivation.

The attitude of young people towards the Party is particularly evident each year at the admission ceremonies. The available reports on the admission of the 1924 and 1925 cohorts to the Party show in general a positive attitude on the part of young people towards the Party. But there are reports from almost all parts of the Reich according to which a not insignificant number of young people have an attitude towards admission to the party which leaves much to be desired. The following detailed observations were made:

Indifference and a lack of inward commitment. Large numbers of young people see joining the Party not as a particularly desirable goal but rather as 'good form', in fact as 'a necessary evil'. 'The opinion was frequently expressed that membership of the Party was the socially correct thing to do and, in addition, was a good springboard for one's career.' 'The young people whose careers do not involve a position of dependence place hardly any value on joining the NSDAP.' 'Young people have a rather indifferent attitude to the Party. Only a very small minority see joining the Party as a mark of distinction. The vast majority regard membership of the Party as a necessity which one simply has to put up with. Thus a young Party comrade remarked: "If one wants to succeed in life one has to be a Party comrade, otherwise one isn't 100%."'

'Many young people believe they absolutely have to be part of the adult world. The comments of an 18-year-old that

as a Party comrade one had to be admitted to everything and be able to make a judgement about everything express the attitude of many young people. Occasionally, young people welcome admission to the Party because then "they were at last free of HJ service"; they hoped the Party would not make so many demands on them.' 'A characteristic remark by young people is: "I don't care in the least whether I'm admitted to the Party or not; it's all rubbish."' Many reports note that the lack of interest in the Party contrasts with a much greater interest in the Wehrmacht.

'Most boys and girls have not the slightest interest in becoming a member of the NSDAP. All attempts by the relevant authorities to get them involved have been in vain. For the boys it's the Wehrmacht which is now the thing not the Party.'

'The example is given that now many young people want to become officers because officers are an attractive role model, a desirable goal. The tasks which the block leader and the local branch leader have to carry out in their fields have little attraction for young people; clearly there is nothing which attracts them "to be in on the action" here in the way that a young man wants to be "in on the action" as a member of an elite military unit or a successful football team.'[2]

Discussion point
'For all the Nazi talk of community, their programme of excluding entire sections of the population fatally weakened Germany.' Assess the validity of this view.

from Romania. Neutral countries such as Sweden and Switzerland did trade with Germany, the former providing urgently needed iron ore supplies. Rationing, introduced in 1939, meant that Germans had less to spend their money on: this meant that they saved more money, which banks could then lend to the government to finance the war effort. It was clear, however, that Hitler needed a quick victory in the west against France and the UK: a prolonged fight in the style of 1914–1918 could not be economically maintained. Economically speaking, Hitler put all his eggs in one basket: a rapid victory over the west in 1940.

This victory was achieved with a speed that left Hitler temporarily hailed as one of the greatest military commanders of all time. France collapsed in 1940, and the British army retreated across the channel, leaving behind large quantities of military equipment. With victory in France, Hitler controlled – directly or through alliances – nearly all of Europe, and began requisitioning supplies from the conquered countries. French industries were particularly badly hit: over the course of the occupation from 1940 to 1944, some 7.7 billion Reichsmarks of goods were transferred from France to Germany, of which around one third was military equipment. The French, Dutch and Belgian railways provided 4260 locomotives to Germany. These war spoils made good the shortages felt so keenly at the end of the 1930s, and provided Hitler with the resources to effect an invasion of the Soviet Union, which he did in June 1941 with Operation Barbarossa.

Operation Barbarossa required vast numbers of tanks which constituted the principal weapon by which the German army could punch through the Soviet lines, supported by mechanised infantry and the Luftwaffe. Throughout late 1940 and early 1941 Germany proved remarkably successful at producing tanks at an incredible rate. Despite rapid success in the autumn of 1941, the German advance ground to a halt in the winter, and the rapid victory that had been hoped for did not materialise. This hit the German economy in two ways. First, heavy casualties in the east required more and more workers to be taken from factories and farms in Germany to fight in the army. Secondly, the campaign required vast resources of munitions and equipment. While the German economy was able to cope in a short campaign, it was not able to maintain its production once the conflict dragged on. A new economic model was needed to keep Germany in the war; the model of total war.

 Thematic link: Society and the economy

Total war and the work of Albert Speer

Fritz Todt, who had served as minister for armaments and war production since 1940, was killed in a plane crash in February 1942. In a surprise appointment, Albert Speer, an architect and Nazi party member from 1931, was appointed to replace him. The step from being Hitler's favourite architect to being a minister might seem a strange one, but it partly reflects Hitler's habit of advancing people close to him. Speer took up his new role for economic leadership following defeats on the eastern front.

ACTIVITY 6.2

Revise your notes on the HJ and other Nazi youth policies. Then make short notes on:

- sense of commitment
- careers
- party membership as a distinction
- the Wehrmacht.

Under Speer at the Ministry of Armaments and War Production the situation improved. Part of the improvement was due to personal access to Hitler and the Führer's active support: Hitler told him that he would sign and approve any document Speer put in front of him without reservation. (See Figure 6.1, too.) Part of Speer's success came through his centralising the operation on his own ministry. Slave labour was extensively deployed to make up for men fighting on the eastern front: millions of workers from across Europe were brought to work on farms and factories, reaching around 20% of the workforce. Less controversially, he encouraged factories to specialise, and prevented the conscription of skilled workers to ensure that the workforce was capable to meeting the demands made on it. Under his leadership war production continued to increase throughout the war, despite Allied bombing.

This was, however, not enough. A series of defeats in early 1943 forced Germany to go to a 'total war' footing in which the entire economy was given over to the war effort. All workers had to register at labour exchanges to see if they could be better utilised, and businesses were examined to see whether they could be used more effectively in the war effort. Non-essential businesses were closed down. These drastic actions worked to increase production further, and ammunition production – the most urgent supply needed on the eastern front – increased by 120% between February 1942 and May 1943. Women were brought into the workplace in order to release men for combat in the east. The economy under Speer seemed to be providing the German army with what it needed to hold back an increasingly aggressive Red Army in the east. These gains, however, were not sustainable, particularly as the main centres of production became the targets of Allied bombing in the west.

Figure 6.1: Albert Speer (right) is awarded an Organisation Todt ring by the Führer, May 1943.

The impact of Allied bombing

The impact of Allied bombing increased significantly from 1942 when the USA joined the war. The USAF and the RAF combined forces to inflict heavy bombing raids on Germany, particularly in the industrial areas of the west. Targets included military formations, military installations and bases, military communications centres, dams, bridges and railways. The most heavily targeted areas were the industrial cities of the Ruhr like Essen. Although railway tracks could be repaired, dams rebuilt and roads repaired, the intensity of the Allied bombing made inroads on the increased rates of production achieved under Speer. Steel production, for example, fell by 200 000 tons in the first three months of 1943. Speer's rapid-reaction teams were now increasingly used to clear rubble and make good bomb damage rather than working on improving production.

Allied bombing continued right up to the end of the war, and civilian casualties were very heavy. The bombing of Hamburg on the night of 27–28 July 1943 resulted in around 40 000 deaths in a massive firestorm. In February 1945, even as the Third Reich was collapsing, the USAF and RAF bombed Dresden, an important transit point for the military as well as a large civilian centre, resulting in over 20 000 deaths. At the outbreak of war Germany had not attempted to evacuate large numbers of civilians from major towns and cities. A voluntary scheme for moving children under the age of ten to the countryside did exist but was small. Following bombing raids in September 1940, Hitler ordered children to be moved from high-risk areas. The HJ were to organise places for them to stay. Numbers of women with infant children also left these areas. Cities such as Cologne,

ACTIVITY 6.3

Make short notes on:

- evacuation of civilians
- gas, water and electricity supplies
- the police
- transport and walking
- the sense of fear.

Düsseldorf and Essen were affected. Because at that stage the government and military high command were expecting a short, successful war, the plans were for only temporary evacuation. Although the intention was good, and the results were broadly positive, many families were reluctant to be divided. As the war went on, and the period of absence therefore longer, willingness to participate declined. The SD reported from Hamburg following heavy bombing in October 1943 that the majority of families had not taken part in the evacuation scheme.

The mobilisation of the labour force and prisoners of war

A key and persistent challenge to the German war effort was manpower. Vast human resources were needed to maintain the war effort. As the war continued the situation became ever more critical. From June 1941 to May 1944, 60 000 men were dying on the Russian front every month. By the autumn of 1941, the Wehrmacht had run out of men in their twenties to conscript. As teenagers reached the correct age, they were conscripted, but this was not enough to make good the losses. In 1942, the desperate Wehrmacht took men out of the munitions industry, previously an area of employment protected from the recruiters, since finding more soldiers at the cost of producing fewer armaments was not a policy anyone thought made sense.

Attempts to mobilise women through calls for volunteers produced inadequate responses, and the leadership was ideologically opposed to conscription of women either into the armed forces or into industry. Even with the contribution made by women, wartime production in Germany turned to another source of labour: slaves. By the spring of 1941, Germany employed 1.2 million prisoners of war, mostly French, and 1.3 million civilians, mostly Poles. That year another 1 million foreign labourers were brought in, mostly from Poland. In 1941 the order was given to construct a number of camps from which slave labourers would be drawn for massive construction projects. The *Generalplan-Ost* (Overall Plan East, GPO) envisaged 400 000–800 000 Jews, Poles and Soviet prisoners of war. By the summer of 1943, the numbers had shot up to 6.5 million. Forced labour from occupied territories gathered pace during 1942. Slave labourers came to make up 20% of the German labour force and they were particularly vital to agriculture and the arms trade. Around 7.6 million foreign labourers worked in Germany in August 1944, of whom nearly 2.8 million came from the Soviet Union, most of those from Ukraine. Altogether, an estimated total of 15 million people were forced to work in Germany during the course of the war. That figure includes all those who were enslaved, including those who died; it does not mean that 15 million people were kept in those conditions at any one time. Many conquered peoples, including French, Greeks, Hungarians and various Slavs including Czechs, Poles and Ukrainians, endured forced labour. Workers brought from the conquered east of Europe were called *Ostarbeiter* (female: *Ostarbeiterinnen*), workers from the east. Workers were treated differently depending on where they came from, in terms of food, accommodation, working conditions and punishment. The best treatment was shown to those from Western Europe (France, the Netherlands and Belgium), while those from the Soviet Union fared worst.

Large numbers died because of the inhuman conditions: poor and inadequate food, disease and cold all took their toll. Others were simply executed, for discipline was murderously severe. Social contact with Germans ('fraternisation') was forbidden. Escape was punishable by death. Germans who had sexual relationships with the foreign labourers were also subject to punishment. Productivity from these forced labourers was low, due in part to their living and working conditions, including poor diet. However, as there was a well-nigh inexhaustible supply of slaves, this was not a major consideration for the organisers and administrators.

 Thematic link: Nazi ideologies

Wartime Policies towards Jews and 'Untermenschen'

The 'Untermenschen'

Untermensch is a German word meaning literally 'underperson' or 'subhuman'. Alfred Rosenberg and other Nazi ideologists argued that the Germans were a warrior people descended from the prehistoric Aryan warriors. This made the Germans the *Herrenvolk*, the 'master race'. The belief was that some were born to be masters and some were born to be enslaved. *Untermensch* was the Nazis' term for those groups they regarded as not equal to the Germans. The division was regarded as scientific and was taught in schools as part of biology lessons. The word had been in their political vocabulary for some time, but it was not purely a racial term. Left-wing revolutionaries were also referred to as *Untermenschen* in Nazi propaganda and theoretical writings. Those targeted by the T4 campaign were also Untermenschen. It was these people who were to suffer most severely under Nazi rule during the Second World War.

Jews were the most prominent example of what the Nazis regarded as *Untermenschen*, because they were the largest such group in Germany itself. Roma and Sinti people were others, because they stood out in society as noticeably different in appearance, costume and lifestyle. Such groups, however, were always a minority in Germany itself. The process of conquest, particularly in Eastern Europe, brought vast numbers of a further group under German rule. German expansionism meant that its racial policies were no longer dealing with an ethnic minority, but an ethnic majority. Germans were now vastly outnumbered by *Untermenschen* in their own empire. This was a political and practical problem.

The Slavs were the majority ethnic group in Eastern Europe. The Nazis decided that they were to be divided into two. Some would be judged Aryan and Germanised. Others would be judged *Untermenschen* and deported further east to make room for German settlement. This was to be ethnic cleansing on a massive scale. The plan was prepared by the RHSA (Reich Main Security Office). The *Generalplan-Ost*, developed between 1939 and 1942, entailed the enslavement, expulsion or extermination of most Slavic peoples. GPO envisaged the elimination of varying percentages of the populations of countries conquered already or targeted, including 50% of Czechs, 50–60% of Russians and 80–85% of Poles.

ACTIVITY 6.4

We have used the expression *Sonderweg* before. Look back over earlier chapters and reread your own notes. Draw up a spider diagram showing:

- what *Sonderweg* means
- some historians who have contributed to the *Sonderweg* debate
- what aspects of the period 1918–1945 the *Sonderweg* debate affects.

Poland

The largest group that NSDAP racial policies had to address was the Poles. Estimates suggest that between 2.7 and 2.9 million Polish people died as a result of Nazi racial policy in addition to the 3 million Polish Jews who were killed. The plan declared in *Mein Kampf* was to remove Slavs. In the run-up to the 1939 invasion, the Nazis drew up a list of over 60 000 notable Poles who were to be arrested and executed. This list contained nobility, political leaders, civil servants and army officers, but also scholars, actors, doctors, lawyers and priests. The intention was to kill the Polish leadership, leaving behind a mass population that could be easily ruled as slaves: relocated or worked to death as necessary. In September 1939, SS leader Reinhard Heydrich set this plan in motion, using Gestapo and SS, but also *Wehrmacht* forces. Heydrich had been a *Freikorps* volunteer in his teens. He was an SS Lieutenant General, in charge of the Reich Main Security Office and Deputy Protector of Bohemia and Moravia.

Slave-labour camps were set up. From October 1939, all Poles over the age of 14 (and Jews over the age of 12) were liable for forced labour, with large numbers moved to Greater Germany for that purpose. Their treatment included wearing a coded 'P' on their clothes to identify them, and working long hours with poor food. Relationships with Germans were forbidden; those found guilty of sexual relationships were executed. Women and girls were vulnerable to sexual enslavement and trafficking for sexual purposes. Polish-language schools were closed. Towns and streets were renamed. Libraries, museums and historic buildings, as part of Polish cultural identity, were destroyed. Children were taught only basic arithmetic, how to sign their name and the Nazi doctrines about race, so that they could understand their place in the new society and follow basic instructions. In addition, the groups victimised in Germany itself were also targeted: Jews, Gypsies, the mentally and physically disabled. Children judged suitable for 'Germanisation' were seized and put up for adoption by German families.

Yugoslavia

Another conquered group to suffer was the Slovenes. They were a southern Slav group, largely found in what is now Slovenia but then lay in northern Yugoslavia. Following the invasion of Yugoslavia by the Axis powers in April 1941, the Slovene-settled areas of Upper Carniola, Lower Styria, and the northern part of Lower Carniola were occupied by Germany. At the same time, other Slovene areas were seized by Italy and Hungary (Figure 6.2). The Nazis planned an 'ethnic cleansing' campaign in northern Slovenia, resettling the German-speaking *Gottsheer* people from the Italian occupation zone. To make way for this, they shipped 46 000 ethnic Slovenes to Germany, where they were used as slave labour on farms and in factories. Slovene resistance led to savage German reprisals.

When the Axis powers invaded Yugoslavia, parts of the country were transferred to Germany, Italy or Hungary, and a new Croat state was set up as an ally. Serbian schools were closed. Serbs, who were Orthodox Christians, were forced to convert to Roman Catholicism; there were a series of massacres of Serbs carried out by Croatia's *Ustase* militias. In addition Nazi policies towards Jews and Gypsies were enforced. In these cases and others, Nazi German forces used existing local conflicts to their own ends. Establishing the exact facts and figures can often be difficult as the situation was complicated then and remains so now. Events can be interpreted in more than one way, and also different groups might exaggerate or minimise figures for their own post-war or contemporary political reasons.

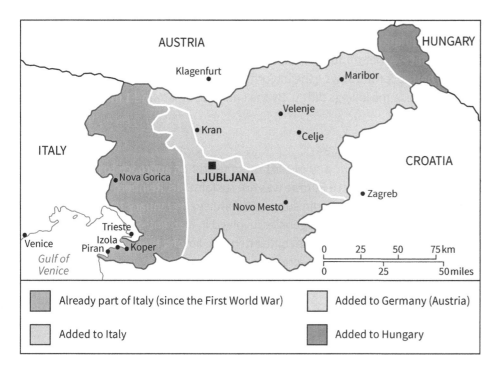

Figure 6.2: Following the Axis invasion of Yugoslavia in April 1941, Slovenia was partitioned.

The Holocaust

As seen in earlier chapters, the Nazis had systematically set out to persecute the Jewish population of Germany between 1933 and 1941. Boycotts of Jewish businesses began in 1933, citizenship was removed in 1935 and widespread pogroms broke out in 1938. Emigration from Germany had been encouraged, with Jewish assets being kept by the State if families chose to leave. The onset of the Second World War removed any restraints on the Nazis. Many Jewish families who had fled Germany now found themselves once again under Nazi rule following German successes in 1939 and 1940. Large populations of Jews now came under German rule, as well as people who were more than willing to support the Nazis in their mission to exterminate the Jews from Europe. As we saw in Chapter 5, Jews in Poland were brought into ghettos – most famously in Warsaw – where disease and hunger were endemic.

It was Operation Barbarossa, however, that marked the transition towards large-scale mass murder. As the first Nazi troops occupied territories in Eastern Europe, they were under orders to execute any 'partisan' opposition. The clear intention here was that 'partisan' be interpreted broadly, and troops on the ground had no difficulty in seeing local Jews as partisans. In some villages in the Baltic states of Lithuania, Latvia and Estonia, as well as Belarus and Ukraine, some local people supported the Nazi troops in rounding up local Jews, and the mass killings began. These killings took numerous forms. In some cases Jews were simply beaten to

ACTIVITY 6.5

Make short notes on the job titles of those who took part in the Wannsee Conference.

What do their official roles tell us about how participants saw the nature of the conference?

death. Many more were shot, often on the edge of mass graves. Where executions were carried out by Nazi soldiers, quite detailed records were kept outlining the number of men, women and children who were murdered. This was grisly work, and some reports began to be raised about the effect mass murder was having on German soldiers, though very few soldiers took the opportunity to be reassigned to different tasks. It is a matter of historical debate just how far the German population supported the Nazi policy of mass murder, but it certainly was the case that – either through a sense of duty, a culture of following orders or a genuine hatred for the Jews – the majority of German soldiers who were ordered to participate in the killings did so. By the end of 1941, around 1 million Jews had been killed.

The Wannsee Conference

It had become clear by the end of 1941 that the ad-hoc approach to mass murder being conducted in Eastern Europe was not sustainable. Reinhard Heydrich thus called a conference in the Berlin suburb of Wannsee in January 1942, at which the many different ministries and agencies involved in Nazi anti-Semitic policy were represented. Fifteen prominent people attended, among them senior members of the NSDAP, SS officers and civil servants (see Figure 6.3).

Gauleiter Dr MEYER and Reichsamtsleiter Dr LEIBBRANDT	Reich Ministry for the Occupied Eastern territories
Secretary of State Dr STUCKART	Reich Ministry for the Interior
Secretary of State NEUMANN	Plenipotentiary for the Four-Year Plan
Secretary of State Dr FREISLER	Reich Ministry of Justice
Secretary of State Dr BÜHLER	Office of the Government General
Under Secretary of State LUTHER	Foreign Office
SS-Oberführer KLOPFER	Party Chancellery
Ministerialdirektor KRITZINGER	Reich Chancellery
SS-Gruppenführer HOFMANN	Race and Settlement Main Office
SS-Gruppenführer MÜLLER SS-Obersturmbannführer EICHMANN	Reich Main Security Office
SS-Oberführer Dr SCHÖNGARTH Chief of the Security Police and the SD in the Government General	Security Police and SD
SS-Sturmbannführer Dr LANGE Commander of the Security Police and the SD for the General-district Latvia, as deputy of the Commander of the Security Police and the SD for the Reich Commissariat 'Eastland'	Security Police and SD

Figure 6.3: Participants in the Wannsee Conference, discussing the final solution of the Jewish question, Berlin, am Grossen Wannsee, 20 January 1942.

The intention was nothing short of planning a more efficient means of eliminating Jews entirely. We know something about the meeting, because Eichmann took minutes, but he was under orders to write them in such a way that they could be misinterpreted by anyone who had not been at the meeting. The talk at the meeting could well have been directly of executions, but the notes record only discussion about moving Jews east. Everyone knew that planning the 'final solution to the Jewish question' meant the extermination of Jews in territories in Europe occupied by the Reich, no less than an attempt to obliterate an entire race. As at any well-run meeting, people were reminded of the story so far: Heydrich summarised actions taken against Jews beginning in 1933, and the numbers of Jews that had emigrated from Greater Germany. Eichmann had prepared some statistics for the meeting. The officials were thus told how many Jews existed in each European country, and how many this added up to (see Figure 6.4). Estonia was marked as *Judenfrei* (free of Jews) because the 4500 Jews who had remained after German occupation had all been exterminated by the end of 1941. Himmler had now banned further emigration. The solution had to be different and it had to be appropriate for the job not just of Germany's Jews, but those in all of Europe. There was discussion regarding the fate of people of mixed Jewish-non-Jewish descent, and people in mixed-race marriages. Göring's representative for the Four-Year Plan, Erich Neurath, did not want Jews whose work was important for the war effort to be rounded up, and he was reassured.

After a two-hour discussion, the 'final solution' reached proposed the creation of death camps around Eastern Europe, particularly in Poland. These camps would exist with the principal purpose of exterminating the Jews of Europe.

Experiments with gas by the *Einsatzgruppen* and in the T4 euthanasia programme confirmed that this was an efficient means of mass murder, and gas chambers were thus to be established in all of these camps. Railways were to bring Jews to the camp. Mass murder could advance at an industrial scale.

The Final Solution

Before 1939 there were around 3.5 million Polish Jews, some 10% of the Polish population. By 1945, about 3 million of these people had been killed in the gas chambers of Auschwitz-Birkenau, Belżec, Majdanek, Sobibór, Treblinka and other extermination camps, much of the killing taking place in the period after 1942. The main means of killing was the use of gas, but the previous methods (starvation, untreated illness and working to death) also continued. The company IG Farben employed 35 000 slave labourers in its Auschwitz factory; 25 000 of them died of maltreatment. Auschwitz-Birkenau is the most famous of the death camps (indeed, of the entire camp system). It was an old army barracks, once used by the Austrians and then the Poles. The SS bought up additional land and evicted local people. The complex of buildings developed over time, but it contained gas chambers and crematoria for burning the dead bodies, but also factories and dormitories for those being worked to death.

Altogether it is estimated that some 6 million Jews were murdered by the Nazis. Of these, perhaps half died in death camps, about 1 million in Auschwitz-Birkenau alone. This campaign of mass slaughter was carried out on an industrial scale, with cattle trucks full of Jews and others destined to die gathering at the railways

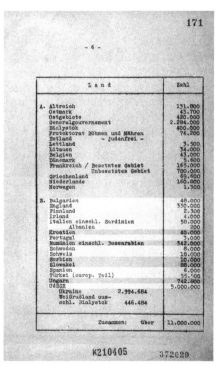

Figure 6.4: A list of Jewish populations in European countries, prepared for the Wannsee Conference, January 1942.

stations that served the camps. Their reception had been carefully planned. They were shouted at, ferocious dogs were barking. They were made to run. There was to be no opportunity to stop, think, negotiate or hesitate. There was an initial sorting process between those who were to be killed immediately and those who were judged capable of working. The journey to the camps itself killed many people. Mass murder and genocide were not invented by the Nazis, nor was the Holocaust the last such set of atrocities. The Holocaust stands out, however, as the largest act of mass murder ever conducted in human history.

At the Nuremberg Trials following the Second World War, a number of the accused said that they could not be held responsible because they were obeying the orders of their superiors. This became known as the 'Nuremberg Defence' and was exactly what Adolf Eichmann declared 15 years later in Jerusalem. 'Superior orders' had been accepted by a German court during a war-crimes trial following the First World War. It was rejected by the international courts conducting war-crimes trials following the Second World War. Do you think that a 'Nuremberg Defence' is sufficient for a court to find someone not guilty?

Opposition and resistance in wartime

It is often asked why more people did not resist the Nazi regime. There certainly was opposition, and in Chapter 4 we saw what forms this opposition took before 1939. As the Second World War advanced, and particularly once Germany began to lose, opposition was not just a political threat to Germany: it was seen as an act of treason in a time of war, and punishments were especially brutal.

Churches

The Churches were often supportive of the law-and-order programme that the Nazis superficially offered. They were also protective of church members. As a result, they were generally compliant with the Nazi regime, but only within certain limits. The largest Protestant Church was the German Evangelical Church. Historically it regarded itself as one of the pillars of German (especially north German) society and culture. By the outbreak of the Second World War, a split had already occurred within this church between those clergy and laity who accepted Nazi thinking and ideas and those who did not. The former created a Reich Church in 1933 when the Nazis came to power in Germany. Opposition to this group came from the Confessing Church (*Bekennende Kirche*), which declared that its allegiance was to God and scripture, not to a worldly Führer.

The Lutheran pastor Dietrich Bonhoeffer was a member of the Confessing Church. He was a well-known opponent of the regime over the issue of the euthanasia programme and anti-Semitism. Arrested by the Gestapo in April 1943, he was sent to prison in Berlin. After allegedly being implicated in the July 1944 plot to assassinate Hitler (discussed below), he was secretly transferred to the Buchenwald concentration camp and then to the camp at Flossenbürg in Upper Bavaria near the border with Czechoslovakia. Here he was executed by hanging early in April 1945, just weeks before the camp was liberated.

The Roman Catholic Church was smaller and historically less powerful in German politics than the Protestant churches. Nevertheless, it was of enormous importance in certain parts of Germany, such as the Rhineland and Bavaria, as well as in Hitler's birthplace Austria, since 1938 part of Greater Germany. The *Reichskonkordat* of July 1933 had given the Nazi regime considerable authority over the Church. Despite this, the Catholic Bishop of Münster, Clemens von Galen, provided a notable example of clergy condemning in public certain Nazi policies. His August 1941 sermon condemning the secret forced euthanasia programme was brave and widely noted.

Student opposition

Student opposition to the Nazi regime was limited in wartime – most students and university professors of military age were away with the Wehrmacht and any form of opposition was extremely dangerous in Nazi Germany. However, one group of students from the University of Munich formed a non-violent resistance group calling themselves the **Weisse Rose**.

They were joined by their philosophy professor, Kurt Huber. This 'White Rose' movement contained Christians from different churches and traditions. They distributed anonymous leaflets and wrote graffiti calling for active opposition to the Nazi state. Their first five leaflets were distributed safely in Munich within academic circles between June 1942 and February 1943, but the sixth (reproduced below), more widely distributed throughout southern Germany and therefore much more risky, caused their discovery, arrest by the Gestapo and trial for treason. Three of their best-known leaders – brother and sister Sophie and Hans Scholl and Christoph Probst – were executed for treason towards the end of February 1943. Two further trials and executions followed. Wili Graf was a former member of Roman Catholic youth organisations; he had refused to take part in HJ activities and so had already served a prison sentence for opposition. Serving as a Wehrmacht medical officer, he had been decorated for his courage. In the White Rose, he took responsibility for graffiti and for recruiting further members. He was arrested in February 1943, tried by the *Volksgerichtshof* for treason and beheaded in October 1943 after months of Gestapo interrogation.

Civilian critics and the Elser assassination attempt

The German civilian population in wartime began the Second World War apparently enthusiastic and patriotic. However, historians have found that there was considerable discontent hidden behind the façade of enthusiasm, and this worsened as the war went on and defeats began to outnumber victories. The main general complaints concerned the state of the economy and the corruption of Nazi officials. These only became worse as Allied bombing from 1942 disrupted everyday life and food shortages became more common as the ration was reduced. The sweeping military successes for Germany 1939 to 1941 damped down any resistance or even civilian discontent. There was, for example, just one public show of opposition to the vicious Nazi persecution of German Jews. In February 1943 the *Rosenstrasse Protest* gathered a large crowd outside the Berlin building where 1800 Jewish men married to non-Jewish women were being held prior to shipment to the extermination camps in Poland. Their wives rallied and protested outside for over a week. The Nazis eventually relented and the men were released, an unusual success and a unique event.

Key term

Weisse Rose: German expression meaning `White Rose', an anti-Nazi student group which in 1942 -1943 campaigned for the end of the war and the end of Nazi rule.

Even so, one of the first assassination attempts on Hitler (and one of those that came closest to success) was carried out not by a conspiracy or an opposition group but by a single individual. It was carried out specifically because of the outbreak of war. Johann Georg Elser was a carpenter from Württemburg. He concealed a time bomb in a Munich beer hall in November 1939 where Hitler was due to speak, set it and then headed for the Swiss border. However, Hitler made a much shorter speech than planned and had already left when the bomb exploded 13 minutes later. Eight people were killed. Elser was arrested, interrogated and sent to Buchenwald concentration camp, where he was executed in 1945. Elser's family declared that he was non-political. However, the police interrogations discovered that he had attended political meetings perhaps three times, had

 Voices from the past

Die Weisse Rose

This White Rose text was smuggled out of Germany. The RAF dropped copies over Germany in July 1943.

A Call to All Germans!

The war is approaching its destined end. As in the year 1918, the German government is trying to focus attention exclusively on the growing threat of submarine warfare, while in the East the armies are constantly in retreat and invasion is imminent in the West. Mobilisation in the United States has not yet reached its climax, but already it exceeds anything that the world has ever seen. It has become a mathematical certainty that Hitler is leading the German people into the abyss. Hitler cannot win the war; he can only prolong it. The guilt of Hitler and his minions goes beyond all measure. Retribution comes closer and closer.

But what are the German people doing? They will not see and will not listen. Blindly they follow their seducers into ruin. Victory at any price! is inscribed on their banner. "I will fight to the last man," says Hitler – but in the meantime the war has already been lost.

Germans! Do you and your children want to suffer the same fate that befell the Jews? Do you want to be judged by the same standards as your traducers? Are we to be forever the nation which is hated and rejected by all mankind? No. Dissociate yourselves from National Socialist gangsterism. Prove by your deeds that you think otherwise. A new war of liberation is about to begin. The better part of the nation will fight on our side. Cast off the cloak of indifference you have wrapped around you. Make the decision before it is too late! Do not believe the National Socialist propaganda which has driven the fear of Bolshevism into your bones. Do not

believe that Germany's welfare is linked to the victory of National Socialism for good or ill. A criminal regime cannot achieve a German victory. Separate yourselves in time from everything connected with National Socialism. In the aftermath a terrible but just judgment will be meted out to those who stayed in hiding, who were cowardly and hesitant.

What can we learn from the outcome of this war – this war that never was a national war?

The imperialist ideology of force, from whatever side it comes, must be shattered for all time. A one-sided Prussian militarism must never again be allowed to assume power. Only in large-scale cooperation among the nations of Europe can the ground be prepared for reconstruction. Centralised hegemony, such as the Prussian state has tried to exercise in Germany and in Europe, must be cut down at its inception. The Germany of the future must be a federal state. At this juncture only a sound federal system can imbue a weakened Europe with a new life. The workers must be liberated from their condition of down-trodden slavery under National Socialism. The illusory structure of autonomous national industry must disappear. Every nation and each man have a right to the goods of the whole world!

Freedom of speech, freedom of religion, the protection of individual citizens from the arbitrary will of criminal regimes of violence – these will be the bases of the New Europe.

Support the resistance. Distribute the leaflets![3]

Discussion point
Use your knowledge of the historical context to comment on this source.

joined the communist RFB and voted KPD in elections. He came to believe that Hitler was leading Germany into disaster and the war could only be ended if Hitler was assassinated. He had started attending church more often, having decided to attempt the assassination. His overwhelming motive, he told the police, had been to stop the war. The Gestapo was convinced he was part of a larger conspiracy, but it seems certain that he was acting on his own, just as he said.

After the German invasion of the USSR, German communists were encouraged to form resistance cells. Exiled communists returned secretly from Russia to enable this and undertook a limited number of activities. Two groups were jointly dubbed the 'Red Orchestra' by the Gestapo. One group concentrated on espionage, gathering information on the military and industrial situation. It was betrayed to the Gestapo in 1942 and the leaders secretly executed. The other group avoided direct contact with the USSR and involved communists but also conservatives, Catholics and Jews. It helped individuals in danger to leave the country secretly. It released anti-Nazi leaflets encouraging civil disobedience. It passed information to a member of the American embassy. This circle too was broken and members were arrested and executed.

Opposition in the army and the July Bomb Plot

Within the Reichswehr a number of officers were covertly active in resistance to the Nazis. In the years before the war, some officers believed that the outbreak of war would be a disaster for Germany. The outbreak of war in September 1939 and the initial German successes made it harder to organise effective opposition. General Carl-Heinrich von Stülpnagel, infantry officer and commander of the 17th Army on the Eastern Front from December 1940 to October 1941, was an active opposition figure in the army. So too was General Erwin von Witzleben, who commanded the 1st Army in France at the start of the war and was in line to become a Field Marshall and Commander-in-Chief of the Wehrmacht if the plot succeeded in deposing Hitler and the Nazis. At the army headquarters at Zossen, south of Berlin, a group of officers planned a coup, calling themselves Action Group Zossen.

Of the 20 or so attempts to assassinate Hitler between September 1939 and July 1944, over half involved army officers, some of high rank, with good access to the Führer. The best known of these plots, because it was the one which came closest to success, was led by Colonel Claus von Stauffenberg and took place at Hitler's military command centre for the Eastern Front, the *Wolfsschanze* (Wolf's Lair) in East Prussia, a military headquarters for the Eastern Front in the Masurian woods about 8 km from the small town of Rastenburg. Stauffenberg was due to attend a meeting there in his capacity as chief of staff to the Commander of the Reserve Army. His intention was to place a bomb in a conference room where Hitler would be sitting and then slip away. With Hitler dead, the conspirators would then seize control of Germany and aim to negotiate an end both to Nazi rule and to the war. The bomb went off, but it did not have the expected effect. It seems that after Stauffenberg had left the room, the suitcase containing the bomb was moved underneath the large, heavy conference table, which took the force of the blast (Figure 6.5). Four people were killed and two were seriously injured. Almost all of the 24 present had perforated ear drums after the bomb exploded. Hitler had over 200 wooden splinters removed from his legs, his hair was singed and his uniform shredded, but he survived. After the failure of the plot, not only were Stauffenberg and other ringleaders executed but also the Gestapo arrested some 7000 others, nearly 5000 of whom were killed; few if any of them had anything to do with the plot.

Members of the Kreisau Circle were connected to the July 1944 Bomb Plot, and some of them, including Peter Graf Yorck von Wartenburg, a member of an aristocratic army family, were picked up by the security services, quickly tried, found guilty and executed in August 1944. Helmuth von Moltke had been arrested in January 1944 and tried by the *Volksgerichtshof*. Already in custody, he was found guilty of treason and executed in January 1945.

Figure 6.5: Aftermath of the bomb plot at the Wolf's Lair, 20 July 1944.

The end of Nazi Germany

Allied forces landed on the Normandy beaches in north-west France in June 1944. After months of heavy fighting, they crossed the River Rhine and into western Germany in March 1945. They encountered a less fierce opposition than expected, which they took to mean that the German army's ability to fight was fatally undermined. Meanwhile, Soviet troops had slowly pushed German forces out of the USSR, back into eastern Germany until the fighting was going from street to street in the streets of Berlin itself. Various leading Nazis knew that Germany had lost and sought to negotiate an end. Hitler had refused to contemplate any surrender. On hearing that Himmler was attempting to open negotiations with the American commander Dwight D. Eisenhower, Hitler ordered his execution. News came that Göring wanted to know whether Hitler was still in charge or whether, as Deputy Führer, he should now take charge; Hitler ordered his execution. Both were out of reach of Hitler's remaining forces, however, and they survived a little longer, committing suicide in the weeks and months that followed.

All through the earlier part of the year the economic situation had grown worse. Rations had been cut more than once, so that the black market had grown in importance. The crime rate had been rising anyway during the war; now it was out of control. The police were unable to keep order. Death sentences were increasingly handed out in an attempt to regain control. There was a major refugee problem. People in their millions, mostly ethnic Germans from the eastern territories of the Reich, had been moving west, deeper into a badly damaged Germany, fleeing the rapidly advancing Red Army. These Displaced Persons (DPs) running from the fighting, ethnic cleansing, revenge killings and so on were Germans from everywhere that German forces had occupied in the Second World War, but also from those parts of Germany in Eastern Europe. These people had little hope of being repatriated to their original homes because of fear of persecution.

In addition to the numerous German refugees there were the vast numbers of slave and forced labourers, taken from every country Germany had occupied. These were now gradually being released, sometimes by the arrival of conquering armies, sometimes just by the breakdown of the system which had held them captive. They too were on the move, trying to avoid the remaining German authorities, to avoid getting caught up in the last weeks of fighting, and to plan their return home to France, Greece, Poland, the USSR or wherever else they had been taken from. It was economic chaos and a catalyst for mass starvation.

At the same time, there were shortages of labour in several places, both in cities and in agriculture, because of the collapsed transport infrastructure preventing the workforce travelling from places of unemployment to places of work. Germany's cities had been badly bombed, especially in industrial areas. Rail and road infrastructure was extensively damaged. Bridges and docks had often been Allied targets in the war. The same infrastructural problems meant that fuel was not being taken to factories, so that they were inactive and closing down. The fragmented road, rail and telephone communications also meant that military commanders, as well as local government officials and police, were often out of contact with central government – and gradually with all authority.

Then on 1 May 1945 German radio played solemn music. Grand Admiral Karl Dönitz came on air to announce that Hitler was dead. The official news was that he had died in street fighting in Berlin, opposing the Red Army: in fact he had committed suicide. Following the death of Hindenburg in 1934, Hitler had held two state posts. Dönitz now became the German president for 20 days. Goebbels was chancellor for a day. Following his suicide, Johann Ludwig Graf Schwerin von Krosigk, a non-party conservative who had been finance minister and then leading minister in the government, became chancellor for the days afterwards. The government sat in the north German town of Flensburg. Dönitz claimed his was a non-political government, but it showed a lot of continuity, retaining many of the people who had been in office under Hitler, such as Schwerin von Krosigk and Speer. They thought they could play a role in managing a period of transition. They thought their experience would be needed. The Allies were not interested.

ACTIVITY 6.6

What similarities and differences do you notice between Germany in 1945 and how Germany was in 1918? Draw up a two-column table, headed '1918' and '1945', and note points under headings such as political, economic, social and military.

ACTIVITY 6.7

Read through your notes on Germany under Nazi rule. Make further notes on the strengths and weaknesses of Hitler's leadership of the Nazi state over time. Discuss why the regime collapsed in 1945. Consider, for example, how far the Nazi party had achieved its aims.

All that was required was surrender. Dönitz and his colleagues thought it might be possible to surrender to the Western Allies but maintain the fight against the Soviets. Again, the Allies were not interested.

The commanders on the front line continued sending in reports that they did not have enough men and ammunition to keep fighting, and the troops that were left were facing annihilation. After a short period of attempts to negotiate a ceasefire, Dönitz's interim government agreed an unconditional surrender on 7 May 1945. It became effective the following day. The last major surrender of German troops happened at Prague three days later. On 23 May, the Allies dissolved the Flensburg government and arrested its members. For two weeks, there was no official government authority. Then on 5 June, the Allies – UK, USA, USSR and France – signed a 'Declaration Regarding the Defeat of Germany and the Assumption of Supreme Authority by Allied Power' in which they took full powers to run Germany directly themselves.

Timeline

1939	
September	Invasion of Poland; introduction of rationing; Kriegswirtschaftsordnung (War Economy Decree); Napola schools under the influence of the SS
1940	Der ewige Jude (The Eternal Jew), anti-Semitic propaganda film, released
1941	
April	Invasion of Yugoslavia
June	Invasion of the Soviet Union
July	Göring wrote to Heydrich to prepare a set of plans for the Final Solution (die Endlösung der Judenfrage)
December	Germany declared war on USA
1942	
August	Battle for Stalingrad; White Rose distributed leaflets – group members executed for treason
1943	
February	Goebbels' 'total war' speech; Rosenstrasse protest succeeded
April	Arrest of Dietrich Bonhoeffer
1944	
June	Allied troop landings in Normandy
July	Bomb plot attempt to assassinate Hitler
1945	
February	Allied bombing of Dresden
April	Dietrich Bonhoeffer hanged; Potsdam Conference

May	Hitler's death announced; Germany surrendered
June	Germany split into four Zones of Occupation; East Prussia and Silesia put into the hands of Poland; North-East Prussia and Memel passed to the USSR
November	Nuremberg trials began

Practice essay questions

1. 'Only the German military posed a serious threat to Hitler's position as Fuhrer between 1939 and 1945.' Assess the validity of this view.
2. 'The Second World War required a change of attitude towards the role of women in Nazi society.' Assess the validity of this view.
3. To what extent did the Wannsee Conference mark a change in direction for Nazi racial policy?
4. 'The outbreak of the Second World War in 1939 changed nothing about Nazi economic policy; the only practical change was the availability of slave labour.' Assess the validity of this view.
5. 'The small numbers active in the Resistance to the Nazis, together with the ineffectiveness of opposition groups, show us that most Germans supported Hitler and his policies.' How far do you agree?
6. With reference to the sources below and your understanding of the historical context, assess the value of the three sources to a historian studying the economic policies of Nazi Germany during the Second World War.

Source A

Heinrich Himmler speaking at a meeting of senior SS leaders in the summer of 1942 (from Shulte, J.E., *Vom Arbeits – zum Vernichtungslager: Die Entschungsgeschichte von 1941/1942 Auschwitz-Birkenau*, VfZ 50, 2002; in Tooze, A., *The Wages of Destruction* and Ferencz, B., *Less Than Slaves*, Cambridge: Harvard University Press, 1979).

If we do not fill our camps with slaves – in this room I mean to say things very firmly and clearly – with worker slaves, who will build our cities, our villages, our farms without regard to any losses, then even after years of war we will not have enough money to be able to equip the settlements in such a manner that real Germanic people can live there and take root in the first generation.

Source B

Albert Speer speaking to the Gauleiter of the different regions in October 1943 (in Sereny, G., *Albert Speer: Sein Ringen mit der Wahrheit*, Leipzig: Goldmann Verlag, 2001).

We have lived through times in army equipment when our tanks were inferior to those of the Russians. … The Luftwaffe in the course of the last two years has quite indubitably suffered from an absolute inferiority, a technical inferiority to the weapons the enemy.

185

And you can see from this example what it means to be able to procure the quantity and to be qualitatively inferior. This is quite insupportable in our situation.

Source C

Field Marshall Erhard Milch speaking to air force engineers and chief quartermasters in March 1944 (from Harvard Law School Library Nuremberg Trials Project: nuremberg.law.harvard.edu).

[Foreign workers] run away. They do not keep to any contract. There are difficulties with Frenchmen, Italians, Dutch. The prisoners of war are… unruly and fresh. These people are also supposed to be carrying on sabotage. These elements cannot be made more efficient by small means. They are just not handled strictly enough. If a decent foreman would sock one of those unruly guys because the fellow won't work, the situation would soon change.

Chapter summary

By the end of this chapter you should understand that, as the Nazi regime took Germany into the Second World War, it maintained its overall policies. It moved the economy onto a war footing, but attempted to minimise the impact on civilians. It used propaganda to persuade people that the war was going well. It introduced the death camps to increase the speed and efficiency of the murder of hated minorities, notably Jews. In particular, you have learned that:

- civilian experience of the Second World War included rationing, was partly shaped by the effectiveness of Nazi propaganda
- the war affected different social groups differently, including women, young people, those that made up the traditional 'ruling class' and those that made up the traditional 'working class'
- the German economy was slow to go onto a total-war footing, and the Four-Year Plan did not achieve its goals; economic leadership passed from Göring to Speer
- Nazi Germany persecuted non-German ethnic groups, notably Jews, as a matter of state policy: having removed civil rights, and treating individuals harshly, the Nazi state now developed a programme of mass murder with the aim of killing all Jews in Europe; large numbers of prisoners were also used as slave labour
- resistance to Nazi rule was difficult and often fatal, yet small numbers of Christians, students, teenagers and soldiers did attempt it.

End notes

1 Petropoulos, J., *Royals and the Reich*.

2 Noakes, J. and Pridham, G. eds., *Nazism 1919–1945, Volume 4*.

3 Scholl, I., 'The Fifth Broadsheet of the White Rose', from *The White Rose: Munich 1942–1943*. © 1983 by Inge Aicher-Scholl and reprinted by permission of Wesleyan University Press.

Glossary

A

Abdication renouncing a position of power or authority, stepping down from such a position

Anschluss The annexation of or union with Austria, from the German term meaning to join something together

Anti-Semitic hostile to Jews

Aristocrat a member of the nobility, from a family with a tradition of owning land and holding political power

Aryan south-central Asian tribe which in pre-history is believed by some historians to have invaded both northern India and Europe; pseudo-scientific classification for pure German

Authoritarian a political point of view or system in which the government has the authority to take decisions without consultation and the power to enforce them, and the population is expected to obey instructions from the government without questioning them

Autocracy a political system in which a single figure possesses unrestrained power

B

Bauhaus A Modernist style of design, art and architecture named after the school that has had a strong and lasting influence on design

Bekennende Kirche German expression meaning 'Confessing Church', Protestant churches and church members who opposed the Nazi regime and argued that the allegiance of the Church should be to God and scripture, not to a worldly Führer

Bund Deutscher Mädel German expression meaning 'League of German Girls'; Nazi youth organisation for girls, part of the Hitlerjugend

Black-marketeer someone who buys and sells goods on the 'black market', dealing in goods in a way that breaks the law, such as not paying an import tariff or without taking account of a rationing system

Blockade a campaign to disrupt trade and communication in order to prevent the movement of imports in such a way as to deprive the targeted place of necessary supplies

C

Camarilla President Hindenburg's group of advisers

Chancellor a figure with authority over certain organisations such as head of government

Coalition a government including members of more than one political party and thus committed to implementing more than one political programme or set of ideas

Communism a left-wing political point of view or party believing in the working class taking political and economic power through revolution

Concentration camp a prison created by a barbed-wire fence and containing huts; a more temporary structure than a traditional prison; built to hold large numbers of prisoners chosen for their membership of specific groups rather than in response to their own specific (criminal) actions

Conservative a political point of view that political and other changes should be avoided, postponed or minimised, especially revolutionary or radical changes

Constitution the written set of rules for how a country is governed; laws can only be passed if they do not conflict with the principles set out in the constitution

Constitutional Convention A conference held to debate and design a reformed constitution

Coup French word meaning 'blow'; the attempt to change government by force rather than persuasion; putsch

D

Dada An artistic movement that produced nonsensical or satirical art in reaction to the traditional values that had enabled the horrors of the First World War

Death camps	Camps in which prisoners were deliberately and systematically killed in huge numbers	**F**		
Decree	a law issued by a head of state, not formulated by an elected government and debated by an elected assembly	**Four-Year Plan**	project for the development of the German economy in readiness for war, with specific production targets; led by Göring
Demilitarisation	removal of armed forces e.g. Army from an area	*Freikorps*	German word meaning 'free corps'; an armed paramilitary group of nationalistic anti-Republicans, usually ex-soldiers, many of which were formed after November 1918
Democracy	a political system in which all citizens are able to choose their government, usually through an electoral process		
Deutsche Christen	German expression meaning 'German Christians', Protestant churches and church members who accepted or supported the Nazi regime	*Führer*	German word meaning 'leader' or 'guide'; a party leader in Weimar Germany; Hitler
		G	
		Gauleiter	German word meaning 'District Leader'
Dolchstoss	German word meaning 'dagger thrust' or 'stab in the back'; the view that the German army was not defeated in the First World War but that left-wing civilians surrendered and signed a peace treaty in an act of treason	**Gestapo**	contraction of *Geheime Staatspolizei*, German expression meaning 'secret state police'
		Ghetto	area or district in which only members of a specified race live
		Gleichschaltung	German word meaning 'coordination' or 'making equal', the policy of bringing all German institutions into line with the NSDAP's aims
E			
Edelweisspiraten	German expression meaning 'Edelweiss Pirates', groups of young Germans who imitated e.g. American clothes and played American music	*Great Depression*	A sustained, severe, worldwide economic downturn that lasted from 1929 until the late 1930s
		H	
		Harzburg Front	a campaigning group including several right-wing groups and parties
Einsatzgruppen	German word meaning 'task forces'; specialist SS and SD units with the responsible for arresting and executing communist leaders and Jews in land taken by the German army on the Eastern Front during the Second World War; death squads	*Hitlerjugend*	German word meaning 'Hitler Youth'; paramilitary youth movement, part of Nazi organisation
		Holocaust	The organised mass murder of Jews by the Nazis
Emigration	movement of people out of a country to live in a different country	**Hyperinflation**	a process by which prices rapidly go up in leaps, making goods and services far more expensive on a day by day basis
Enabling Act	1933 Nazi law abolishing political parties and democratic process		
Eugenics	The attempt to control the characteristics of human populations by controlling breeding	**I**	
		Ideology	set of ideas and ideals that underpins and gives shape to e.g. a policy or political programme
Expressionism	An artistic movement that emphasised the expression of the artist's subjective feelings and experience. Expressionism developed in Germany during the Weimar period	**Industrialisation**	the development of industry and the increasing dependence of a country on industry as opposed to agriculture for income and employment

Inflation The consequence of too much money in the economy compared with the supply of products and services; the obvious effect is that prices rise

Iron Front a left-wing campaigning group including several left-wing groups and parties

Inflation a process by which prices go up over time, making goods and services more expensive on a year by year basis

Infrastructure the services and systems which unpin the economy and society of a state, including bridges, power-distribution networks, railways, roads, telecommunications and water supplies

Internment camps Prisons built as a series of huts surrounded by a barbed-wire fence, rather than as a high-walled building. These were places where anyone considered an enemy or threat of any kind could be sent and held

J

Junker land-owning Prussian nobility with tradition of joining the officer class in the Army and the government's bureaucracy

K

Kaiser German word for emperor

Kaiserreich Imperial Germany (1871–1918), a German state dominated by Prussia and ruled by Prussia's king as emperor

Kreisau Circle group of opponents to the Nazi regime, especially from army and aristocratic backgrounds, largely social conservatives, monarchists, liberals and Christians

Kristallnacht German word meaning 'crystal night' but often translated as 'Night of Broken Glass'; a night in 1938 when Jews were killed and arrested and their property seized and destroyed

L

Labour camps Camps in which prisoners were forced to work and held in harsh and sometimes fatal conditions

Landtag elected assembly for any of the *Länder*

Lebensraum German word meaning 'living space'; territory claimed by Hitler's Germany in eastern Europe

Liberals a 19th-century reform movement which emphasised free trade and a process of constitutional political change

Luftwaffe German air force

M

Marks German currency or money; its name changed after each of a series of currency reforms e.g. Goldmark, Reichsmark, Rentenmark, Deusche Mark etc

Matériel military supplies

Mefo an abbreviation for the German name of government promissory notes, certificates of borrowing

Middle class a social group possessing less property and political power than nobility but more than working class and so in the middle of society; dependant on working to earn a living, so unlike nobility, but works in employment requiring higher levels of education (professions and management of business), so unlike working class

Militarism a belief in the importance of the army; a tendency to depend on the army to solve diplomatic problems

Monarchist political point of view or party believing in monarch e.g. a kingbeing head of state or head of government

Mutiny refusal by armed forces personnel to obey an order or orders

N

Nationalism a political point of view or tradition whereby one's country is prioritised above competing demands on one's time and resources; the belief that one's own country is special – this can take the form of believing it is always best, always right or both

NS-Frauenschaft Nationalsozialistische Frauenschaft, German expression meaning 'National Socialist Women's League', Nazi women's association

Nazis contraction for *Nationalsozialistiche Deutsche Arbeiterpartei*, a German expression meaning 'National Socialist German Workers' Party' (NSDAP)

No confidence	In politics, a leader or government that lacks the confidence of parliament is no longer trusted by a majority of that parliament and is unable to govern. After a vote of no confidence, the government is obliged to resign	*Reichsbanner*	a paramilitary group dedicated to the protection of the Weimar Republic and parliamentary democracy
P		*Reichstag*	the elected federal assembly or parliament of unified Germany; the building where that assembly met
Pragmatism	moral principle favouring choices being based on the relative practicality of the options available than basing them on other moral or religious principles	*Reichswehr*	German armed forces
		Remilitarisation	put armed forces e.g. Army back into an area
Profiteer	someone who takes advantage of a crisis such as a war or famine to make money	**Reparation**	payment made by e.g. state as punishment for wrongdoing e.g. war crimes
Productivity	the amount workers produce in a given time	**Reparations Commission**	In accordance with Articles 231–235 of the Treaty of Versailles, the Reparation Commission was directed to estimate damage done by Germany to Allied civilians and their property during the First World War and to formulate methods of collecting assessments
Propaganda	Publicity or communications material that is deliberately aimed at pushing a particular political (and often simplified) message onto its audience in an appealing and convincing way in order to affect their views and behaviour		
Proportional representation	an electoral system whereby the number of seats a political party holds in an assembly closely reflects the number of votes cast for that party in an election	**Republicanism**	a political point of view preferring an elected or appointed head of state e.g. a president to a hereditary one, e.g. a king
		Revolution	change that takes place suddenly and unexpectedly, often despite opposition, usually by violent means
Protectionism	an economic approach designed to protect the producers in one country against the important of competing produce from any other country, usually through imposing tariffs	**Roman Catholic**	member of largest of the Christian churches with administrative centre in Rome
		S	
Protestant	group of Christian churches stemming from a church-reform movement in the 16th century with a tendency to be more closely linked to individual nationalities and states than e.g. Catholic church	**SA**	abbreviation of *Sturmabteilung*, German word meaning 'storm division'; the NSDAP paramilitary wing
		Social Darwinism	late 19th- and early 20th-century pseudoscience based on applying the scientific ideas and discoveries of Charles Darwin about the natural world to society; in particular, the idea that the strongest human beings would and should succeed and thrive where the weakest would fail and die
Putsch	An attempt to change government by violence rather than democratic methods		
R			
Reactionary	of a right-wing point of view created in reaction to a left-wing expression or course of action; conservative; wishing to re-establish a set of circumstances which have been changed		
		Social democracts	a left-wing political movement campaigning for political reform especially allowing all men, or all adults, to vote in elections; influenced by the ideas of Karl Marx; contains both constitutional and revolutionary traditions
Reform	change that takes place over the course of time, usually with widespread agreement, usually by constitutional means		

Socialist	a left-wing political point of view believing in universal adult suffrage, a welfare state and workers' control of the means of production; different schools of thought believe political change can be achieved through constitutional reform or revolution
SS	abbreviation of *Schutzstaffel*, German word meaning 'protection squadron'
Swastika	The 'hooked cross' symbol of the NSDAP, adopted from Indian traditions to symbolise the Aryan origins of Germans

T

Tariff	a tax applied to goods when they are imported
Third Reich	partial translation of *Dritte Reich* (Third Empire), an expression coined to show Nazi rule as the third stage of German imperial success, following the Holy Roman Empire (which began in the early Middle Ages and ran until the beginning of the 19th century) and the *Kaiserreich* (1871–1918), a German state dominated by Prussia and ruled by Prussia's king as Emperor
Total war	a war in which every part of the economy prioritises the war and the needs of the military
Transit camps	Camps in which prisoners were held while waiting to be moved elsewhere
Tsar	Russian word meaning 'emperor'

V

Volk	German word meaning 'nation', 'people'
Volksgemeinschaft	German word meaning 'nation community'; an ideal community of Germans regardless of social status and based on race

W

Wall Street Crash	A sharp drop in share prices that began in the stock market of Wall Street, New York, on Black Tuesday, 24 October 1929
Weisse Rose	German expression meaning 'White Rose', an anti-Nazi student group which in 1942–1943 campaigned for the end of the war and the end of Nazi rule

Women's rights	women's civil rights as citizens; usually discussed in the context in which it is argued that women ought to possess the same civil rights and the same status of citizenship as men, but don't

Bibliography

Chapter 1

Abel, T., *Why Hitler Came into Power* (New York: Prentice-Hall, 1938).

Berghahn, V.R., *Modern Germany: Society, Economy and Politics in the Twentieth Century* (Cambridge: Cambridge University Press, 1987).

Dickinson, E.R., *The Politics of German Child Welfare from the Empire to the Federal Republic* (Cambridge, Mass: Harvard University Press, 1996).

Evans, R.J., *The Coming of the Third Reich: How the Nazis Destroyed Democracy and Seized Power in Germany* (New York/London: Penguin, 2004).

Feldman, G.D., *The Great Disorder: Politics, Economics, and Society in the German Inflation, 1914–1924* (Oxford: Oxford University Press, 1996).

Hagemann, G., *Reciprocity and Redistribution: Work and Welfare Reconsidered* (Pisa: Pisa University Press, 2007).

Keynes, J.M., *The Economic Consequences of the Peace* (New York: Harcourt Brace Howe, 1920).

Lee, S.J., *Europe 1890–1945* (Hove: Psychology Press, 2003).

Meyer, G.J., *A World Undone: The story of the Great War 1914–1918* (New York/London: Random House, 2006).

Noakes, J. and Pridham, G., eds., *Nazism 1919–1945, Volume 1: The Rise to Power 1919–1934* (Exeter: University of Exeter Press, 1998).

Peukert, D., *Inside Nazi Germany: Conformity, Opposition, and Racism in Everyday Life* (New Haven: Yale University Press, 1989).

Peukert, D., *The Weimar Republic* (New York: Hill and Wang, 2006).

Pine, L., *Education in Nazi Germany* (Oxford: Berg, 2010).

Shirer, W., *The Rise and Fall of the Third Reich* (London: Random House, 1960, 1998).

Stackelberg, R. and Winkle, S.A., *The Nazi Germany Sourcebook: An anthology of texts* (Abingdon: Routledge, 2013).

Taylor, S., *Germany 1918–1933* (London: Duckworth, 1983).

Weitz, E.D., *Weimar Germany* (Princeton: Princeton University Press, 2007).

Chapter 2

Keynes, J.M., *The Economic Consequences of the Peace* (New York: Harcourt Brace Howe, 1920).

Kershaw, I., *The 'Hitler Myth' – Image and Reality in the Third Reich* (Oxford: Oxford University Press, 1985).

Kolbe, E., *The Weimar Republic*, 2nd ed. (Falla, P.S., Park, R.J., translators) (Abingdon: Routledge, 2004).

Paxton, R.O. and Hessler, J., *Europe in the Twentieth Century* (Boston, Mass: Wadsworth, 1975).

Stark, G.D., *Entrepreneurs of Ideology: Neoconservative Publishers in Germany, 1890–1933* (Chapel Hill: University of North Carolina Press, 1981).

Chapter 3

Blackbourn, D., and Eley, G., *Peculiarities of German History: Bourgeois Society and Politics in Nineteenth-Century Germany* (Oxford: Oxford University Press, 1984).

Kershaw, I., *The 'Hitler Myth' – Image and Reality in the Third Reich* (Oxford: Oxford University Press, 1985).

Longerich, P., *Goebbels: A Biography* (New York: Random House, 2015).

Noakes, J. and Pridham, G., eds., *Nazism 1919–1945, Volume 1: The Rise to Power 1919–1934* (Exeter: University of Exeter Press, 1998).

Noakes, J. and Pridham, G., eds., *Nazism 1919–1945, Volume 2: State, Economy and Society 1933–1939* (Exeter: University of Exeter Press, 1998).

Shirer, W., *The Rise and Fall of the Third Reich* (London: Random House, 1960, 1998).

Tooze, A., *The Wages of Destruction: The Making and Breaking of the Nazi Economy* (London: Allen Lane, 1960; 2006).

Taylor, A.J.P., *The Origins of the Second World War* (London: Penguin, 1991).

Wehler, H.-U., *Deutsche Gesellschaftgeschichte* (Munich: Beck, 1987).

Weitz, E.D., *Weimar Germany* (Princeton: Princeton University Press 2007).

Winkler, H., *Germany: The Long Road West, Volume 1: 1789–1933* (Oxford: Oxford University Press, 2006); *Volume 2: 1933–1990* (Oxford: Oxford University Press, 2007).

Chapter 4

Barnett, V., *For the Soul of the People: Protestant Protest against Hitler* (Oxford: Oxford University Press, 1992).

Dietrich, O., *The Hitler I Knew* (republished New York: Skyhorse Publishing, 2010).

Evans, R.J., *The Third Reich in Power: How the Nazis Won Over the Hearts and Minds of a Nation* (New York/London: Penguin, 2006).

Manvell, R. and Fraenkel, H., *Doctor Goebbels: His Life and Death* (New York: Skyhorse Publishing, 2010).

Noakes, J. and Pridham, G., eds., *Nazism 1919–1945, Volume 2: State, Economy and Society 1933–1939* (Exeter: University of Exeter Press, 1998).

Noakes, J. and Pridham, G., eds., *Nazism 1919–1945, Volume 3: Foreign Policy, War and Racial Extermination* (Exeter: University of Exeter Press, 2001).

Trevor-Roper, H.R. (intro), *Hitler's Table Talk 1941–1944* (Oxford: Oxford University Press, 1988).

Turner, H.A., *German Big Business and the Rise of Hitler* (Oxford: Oxford University Press, 1985).

Welch, D., *The Third Reich: Politics and Propaganda* (Abingdon: Routledge, 2002).

Chapter 5

Browning, C., *Ordinary Men: Reserve Police Battalion 101 and the Final Solution in Poland*, (London: Penguin, 2001).

Goldhagen, D., *Hitler's Willing Executioners: Ordinary Germans and the Holocaust* (New York: Abacus, 1997).

Grau, G., ed., *Hidden Holocaust?* (Abingdon/New York: Routledge/Taylor & Francis, 1995).

Hentschel, K., ed., *Physics and National Socialism: An Anthology of Primary Sources* (Boston, Berlin, Basel: Birkhauser, 1986).

Kershaw, I., *The 'Hitler Myth' – Image and Reality in the Third Reich* (Oxford: Oxford University Press, 1985).

Klemperer, V., *I Shall Bear Witness* (London: Random House, 1998).

Mendelsohn, J., ed., *The Holocaust: Selected Documents* (New York: Garland, 1982).

Chapter 6

Bessel, R., *Germany 1945: From War to Peace* (London: Simon and Schuster, 2010).

Davies, N., *Europe at War 1939–1945: No Simple Victory* (London: Macmillan, 2006).

Hilberg, R., *The Destruction of the European Jews* (New York: Holmes and Meier, 1986).

Kershaw, I., *The 'Hitler Myth' – Image and Reality in the Third Reich* (Oxford: Oxford University Press, 1985).

Kershaw, I., *The Nazi Dictatorship, Problems and Perspectives of Interpretation* (London: Hodder Arnold, 2000).

Mason, T., *Social Policy in the Third Reich: The Working Class and the 'National Community'* (London: Bloomsbury, 1993).

Noakes, J. and Pridham, G., eds., *Nazism 1919–1945, Volume 4: The German Home Front in World War II* (Exeter: University of Exeter Press, 1998).

Petropoulos, J., *Royals and the Reich* (Oxford: Oxford University Press, 2008).

Roseman, M., *The Villa, The Lake, The Meeting: Wannsee and the Final Solution* (London: Allen Lane, 2002).

Tooze, A., *The Wages of Destruction: The Making and Breaking of the Nazi Economy* (London: Allen Lane, 1960; 2006).

Acknowledgements

The authors and publishers acknowledge the following sources of copyright material and are grateful for the permissions granted. While every effort has been made, it has not always been possible to identify the sources of all the material used, or to trace all copyright holders. If any omissions are brought to our notice, we will be happy to include the appropriate acknowledgements on reprinting.

The publisher would like to thank the following for permission to reproduce their photographs (numbers refer to figure numbers, unless otherwise stated):

Chapter 1 Opener Alamy Images: The Art Archive, **Figure 1.2** The Everett Collection Historical; **Figure 1.3 REX Shutterstock:** Underwood Archives / UIG; **Figure 1.4 Getty Images:** *Popperfoto;* **Figure 1.7 Mary Evans Picture Library:** ONSLOW AUCTIONS LIMITED, **Figure 1.8 akg-images:** ullsteinbild; **Figure 1.9** Imagno; **Chapter 2 Opener TopFoto:** ullsteinbild, **Figure 2.1** The Grainger Collection; **Figure 2.2 akg-images:** Peter Weiss; **Figure 2.3 Mary Evans Picture Library:** Sueddeutsche Zeitung Photo**; Figure 2.4 Getty Images:** Universal History Archive; **Figure 2.5 Mary Evans Picture Library; Chapter 3 Opener akg-images** Walter Ballhause, **Figure 3.3 Interfoto: Figure 3.5; Figure 3.6 Alamy Images:** Chronicle, **Figure 3.7** Mary Evans Picture Library; **Chapter 4 Opener Corbis:** Stapleton Collection; **Figure 4.1 Alamy Images**: Pictorial Press Ltd; **Figure 4.2, Figure 4.3 akg-Images; Figure 4.4 Mary Evans Picture Library:** Sueddeutsche Zeitung Photo; **Chapter 5 Opener Alamy Images:** World History Archive, **Figure 5.1** CBW; **Figure 5.2 TopFoto:** World History Archive, **Figure 5.3** Ullsteinbild, **Figure 5.4** INTERFOTO; **Figure 5.5 akg-Images; Chapter 6 Opener akg-Images:** Picture-alliance / dpa; **Figure 6.1 Getty Images:** Keystone-France/Gamma-Keystone; **Figure 6.4 Alamy Images:** World History Archive, **Figure 6.5** Chronical

The publisher would like to thank the following for permission to reproduce extracts from their texts:

Chapter 1 The Nazi Germany Sourcebook An Anthology of Texts Edited by Roderick Stackelberg, Sally A. Winkle © 2002 – Routledge. Taylor & Francis Group; **Chapter 2** The Weimar Republic 2nd Edition By Stephen J. Lee © 2009 – Routledge. Taylor & Francis Group; **Chapter 3**, The Nazi Germany Sourcebook An Anthology of Texts Edited by Roderick Stackelberg, Sally A. Winkle © 2002 – Routledge. Taylor

& Francis Group; **Chapter 3** Nazism 1919-1945 Volume 2: State, Economy and Society 1933-39 (A Documentary Reader) Paperback – 1 Aug 2000, by Jeremy Noakes|G. Pridham. Reprinted by permission of Liverpool University Press; **Chapter 3** A Life in Letters, 1914-1982 by Gershom Scholem. Edited and translated by Anthony David Skinner. Reprinted with kind permission of the Scholem family and The National Library of Israel, Jerusalem; **Chapter 3** Nazism 1919-1945 Volume 1: The Rise to Power 1919-1934 (Exeter Studies in History (Book 1) paperback March 1998 by Jeremy Noakes|G. Pridham. Reprint with permission of Liverpool University Press; **Chapter 4** Excerpt from: Gershom Scholem, A Life in Letters: 1914-1982. All rights reserved by and controlled through Suhrkamp Verlag Berlin; **Chapter 4** Nazism 1919-1945 Volume 2: State, Economy and Society 1933-39 (A Documentary Reader) Paperback – 1 Aug 2000, by Jeremy Noakes|G. Pridham. Reprinted by permission of Liverpool University Press; **Chapter 4** The Third Reich: Politics and Propaganda by David Welch, Routledge 2002. Taylor & Francis Group; **Chapter 4** The Third Reich in Power, 1933 - 1939: How the Nazis Won Over the Hearts and Minds of a Nation– 25 May 2006 by Richard J. Evans. Penguin; First Edition (25 May 2006); **Chapter 5** I Shall Bear Witness: The Diaries Of Victor Klemperer 1933-41: I Shall Bear Witness, 1933-41 Vol 1 Paperback – 20 Aug 2009 by Victor Klemperer. W&N; New Ed edition (20 Aug. 2009). Orion Publishing Group; **Chapter 6** I Shall Bear Witness: The Diaries Of Victor Klemperer 1933-41- ISBN: 9780753806845. Publication date: 20 Aug 2009. Page count: 672. Imprint: W&N. Aufbau Verlag GmbH & Co; **Chapter 6** Nazism 1919-1945, Volume Four: The German Home Front in World War II - A Documentary Reader: Vol. 4 (Exeter Studies in History) 1 Sep 1998 by Jeremy Noakes. Reprinted with permission of Liverpool University Press; **Chapter 6** Source of English translation: Inge Scholl. "The Fifth Broadsheet of the White Rose" from The White Rose: Munich 1942-1943. © 1983 by Inge Aicher-Scholl and reprinted by permission of Wesleyan University Press;

Sources to cite

Chapter 1 From Documents of German History © 1958 by Louis L. Snyder. Rutgers University Press; **Chapter 1** Catholic Citizens in the Third Reich: Psycho-Social Principles and Moral Reasoning. New Brunswick, NJ, Transaction Books, Rutgers University, 1988; **Chapter 2** By John_Simkin (john@spartacus-educational.com) ©

September 1997 (updated August 2014); **Chapter 3** Political Violence Under the Swastika: 581 Early Nazis by Peter H. Merkl. Princeton University Press (March 8, 2015); William Sheridan Allen, The Nazi Seizure of Power: The Experience of a Single German Town, 1930—1935, Quadrangle, Chicago 1965, pp. 1116; **Chapter 4** C N Trueman ""Nazi Education"" historylearningsite.co.uk. The History Learning Site, 9 Mar 2015. 16 Nov 2015."; **Chapter 5** Source of English translation: Stenographic Report of the Meeting on —the Jewish Question‖ under the Chairmanship of Field Marshall Goering in the Reichs Air Force (12 November 1938 – 11 o'clock), in United States Chief Counsel for the Prosecution of Axis Criminality, Nazi Conspiracy and Aggression, Volume IV. Washington, DC: United States Government Printing Office, 1946, Document 1816-PS, pp. 425-57; **Chapter 5** Source of English translation: Law for the Prevention of Offspring with Hereditary Diseases (July 14, 1933). In US Chief Counsel for the Prosecution of Axis Criminality, Nazi Conspiracy and Aggression. Volume 5, Washington, DC: United States Government Printing Office, 1946, Document 3067-PS, pp. 880-83. (English translation accredited to Nuremberg staff; edited by GHI staff.); **Chapter 5** Source of original English text: American Consul Samuel Honaker's description of Anti-Semitic persecution and Kristallnacht and its aftereffects in the Stuttgart region (November 12 and November 15, 1938), State Central Decimal File (CDF) 862.4015/2002, Records of the Department of State in the National Archives, Record Group 59, General Records of the Department of State; reprinted in John Mendelsohn, ed., The Holocaust: Selected Documents in Eighteen Volumes. Vol. 3, New York: Garland, 1982, pp. 176-89;

Index

The publisher would like to thank
Indexing Specialists (UK) Ltd for
supplying the index.